Windows Home Server User's Guide

Andrew Edney

Apress®

Windows Home Server User's Guide

Copyright © 2007 by Andrew Edney

ISBN-13 (pbk): 978-1-59059-898-6

ISBN-10 (pbk): 1-59059-898-9

Printed and bound in the United States of America 9 8 7 6 5 4 3 2 1

Lead Editor: Jonathan Hassell
Technical Reviewers: Joel Burt, Tony Campbell, Terry Walsh
Editorial Board: Steve Anglin, Ewan Buckingham, Tony Campbell, Gary Cornell, Jonathan Gennick,
    Jason Gilmore, Kevin Goff, Jonathan Hassell, Matthew Moodie, Joseph Ottinger, Jeffrey Pepper,
    Ben Renow-Clarke, Dominic Shakeshaft, Matt Wade, Tom Welsh
Project Manager: Beth Christmas
Copy Editors: Bill McManus, Marilyn Smith
Associate Production Director: Kari Brooks-Copony
Production Editor: Candace English
Compositor: Patrick Cunningham
Proofreader: Patrick Vincent
Indexer: Julie Grady
Artist: Kinetic Publishing Services, LLC
Cover Designer: Kurt Krames
Manufacturing Director: Tom Debolski

Distributed to the book trade worldwide by Springer-Verlag New York, Inc., 233 Spring Street, 6th Floor, New York, NY 10013. Phone 1-800-SPRINGER, fax 201-348-4505, e-mail orders-ny@springer-sbm.com, or visit http://www.springeronline.com.

For information on translations, please contact Apress directly at 2855 Telegraph Avenue, Suite 600, Berkeley, CA 94705. Phone 510-549-5930, fax 510-549-5939, e-mail info@apress.com, or visit http://www.apress.com.

For Katy.
Thanks for all of the support and for once again putting up with the long hours of work
that go into writing a book.

Contents at a Glance

Contents

Foreword

Windows Home Server is a key ingredient in Microsoft's quest to build a broad platform for the home that is enabling consumers to both simplify their digital lifestyles and expand what is possible. I am very excited to have managed and worked with a great team to build Windows Home Server, a product that provides such powerful and useful capabilities but in such a simple way. And, I am even more excited to see books like this one that complement it.

I was fortunate to have the opportunity to drive Windows Home Server from inception to release. One of the most gratifying things for me is seeing the multiplier effect that occurs when others outside of Microsoft "get it" and become independent proponents. In a sense these individuals and companies become extensions of my team at Microsoft.

Hats off to Andrew for creating this very informative and useful companion to Windows Home Server.

Charlie Kindel
General Manager Windows Home Server
Microsoft Corporation

About the Author

ANDREW EDNEY has been an IT professional for more than 12 years and has, over the course of his career, worked for a range of high-tech companies such as Microsoft, Hewlett-Packard, and Fujitsu Services. Andrew has a wide range of experience in virtually all aspects of Microsoft's computing solutions, having designed and architected large enterprise solutions for government and private-sector customers. Over the years, Andrew has made a number of guest appearances at major industry events, presenting on a wide range of information systems subjects, such as an appearance at the annual Microsoft Exchange Conference in Nice where he addressed the Microsoft technical community on mobility computing. Andrew is currently involved in numerous Microsoft beta programs, including next-generation Windows operating systems and next-generation Microsoft Office products, and he actively participates in all Windows Media Center beta programs and was heavily involved in the Windows Home Server beta program. Andrew also has a number of qualifications; he has an MSc in Network Technologies and Management, he is an MCSE and has numerous MCPs, and he is a Certified Information Systems Security Professional (CISSP) and a Certified Ethical Hacker.

In addition, Andrew has written a number of books on topics such as Windows Media Center, Live Communications Server, PowerPoint 2007, networks, Windows Vista, and the Xbox 360. These include *Pro LCS: Live Communications Server Administration* (Apress, 2007), *Getting More from Your Microsoft Xbox 360* (Bernard Babani, 2006), *How to Set Up Your Home or Small Business Network* (Bernard Babani, 2006), *Using Microsoft Windows XP Media Center 2005* (Bernard Babani, 2006), *Windows Vista: An Ultimate Guide* (Bernard Babani, 2007), *PowerPoint 2007 in Easy Steps* (Computer Step, 2007), *Windows Vista Media Center in Easy Steps* (Computer Step, 2007), and *Using Ubuntu Linux* (Bernard Babani, 2007).

You can reach Andrew at andrew@firebirdconsulting.co.uk. You can also view his blog at http://usingwindowshomeserver.com/.

About the Technical Reviewers

TONY CAMPBELL is an experienced Microsoft consultant specializing in the architecture and design of secure Microsoft-centric business solutions. He also has vast experience in many other industry niches such as networking, collaboration, multimedia, security, business logic, and disaster recovery. Tony has been involved in all sizes of business, from the very small to the very large, and has to date written and published nine IT books, three of which he has written or co-written for Apress, including *Windows Vista: Beyond the Manual* and *Outlook 2007: Beyond the Manual*. Tony started his career back in the 1980s as a "green screen" main-frame programmer for the British Meteorological Office, finally arriving after a long journey in his current role as a self-employed IT consultant. Tony is a regular contributor to a variety of IT magazines distributed worldwide and has been involved in the production of software manuals, user guides, white papers, hardware manuals, and training courses for many of his clients during the past decade. Tony's love of writing has also led to the publication of some fiction in a variety of small presses and magazines.

TERRY WALSH is an Innovation Consultant at ?What If! in London, UK, where he specializes in developing new user and customer experiences for a wide range of global retail, service, and product brands. Terry has been active in the Microsoft Beta Testing community for the past five years, and has focused on operating system testing on Windows XP, Windows Media Center, and Windows Vista, where he led beta testing efforts with the highest number of sub-mitted bugs across 25,000 testers worldwide. That's not to say that Microsoft fixed them all. Most recently, Terry has been enjoying putting Windows Home Server through its paces.

In February 2007, Terry started We Got Served (http://www.wegotserved.co.uk), which was the first and is still the largest Windows Home Server community web site on the Internet, with news and reviews of the latest hardware and software add-ins available for the platform, as well as detailed walkthroughs and tutorials to help you get the most out of Windows Home Server. He's looking forward to seeing you there soon.

Acknowledgments

First I want to thank my partner, Katy, for putting up with me writing yet another book! It takes quite a lot of patience and dedication to write a book and probably takes just as much to live with someone who is writing one, so thanks! I also want to thank Starbuck and Apollo for keeping me sane and for trying to help—well, eating or sitting on my notes while I was trying to write things up.

I also want to extend a big thank you to everyone at Apress who made this happen— Jonathan and Beth, once again, it's been great working with you both on another book. Also to Bill and Marilyn for turning what I wrote into something easier on the eyes. Also thanks to Candace and Terry, and everyone else who did a fantastic job taking what I put together and turning it into what you now have in your hands. These guys never get enough credit as far as I'm concerned.

I would also like to say a big thank you to Todd Headrick and Joel Burt at Microsoft for their help in answering questions, getting software, and generally doing whatever they could to help. The same goes for Tommy Tse and Joel Sider—thanks guys! Also thanks to Charlie Kindel, not only for writing the foreword to this book, but also for coming up with Windows Home Server, because without his efforts, this book never would have existed.

I would also like to thank anyone else who has helped along the way but hasn't had a specific mention—you know who you are, and I thank you.

And, finally, thanks to you, the reader, for buying the book; I hope you like it.

Introduction

A lot of homes have a personal computer in them; in fact, a lot of homes have multiple personal computers in them, especially if there are children in the home and they have their own computers for schoolwork and such. Many of the people who own multiple computers might find it hard to manage the digital content stored on them, including schoolwork, vacation photographs, home movies, music, and more. Often, family or friends might take turns sitting in front of a single computer to view some of their favorite vacation or holiday photos, when in fact they could easily each view them from their own computers, if only it were simple to share the content. And what about backing up the computers? We have all been there—something really important gets deleted or overwritten, or we have a hard drive failure and lose something that really was irreplaceable. How often have you sat there and thought to yourself, "I really should be backing up my important files"? And more often than not the reasons you don't do it are that it's time consuming, difficult, takes up too much space, requires visiting each computer, and so on. I am sure you have plenty of other excuses—I know I do! How many times have you been away from home and wanted access to something on your computer, or even wanted to copy something to your computer?

Microsoft has developed a new product called Windows Home Server, the reason you are reading this introduction now. Windows Home Server takes all the complexity and effort out of sharing media, backing up computers, and much more. Windows Home Server makes it very easy to perform numerous tasks that once may have been considered beyond the knowledge and skills of a "normal" home user. Windows Home Server provides numerous wizards (no, not the Harry Potter kind of wizards) to walk you through most of the tasks you might need to perform, including creating backups of your data, creating and sharing folders for storing your digital content, creating and enabling users to access the data, and more.

Backing up your data is easy with Windows Home Server, but the really great thing is that restoring your data, if you ever need to, is just as easy. You can choose to restore a single file, multiple folders, or even have Windows Home Server restore your entire computer for you, which does not require you to reinstall the operating system and all the drivers, software, and data you had on there before—and believe me, this can save you a lot of time and effort. Windows Home Server even provides you with your own unique domain name so that, if you choose, you can access your Windows Home Server and any data stored on it when you are away from home—all from an Internet browser. You can even easily add more storage space to your Windows Home Server without all the usual problems of adding drive letters. And to give you even more peace of mind, you can have Windows Home Server duplicate your folders onto other hard drives so that if you do have a hard drive failure, you won't actually lose any data. How cool is that? But that's not all; carry on reading this book, and you may be surprised just how much this one product can actually do for you.

So now that you know a bit about all the great features Windows Home Server offers, wouldn't it be useful to have a single source of information and guidance for Windows Home Server? Well, you have it right here in your hands. Yes, that's right, this very book is your guide to everything that Windows Home Server has to offer, including how to install, configure, use, and troubleshoot it. This book is packed with advice and guidance to help you get the most out of Windows Home Server so that you can start benefiting from its use immediately.

■ ■ ■

CHAPTER 1

What Is Windows Home Server?

Microsoft's intention to release Windows Home Server was first announced on January 7, 2007 by Bill Gates at the 2007 International Consumer Electronics Show (CES) in Las Vegas. (For anyone who is interested, Microsoft referred to Windows Home Server as both Code Name Q and Quattro during its development. It was dubbed Quattro by the leader of the project, Charlie Kindel, because it was his fourth attempt at building a home server.) Soon after the announcement, Microsoft released a beta version to approved testers, and by early June 2007, over 60,000 people were testing Windows Home Server worldwide.

So, what is Windows Home Server? You likely have some idea, because you are reading this book. But just in case you are not sure what it is, or you want to make sure you know everything that it is supposed to do for you, this chapter provides an introduction. First, this chapter gives you an overview of Windows Home Server. It then describes the system requirements for running Windows Home Server, reviews the option of buying a ready-made Windows Home Server, and details what software you get with Windows Home Server.

Windows Home Server Overview

In a nutshell, Windows Home Server is a server running Windows for your home. Yes, I know that is obvious, but bear with me.

When most people think of servers, they think of those big machines that sit in secured rooms somewhere in the workplace and do things such as run databases or e-mail programs; most people typically don't think of a server as something that they might have at home. Of course, because you are reading this book, you realize that having a server at home not only is possible but is a great idea (indeed, you may already have a server at home).

According to Microsoft, by the year 2009 there will be over 70 million multi-PC networked households in the world. That is quite a large number! Obviously Microsoft would like to take advantage of this opportunity by providing a product that will benefit all of those households, and that is where Windows Home Server comes into play.

It is very likely that the residents of each of those 70 million households have some data that they will want to share among their PCs, be it digital photographs, home movies, songs, or some other type of media. It is extremely likely that each of those households will want to be able to easily back up and restore those computers with as little effort as possible. (I don't know about you, but if I had a dollar for every time I wished I had performed that backup when something later went wrong, I probably could have bought a new computer by now.)

It's not that I don't back up my data—far from it—it's just that I occasionally forget to back it up, or sometimes I just can't be bothered.) Also, each one of those computers in those households will need to be updated with security patches and updated virus definition files to ensure that they are protected from the many threats that exist on the Internet.

Windows Home Server has features that address each of these scenarios to some extent, most of which can be set up initially with a few clicks of the mouse and then left to run quietly in the background. The only one of these scenarios that Windows Home Server does not really address adequately is the need to obtain security patches and virus updates. Windows Home Server will inform you that your computers are not patched or have out-of-date protection, but it will not handle the updates for you. You still have to visit each computer and take care of this issue yourself. Let's hope Microsoft plans to include that functionality in Version 2 of the product!

Microsoft wants you to take away one message from using Windows Home Server: "Protect, Connect, and Organize." Using Windows Home Server enables you to protect, connect to, and organize your digital data with very little effort.

Essentially, your Windows Home Server will become the central hub of your home network, performing and storing all of your computer backups, storing and sharing all of your digital files, and monitoring the health of your home computers on your network. It can also provide you with remote access to your computers and your files for when you are away from your home.

Note There are certain things that Windows Home Server cannot do. For example, you cannot use Windows Home Server to share your Internet connection with all of your home computers. If you are currently using Internet Connection Sharing provided by Windows XP, for example, then you will still have to use it!

The following list gives you an idea of what you can do with some of the features of Windows Home Server:

- *Back up automatically any connected and supported Windows home computer.* During the Windows Home Server Connector software installation process on each of your home computers, an automated backup schedule is created. All you have to do is ensure that your computer is switched on and connected to your home network when the backup time arrives, and your backups will be performed automatically.

- *Easily restore any backed up files:* You can easily and quickly restore any number of files, from a single Word document to an entire hard drive full of data, with just a few clicks of the mouse.

- *Easily restore a backed up computer.* You can easily restore an entire computer in the event of a failure or other problem just by inserting the Windows Home Server Home Computer Restore CD and selecting a backup.

- *Share digital files:* You can share any of your digital files, be they movies, photos, songs, or other digital media, just by copying them to any shared folder and ensuring that others have access to that folder. Giving access to shared folders is as simple as clicking the mouse.

- *Access computers and files from anywhere*: You can access any of your shared files or computers from anywhere in the world by connecting to a Microsoft Windows Live web site, which in turn connects to your Windows Home Server. Not only can you view or download files, you can also upload files.

- *Centralize storage*: All of your shared storage can be accessed in one single place. Instead of seeing drive letters, you just see shared folders.

- *Expand the storage as your needs increase*: If you start to run out of hard disk storage space on your Windows Home Server, you can easily add more hard drives, either internal drives, if your hardware can support any more, or external drives. It's just as simple as plugging them in! This is called the Windows Home Server Drive Extender.

- *Protect your shared files*: If you want to ensure that your shared files are available to you even if one of the hard drives in your Windows Home Server fails for any reason, you can choose to duplicate folders over multiple hard drives, again just by a click of the mouse.

- *Monitor the health of the computers on your network*: By using the Windows Home Server Console, you have a single place to view the state of your computers so that you don't have to visit every machine to check its health.

- *Add and remove users*: You can easily add and remove users and grant them privileges.

- *Easily connect your home computers*: You can connect up to ten home computers and create up to ten user accounts.

- *Use less space for backups*: Windows Home Server reduces the amount of disk space used for backups by utilizing single-instance storage, which requires only one copy of any file, no matter how many times it appears on computers within your home network.

- *Stream media across your network*: You can stream media to devices on your network that support Windows Media Connect, such as a Microsoft Xbox 360.

Note Each of these elements of Windows Home Server will be covered in depth in subsequent chapters in this book.

If you are thinking that similar software is available from Microsoft, you are right, sort of. You could run Microsoft Windows Server 2003 with Active Directory at home and have all of your computers as part of your home domain, which, with the correct additional software, could help you to back up and monitor your computers and provide shared folders. Obviously, though, the average home user likely does not have the knowledge to set up, configure, and maintain a potentially complex network such as this and really wants only the simple functionality of being able to monitor computers and back up and share data easily—which is exactly what Windows Home Server is designed for. And besides the complexity involved in this setup, it potentially is very expensive for a household with only a few computers.

Note Active Directory is Microsoft's directory service that was first introduced in Windows 2000. Think of it as a giant phone book that includes entries for a number of different elements, including users, computers, printers, and more.

Another piece of software from Microsoft that provides some similar functionality to Windows Home Server is Small Business Server 2003. Unlike the Windows Server 2003/Active Directory combination, Small Business Server 2003 is a single piece of software that comes with a number of additional applications out of the box, enabling small businesses and home users to set up and configure only the components that they need to use. For example, Small Business Server 2003 contains a simplified version of Microsoft Exchange so that you can run your own e-mail server. It also contains a number of wizards that walk you through setting up each of the components, which means you don't have to be an expert at numerous applications. This is a far easier and less expensive option than purchasing Windows Server 2003, creating an Active Directory, and then purchasing any additional software that you might need, such as ISA Server or Exchange, which are really aimed at the enterprise market. However, Small Business Server 2003 still involves more hassle and expense than most average home users are willing to accept, and in most cases, average home users are not interested in running their own e-mail server and want something even simpler to use.

Windows Home Server is intended to overcome home users' reluctance to set up a home server. It is relatively inexpensive (depending on the hardware you purchase) and is incredibly simple to set up and use. In fact, once you have it set up and running how you want it, you may even forget it's there. It is designed to be set up and used by anyone, not just those people who are computer experts.

Windows Home Server is actually built on the Windows Server 2003 platform, but many of the more complex elements have been hidden away, leaving just the simple elements that are needed to perform the job in question; for example the number of options on the Start menu is dramatically reduced from what you would expect to see. This is because you don't need them!

Windows Home Server is designed to run on a small form factor set of hardware, meaning that instead of a big box with multiple hard drives, CD and DVD drives, and more ports than you can shake a stick at, it has only exactly what it needs to run, nothing more, nothing less. In fact, you will probably find that most prebuilt Windows Home Server machines don't even have ports for a keyboard, mouse, or monitor. But don't worry, you can do everything you need to do on your Windows Home Server from the Windows Home Server Console—more on that later.

Note Having no keyboard, mouse, or monitor is also referred to as being *headless*.

One of the reasons for making the form factor so small is that most people don't want yet another bulky computer in their home. Windows Home Server can run on a computer that is small and relatively quiet, and you can set up your system so that the computer doesn't need to be connected to anything other than an AC power socket and an Ethernet cable, meaning you can tuck it away in a corner or some other unobtrusive spot.

■**Caution** If you decide to put your Windows Home Server somewhere out of the way, make sure it has enough ventilation so that it doesn't overheat!

Prices for Windows Home Server hardware will vary depending on the manufacturer or system builder, the specification of the hardware, and other factors such as additional software that might come with the machine, but Microsoft's ultimate vision is to see Windows Home Servers selling for around $500.

Microsoft produced a prototype Windows Home Server, shown in Figure 1-1, lovingly referred to as "the hockey puck" by anyone who has seen it. Unfortunately, it is unlikely that this particular piece of hardware will ever see the light of day in the stores, although you might see something similar from some manufacturers and systems builders.

Figure 1-1. *Microsoft's prototype Windows Home Server hardware*

There are a number of specific language versions of the Windows Home Server software:

- English

- German

- Spanish

- French

Other language versions may be released at a later date, so keep checking the Microsoft Windows Home Server web site for updates if you need a version in another language.

■**Note** The Microsoft Windows Home Server web site is at `http://www.microsoft.com/windows/products/winfamily/windowshomeserver/default.mspx`.

Windows Home Server is also designed to enable additional software to be integrated with it. This additional software could be installed in the same way as you would install software now, such as antivirus software, or it could be installed as an add-in, with the software's features available within the Windows Home Server Console. The possibilities are endless for the different types of software that could be available. For example, software might be offered that provides home automation through your Windows Home Server.

Note For more information on add-ins and additional software for Windows Home Server, take a look at Chapter 13.

Requirements for Running Windows Home Server

The minimum requirements for running Windows Home Server are lower than the requirements for running a current home computer, because Windows Home Server is not used in the same way that a normal home computer is used.

This statement may lead you to think that you can reuse an older computer rather than buy a new one for Windows Home Server, and for the most part you probably can do this. However, if you attempt to do so, you will need to find hardware drivers for those components you wish to reuse. Because Windows Home Server is built upon the Windows Server 2003 platform, you need to find drivers for your hardware for Windows Server 2003. If you cannot locate drivers for this platform, then your hardware will not work with Windows Home Server.

Note Windows Home Server does not support USB 1.1—it supports only USB 2.0. This does not affect you unless you plan to use external storage, in which case you must make sure that your motherboard supports USB 2.0 or it won't work.

The minimum hardware requirements and the recommended hardware requirements are listed and described in Table 1-1. These requirements are found in the *Windows Home Server Getting Started* guide (accessible from the Windows Home Server web site) and may be subject to change, so check the latest version of the document if you are not sure. The recommended hardware requirements are those that will ensure you have a better Windows Home Server experience.

Note You can certainly run Windows Home Server on a computer that meets the minimum hardware requirements. However, if you plan to do more with your Windows Home Server than just use the features provided, you really should consider meeting the recommended requirements or even plan on exceeding them. Don't go overboard, though, because you may not get as much of a return on your investment.

Table 1-1. *Windows Home Server Hardware Requirements*

Requirement	Minimum	Recommended
CPU	1 GHz Pentium 3 (or equivalent)	Pentium 4, AMD x64, or newer processor. Windows Home Server includes a 32-bit operating system, which runs on 32-bit and 64-bit (Intel EM64T and AMD x64) architectures. Future versions of Windows Home Server may support 64-bit processors only, so it is recommended that you use a 64-bit compatible processor in order to make sure that you can upgrade to future versions.
RAM	512 MB	512 MB
Hard drives	70 GB internal (ATA, SATA, or SCSI) hard drive as the primary drive, and any number of additional hard drives of any capacity. The primary (system) hard drive should be as large as possible to ensure that you can copy a large number of files or multiple large files to your home server at the same time.	At least two internal hard drives with 300 GB as the primary (system) hard drive.
Network interface card	100 Mbps Ethernet network interface card.	100 Mbps (or faster) Ethernet network interface card.

■**Caution** Microsoft has stated that future versions of Windows Home Server may support 64-bit processors only. It is recommended that you use a 64-bit compatible processor to make sure that you can upgrade to future versions.

You may also need the devices listed and described in Table 1-2 to install Windows Home Server, depending on the computer manufacturer and whether you are building your own Windows Home Server. These requirements are also found in the *Windows Home Server Getting Started* guide.

■**Tip** For information on the components needed to build your own Windows Home Server, take a look at Appendix A.

Table 1-2. *Other Device Requirements*

Requirement	Description
DVD drive	Internal or external DVD drive. Your home server must be capable of booting from this internal or external DVD drive in order to install Windows Home Server. Follow the computer manufacturer's instructions to configure the computer's BIOS to boot from the DVD drive.
Display	Compatible monitor.
Other devices	Keyboard, mouse, or other compatible pointing device.

There are also a number of network requirements that you must meet in order to use and get the most out of Windows Home Server. These requirements, found in the *Windows Home Server Getting Started* guide, are listed and described in Table 1-3.

Table 1-3. *Windows Home Server Network Requirements*

Requirement	Minimum
Server connection	100 Mbps wired connection.
Home computers	One or more computers that are running a supported operating system, with either a wired or a wireless network connection.
Internet connection	Broadband connection.
Broadband router/firewall device	An external Internet broadband router/firewall device with 100 Mbps wired Ethernet connection.
	Additionally, Windows Home Server assumes that your home computers get their IP address from the router/firewall device on your home network.

■**Note** To see a list of supported home computer operating systems, take a look at Chapter 4.

■**Note** Your Windows Home Server must be connected to your home network via a wired connection—wireless is not supported. See Appendix A for more information about home networking.

Buying a Windows Home Server System

By the time you are reading this book, there should be a number of Windows Home Servers on the market from different manufacturers, with that number increasing as time goes on.

Buying a Windows Home Server rather than building one yourself has numerous advantages, including the following:

- The hardware is all prebuilt for you and you will have confidence that it will all work with the Windows Home Server software.

- You will get support from the manufacturer.

- The form factor of the Windows Home Server could be a lot smaller than one you build yourself.

- Buying one might actually work out to be cheaper than building one.

- Sometimes it is just plain easier to buy one thing that has everything you need!

Hewlett-Packard was one of the first manufacturers to announce its intent to release a machine that runs Windows Home Server software—the HP MediaSmart Server, shown in Figure 1-2. The MediaSmart Server is essentially a Windows Home Server that has a reduced form factor that HP describes as "a powerful home server allowing access to personal documents and digital entertainment from anywhere in the world."

Figure 1-2. *The HP MediaSmart Server*

This product, one of the first variants of a Windows Home Server, has the capability to support four separate SATA hard drives, as you can see in Figure 1-3. This should give you a real indication of the actual size of the HP MediaSmart Server, because it is not much taller than those four hard drive bays.

The specification of the HP MediaSmart Server is as follows (although it is important to note that this specification might be different by the time you are reading this):

- AMD 1.8 GHz 64-bit Sempron processor

- 10/100/1000 RJ45 Ethernet

- SATA 7200 RPM hard disk drives

- Size: 14cm (W) × 25cm (H) × 23cm (D)

- Four internal hard disk drive bays

- Up to 7.5 terabytes storage

- 4 USB 2.0 ports

- Internal universal power supply

You may notice from the preceding specification that there is no CD or DVD drive; that's because one is not needed on this particular machine! If you needed one, you could always connect a USB DVD drive in order to install additional software.

Figure 1-3. *A better view of the HP MediaSmart Server*

So that was a very quick look at one Windows Media Server. You should take a look at what is available currently and make a decision whether to buy one or build one. If you decide to buy one, make sure it is the right one for you. Only you will know what else you might want to use the Windows Home Server for, so keep that in mind when shopping around.

Windows Home Server Software

Depending on the Windows Home Server you may have purchased or built, you should have some Windows Home Server software. That software will include specific Windows Home Server media:

- *Windows Home Server Installation DVD*: The DVD you use to install the Windows Home Server software on the Windows Home Server computer

- *Windows Home Server Connector Software CD*: The CD that you use to install the Windows Home Server Connector software onto each of your home computers

- *Windows Home Server Home Computer Restore CD*: The CD that you use if you need to perform a system restore on one of your home computers

---

■**Note** During the installation of the Windows Home Server software, a Software shared folder is created on the Windows Home Server that contains both the Windows Home Server Connector software and the Windows Home Server Home Computer Restore CD software. For more information on the Windows Home Server Connector software, take a look at Chapter 4, and for more information on using the Windows Home Server Home Computer Restore CD, take a look at Chapter 7.

Summary

So now you have a high-level view of what Windows Home Server is and what it can do for you. In the upcoming chapters, each of the elements of Windows Home Server will be examined in detail. You have also seen what software you actually get as part of Windows Home Server and the different requirements for running Windows Home Server.

CHAPTER 2

■■■

Windows Home Server Installation

This chapter leads you step-by-step through the process of installing (or reinstalling) Windows Home Server. If you intend to install Windows Home Server fresh on a new or used computer (or one that you built yourself) that doesn't have Windows Home Server preinstalled, you should first read the "Checking the Prerequisites" section to make sure the computer is capable of running Windows Home Server, and then go through the installation procedure in the "Installing Windows Home Server" section. If you purchased a computer with Windows Home Server preinstalled but need to reinstall it for one reason or another, begin with the section "Reinstalling Windows Home Server." Also go to that section if you install Windows Home Server yourself and later need to reinstall it. This chapter also provides a "Troubleshooting the Setup" section if you run into problems during the installation of Windows Home Server.

■**Note** If you purchased a computer with Windows Home Server preinstalled and aren't having any problems, you can skip this chapter. If you ever need to reinstall Windows Home Server, you can come back to this chapter for guidance and assistance. Note that each computer manufacturer may have a different way of reinstalling Windows Home Server, so you should check the manual that came with your Windows Home Server computer. For example, a manufacturer might have built-in flash memory that contains all the installation software and drivers, in which case reinstallation might be as simple as pushing a button.

Checking the Prerequisites

Before you install Windows Home Server, you should ensure that you have the following available (see Chapter 1 for more information on system requirements):

- A computer capable of running Windows Home Server.

- A mouse, keyboard, and monitor, all connected to the Windows Home Server.

■**Note** As stated in Chapter 1, Windows Home Server does not need to have a mouse, keyboard, or monitor connected in order to run. However, you may need to connect them to install Windows Home Server; if you do, make sure you connect them now. Some Windows Home Servers may not have any ports on them, requiring that you install or reinstall the Windows Home Server software via another computer connected to your network; if you're in that situation, consult the manual that came with your Windows Home Server to find out what you need to do.

- A working network connection connected to the Windows Home Server. This network connection must be wired, because Windows Home Server does not support using a wireless connection. If you are new to networking concepts or would just like a little refresher, please take a look at Appendix A.

- The Windows Home Server installation DVD, if required, depending on the installation options available from the manufacturer of the Windows Home Server.

- A Windows Home Server product key, which you need during the installation or during the product activation, depending on the installation options available from the manufacturer of the Windows Home Server.

■**Note** Your computer must be capable of booting from DVD; otherwise the installation will not be able to take place. You may need to go into the BIOS of your computer to set the boot priority so that the DVD is first in the list. Consult the documentation that came with your computer if you are unsure how to do this.

Installing Windows Home Server

You must complete the following steps to successfully install Windows Home Server. As you will see, the majority of the installation does not require any input from you, but to help you understand what is being performed, I have included screenshots and descriptions so that you know what is happening at each step of the installation.

■**Caution** If you plan to use a hard drive that already contains some data on it, you should back up that hard drive before you go any further, because it will be formatted during the setup process and all data will be lost.

1. Ensure that the computer on which you will be installing Windows Home Server is connected to the power, monitor, keyboard, mouse, and network.

2. Power on the computer and place the Windows Home Server installation DVD in the computer's DVD drive (you may need to power off the computer and power on again after you have loaded the DVD into the drive if the boot check happens too quickly to read the DVD when you first put it in the DVD drive).

You should see a screen displaying "Windows is loading files," as shown in Figure 2-1. At this point there is nothing for you to do other than wait—but don't worry, this should only take a few moments. If you see this screen, at least you know that setup is starting.

Figure 2-1. *Windows is loading the setup files.*

After the setup files are loaded into memory, you should see the "Setup is initializing" screen, as shown in Figure 2-2.

■**Note** This is the point where problems may occur due to issues with hard drives, memory, and other components. If you get an error message at this point (or any other in the setup), go to the "Troubleshooting Setup" section toward the end of this chapter for more information, and then return to Step 3 after you have resolved the issue.

Figure 2-2. *Setup is initializing.*

3. After initialization is complete, you are presented with the Welcome to Windows Home Server Setup screen, shown in Figure 2-3. Click Next to continue.

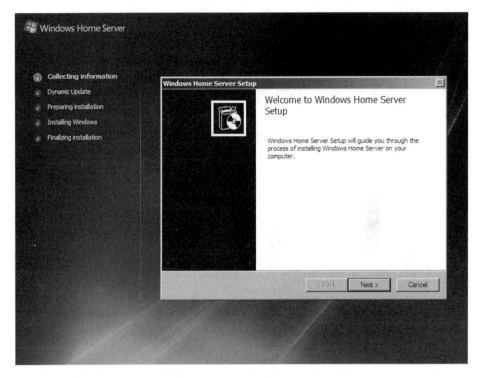

Figure 2-3. *The Welcome to Windows Home Server Setup screen*

4. On the Load Additional Storage Drivers screen, shown in Figure 2-4, you need to ensure that all of your hard drives are listed. For example, Figure 2-4 shows a single 66 GB ATA drive attached.

5. If all of your drives are shown, click Next to continue. If for some reason one (or more) of your hard drives is not displayed here, you might need to load an additional driver. See the troubleshooting section "Unlisted Storage Driver," later in the chapter, for instructions on what to do.

Note You should keep the USB flash drive or floppy disk connected during the remainder of the installation process to ensure that the drivers are accessed whenever they are needed.

---

6. When you see the next screen, Select an Installation Type, shown in Figure 2-5, select New Installation, the default choice for a new, clean installation of Windows Home Server. If the Server Reinstallation option is available in the Installation Type dropdown list, then you already have Windows Home Server installed, in which case you should be following the instructions in the "Reinstalling Windows Home Server" section, later in the chapter. Start at Step 5 in that section.

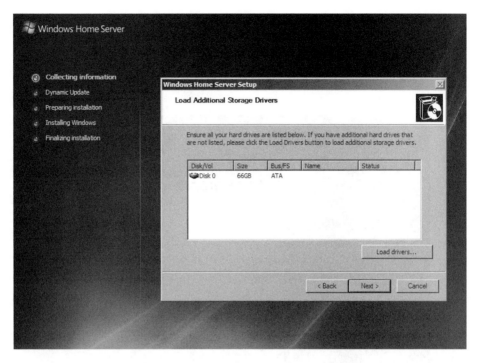

Figure 2-4. *Confirm that all of your hard drives are visible to the Setup program.*

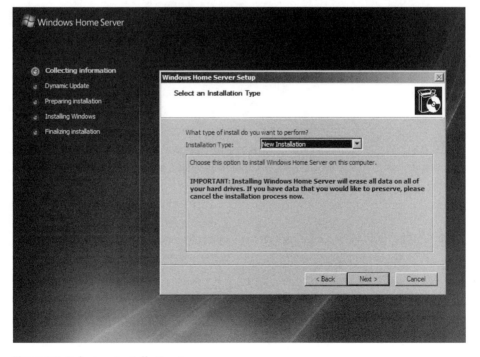

Figure 2-5. *Select an installation type.*

7. On the Select Your Regional and Keyboard Settings screen, shown in Figure 2-6, set the Time and Currency Format option to the area you are in; for example, English (United States). Set the Keyboard or Input Method option to your location; for example, choosing US sets the keyboard for the U.S. format. When you have selected both settings, click Next to continue.

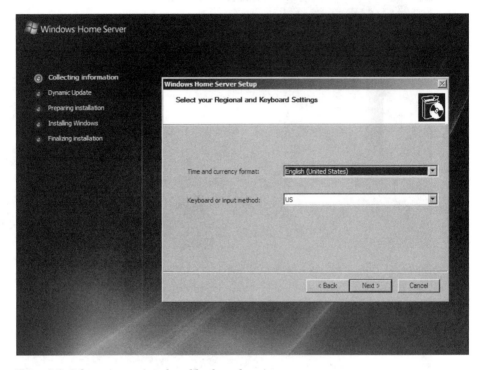

Figure 2-6. *Select your regional and keyboard settings.*

■**Note** If an option for your location and language is not available, try selecting one that you are comfortable using for now and consider contacting Microsoft to find out if and when they might release a version of Windows Home Server that supports what you need.

8. On the End-User License Agreement screen, shown in Figure 2-7, carefully read through the License Agreement (sometimes referred to as the EULA). If you agree to its terms (if you don't, you won't be able to install and use Windows Home Server), click the I Accept This Agreement radio button and then click Next to continue.

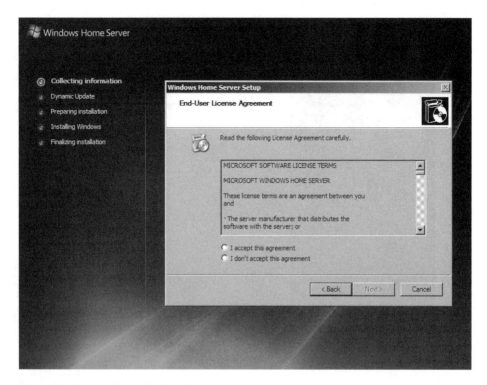

Figure 2-7. *Review the End-User License Agreement.*

■**Note** You will not be able to click the Next button until you have clicked the I Accept This Agreement radio button.

9. The next screen asks you to enter your Windows Home Server Product Key, as shown in Figure 2-8. The Windows Home Server Product Key should be located either inside the DVD case or on a sticker on the actual computer if you have purchased a Windows Home Server computer. Type in the Product Key carefully and then click Next to continue.

■**Note** If the Product Key is not accepted, try entering it again, checking each entry as you type it. If you have entered the Product Key correctly, and you have checked it, and it still does not work, either contact Microsoft or contact the place you purchased the software or hardware and discuss the problem with them.

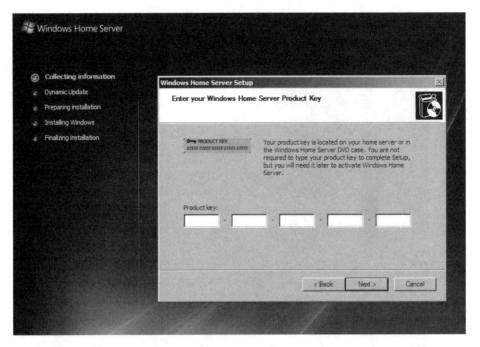

Figure 2-8. *Enter your Windows Home Server Product Key.*

■**Caution** You should always purchase software from a reputable source. If the product key does not work and you did not obtain the software from a reputable source, then you could have a pirated copy of Windows Home Server. To find out whether your copy is licensed by Microsoft, contact Microsoft, who can advise you whether it is legal or not.

---

10. The next stage is to actually name your Windows Home Server, as shown in Figure 2-9. By default, the Home Server name is SERVER and you could quite easily just leave it as that. However, you should name it something else so that you remember it better and to add an additional layer of security—there will be a lot of Windows Home Server computers called SERVER. If you don't intend to set up remote access to your Windows Home Server, then this is not really much of an issue. Enter the name for your Windows Home Server and then click Next to continue.

■**Note** The Windows Home Server name can contain

- Up to 15 characters with no spaces in it.

- Letters, numbers, and hyphens, although you need to have at least one letter in the name.

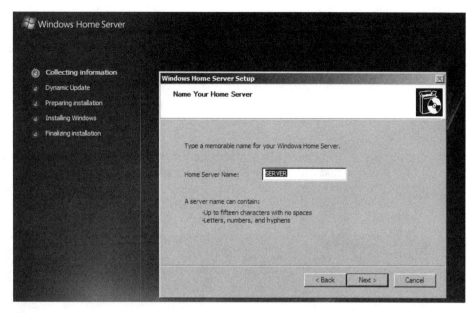

Figure 2-9. *Name your Windows Home Server.*

11. The Formatting Hard Drives screen, shown in Figure 2-10, lists all the hard drives and volumes and reminds you that all the data will be lost on those drives when the installation begins and the drives are formatted. To continue with the installation, select the I Acknowledge That All Data on These Drives Will Be Lost check box and then click the Next button to continue.

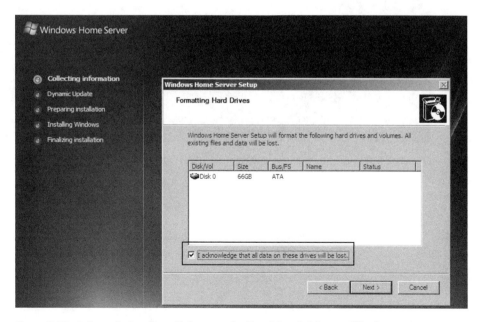

Figure 2-10. *Acknowledge that all data on the listed hard drives will be lost.*

■**Caution** This really is the point of no return for the drive or drives on which you are installing Windows Home Server. If there is any data on those drives that you want to keep, now is the time to make a copy of that data before continuing with the installation. If you need to back up any data, just click the Cancel button and shut down the computer. After you have copied or backed up your data, start the installation process again from Step 2.

---

12. You are warned again that all data on your hard drives will be deleted, and asked once again to confirm that you are sure you want to continue, as shown in Figure 2-11. You may also be asked to remove any external drives you currently have attached. If you are really sure at this point that you want to continue, click the Yes button.

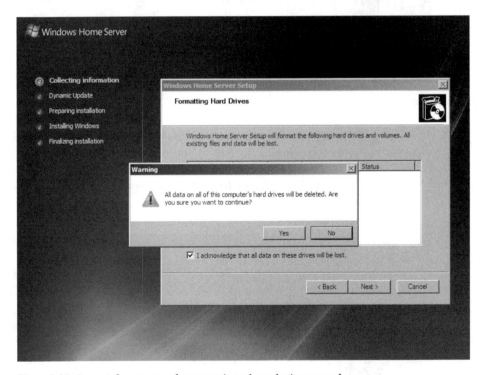

Figure 2-11. *Respond to yet another warning about losing your data.*

■**Note** If you need to back up any data, just click the No button and shut down the computer. After you have copied or backed up your data, start the installation process again from Step 2.

---

13. You should now see the Ready to Install Windows Home Server screen, shown in Figure
2-12. Click the Start button to begin the actual installation.

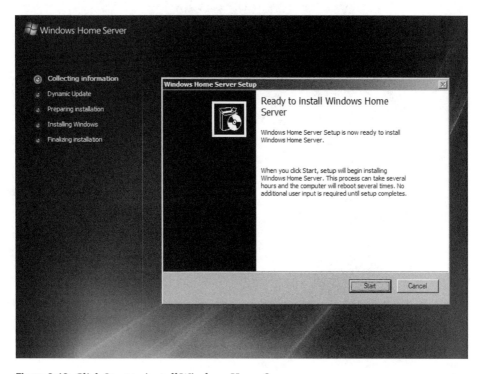

Figure 2-12. *Click Start to install Windows Home Server.*

The installation itself can take several hours to complete. How long it takes depends on
the type of hardware you are using, but on the whole the process is likely to take somewhere
between 45 minutes and an hour to complete, so just be patient. Also, the computer will
reboot several times; don't be alarmed, it's supposed to do that.

At this stage, you can either sit and watch the installation happen (I did the first time) or
go make yourself a cup of coffee and come back in a little while. You will know that the installation has completed successfully when you see the Windows Home Server Welcome screen,
shown in Figure 2-13.

And that is it for installation of Windows Home Server. Next, you need to perform a number of configuration tasks, which are covered in Chapter 3. The rest of this chapter covers
server reinstallation, upgrading, and troubleshooting, so if you don't need any of that information at this point, feel free to move on to Chapter 3.

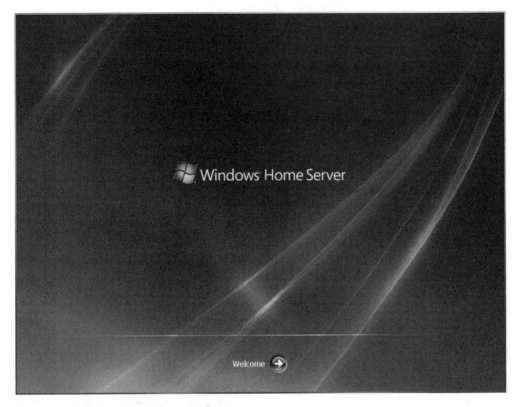

Figure 2-13. *Windows Home Server Welcome screen*

Reinstalling Windows Home Server

You need to completely reinstall Windows Home Server if, for example, your system drive has become corrupted, you have forgotten the Windows Home Server password, or you want to replace the primary system hard drive with a larger one. This section takes you through the reinstallation process.

You have two options open to you:

- Completely reinstall the Windows Home Server from scratch, losing all data but starting from a completely clean Windows Home Server installation. If you want to use this option, go to Step 6 in the "Installing Windows Home Server" section, earlier in the chapter, and follow the instructions from there.

- Perform a Windows Home Server reinstallation and preserve your shared folders and backups. This option is the focus of this section. Note that all server settings and user accounts will be deleted. You will need to reset the server settings and re-create the user accounts. It would be a good idea at this point to create a record of any specific settings changes you made and a list of all the user accounts you will need to re-create—it will save you time later!

To perform a Windows Home Server reinstallation, follow these steps:

Note The following steps might be different if you are reinstalling a purchased Windows Home Server. For example, you may be able to completely restore your Windows Home Server from a special hidden partition on the hard drive, or from flash ROM installed in the hardware itself. Check the documentation that came with your Windows Home Server to find out what you need to do.

---

1. Ensure that the computer on which you will be reinstalling Windows Home Server is connected to the power, monitor, keyboard, mouse, and network.

2. Power on the computer and place the Windows Home Server installation DVD in the computer's DVD drive (you may need to power off the computer and power on again after you have loaded the DVD into the drive if the boot check happens too quickly to read the DVD when you first put it in the DVD drive).

3. You may need to set the DVD drive as the primary boot device in the BIOS to get it to boot directly from the installation DVD or you might be able to select the boot device on the computer—consult your computer manual to check how to do this if you are not sure. If the computer boots from the DVD, you should see a screen similar to the one shown in Figure 2-14. Press any key to boot from the DVD.

Note You may have to be quick here because this screen does not stay on for long. If you miss your opportunity, just reboot the computer and start again.

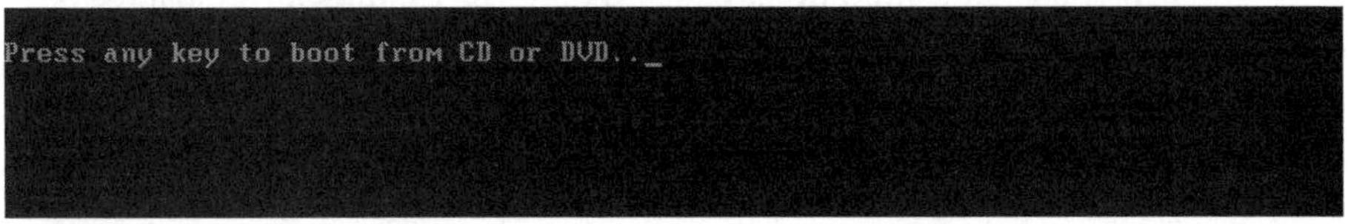

Figure 2-14. *Press any key to boot from CD or DVD.*

After the setup files are loaded into memory, you should see the "Setup is initializing" screen, shown in Figure 2-15.

Figure 2-15. *Setup is initializing.*

4. After initialization is complete, you are presented with the Welcome to Windows Home Server Setup screen, shown in Figure 2-16. Click Next to continue.

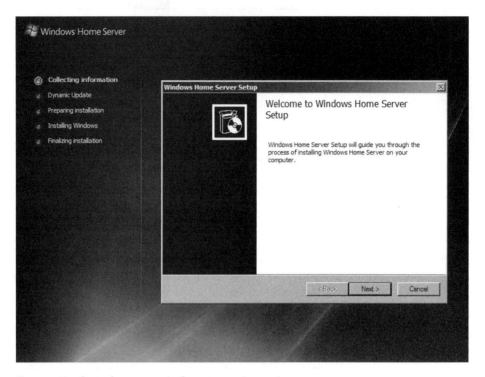

Figure 2-16. *The Welcome to Windows Home Server Setup screen*

5. The next screen is the Load Additional Storage Drivers screen, shown in Figure 2-17. You will notice that there are two volumes shown in the example (you may have more than this depending on your particular setup). The volumes are as follows:

- *Vol 1*: This is the SYS volume and contains all the files and settings for your Windows Home Server. This is the volume that will be deleted and re-created during the server reinstallation process.

- *Vol 2*: This is the DATA volume and contains all of your shared folders and computer backups. This volume will remain untouched during the server reinstallation process.

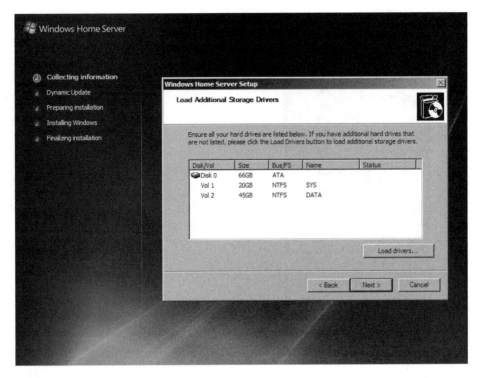

Figure 2-17. *Confirm that your drives and volumes are listed.*

6. If all of your drives are listed, click the Next button to continue. If all of your drives are not listed, see the troubleshooting section "Unlisted Storage Driver," later in the chapter, for instructions on what to do.

7. The next screen, Select an Installation Type, shown in Figure 2-18, presents a default installation type of Server Reinstallation. Click Next to continue. (If you decide at this point to choose New Installation, in which you will lose all data but start from a completely clean Windows Home Server installation, go to Step 6 in the "Installing Windows Home Server" section, earlier in the chapter, and follow the instructions from there.)

■**Note** If you select Server Reinstallation, the system partition (the area of the hard drive on which the Windows Home Server system files are stored) will be formatted and Windows Home Server will be reinstalled onto the cleanly formatted drive. This means that all of your server settings and user accounts will be deleted and you will need to re-create them, so make sure you have made a list of all the user accounts to be re-created. Your shared folders and backups are not affected by the Server Reinstallation option, so you don't have to worry about losing them!

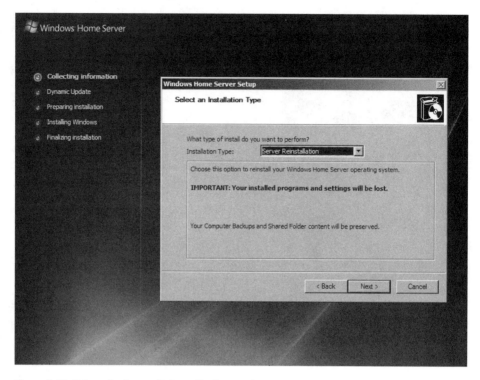

Figure 2-18. *Select the Server Reinstallation option.*

From this point, the reinstallation steps are exactly the same as those for a clean installation, so go to Step 7 in the "Installing Windows Home Server" section earlier in this chapter and continue the reinstallation from there.

■**Note** Don't forget that once the Windows Home Server reinstallation process has completed, you will need to re-create all of your user accounts and perform all of your settings changes in order to get your Windows Home Server back into the working state you had it in before you needed to perform the reinstallation. This includes giving each user their access rights back to any folders that they previously had access to.

Upgrading Windows Home Server

The only upgrade option available is if you are currently running the 120-day evaluation copy of Windows Home Server. Rather than start from scratch and lose all of your shared folders and backups, you can follow the steps in the "Reinstalling Windows Home Server" section and enter the product key from the fully licensed Windows Home Server software. This will result in the 120-day evaluation version being replaced with a fully licensed version, and then all you have to do is re-create the accounts and permissions and install any applications that you had running on your Windows Home Server before performing the reinstallation.

Troubleshooting the Setup

This section helps you to troubleshoot some of the more common problems you might have encountered during installation or reinstallation of Windows Home Server, including insufficient memory, a failed setup, an unlisted storage driver, or hard drive problems.

Insufficient Memory

As Chapter 1 pointed out, Windows Home Server requires a minimum of 512 MB of RAM in order to run, and this is required to perform the installation process. If you do not have sufficient RAM installed in the computer, you will see an error message similar to that shown in Figure 2-19.

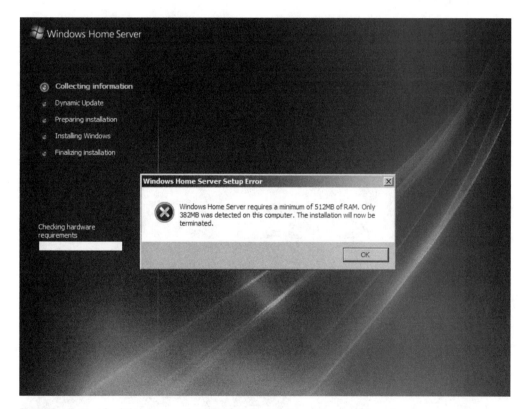

Figure 2-19. *You don't have enough RAM installed in the computer to continue.*

The solution to this problem is simple—add additional RAM until you meet the 512 MB requirement.

■**Note** Although you can run Windows Home Server with 512 MB of RAM, that is the minimum that is needed. If you want your Windows Home Server to run smoothly and not run low on system resources, you should consider increasing the RAM to at least 1 GB or possibly even 2 GB, although this may be completely dependent on what else you want to use the computer for. However, at the time of writing, the cost of RAM is very low, so consider putting in enough not only for what you want to do today, but also a little more for what you might want to do tomorrow.

Failed Setup

If the Windows Home Server setup fails for any reason, you will see an error message displayed similar to the one shown in Figure 2-20 (for example, you see this error message after you click OK in Figure 2-19).

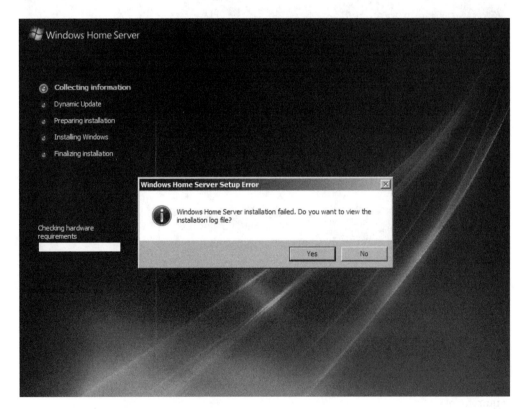

Figure 2-20. *The Windows Home Server installation has failed.*

At this point you have the option to view the installation log file. If you know exactly why the setup has failed, then you may not gain anything from reviewing the log. If you are not sure why the setup failed, or if you are just curious, then click the Yes button to display the installation log file.

The installation log file is just a simple text file that shows all of the setup information, as shown in Figure 2-21.

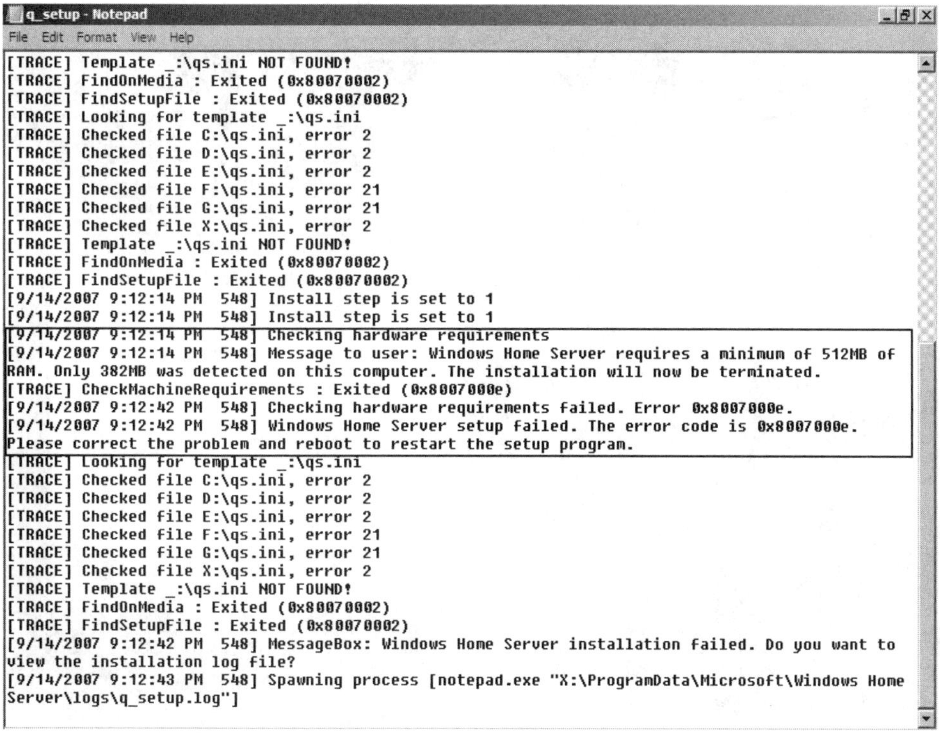

Figure 2-21. *The installation log file*

There may be a lot of information contained within the log file, depending on where the installation failed. Most of the information may mean nothing to the casual observer, but you may be able to glean some information from it. In the example in Figure 2-21, you can see that the failure happened when the installation program checked the hardware requirements and found insufficient RAM. The log files shows that a message was then displayed to the user to inform them that Windows Home Server requires a minimum of 512 MB of RAM and that the installation will be terminated (shown in Figure 2-19).

■**Note** You will notice a series of error codes in the log file; for example, 0x8007000e. If the information contained in the installation log file is not very helpful, you might try doing a search on the Internet for that error code, or contacting Microsoft Product Support and telling them the error code and asking for some assistance.

When you have finished reviewing the installation log file, close it either by choosing File ➤ Exit or by clicking the X button in the top-right corner of the window. You then see the Cannot Complete Windows Home Server Setup Wizard screen, shown in Figure 2-22. Click the Finish button and then attempt to resolve whichever problem you experienced. After you have resolved the problem, start the installation all over again.

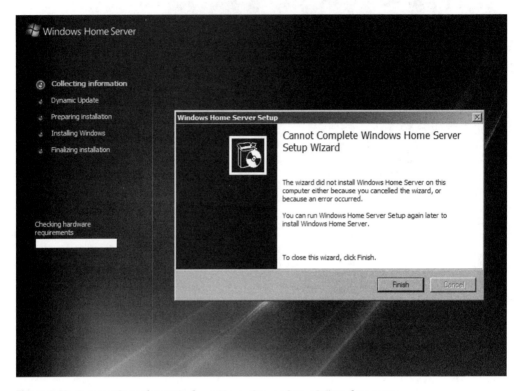

Figure 2-22. *Cannot Complete Windows Home Server Setup Wizard message*

Unlisted Storage Driver

During the setup process, if one (or more) of your hard drives is not listed on the Load Additional Storage Drivers screen (refer to Figure 2-4), you might need to load an additional driver. Follow these steps:

1. Click the Load Drivers button and then locate the device driver file, as shown in Figure 2-23. If you don't see the device driver file, check the manufacturer's web site for an updated device driver. If there is one, download it and write it to a CD so that you can then use the CD when searching for the new driver.

2. Select the relevant device driver file and click Open to continue.

3. When you have loaded the additional device driver file or files, all of your hard drives should appear in the list on the Load Additional Storage Drivers screen. If this is the case, click Next to continue, and return to Step 6 in the "Installing Windows Home Server" section or Step 7 in the "Reinstalling Windows Home Server" section, whichever is appropriate.

4. If one or more hard drives are still not shown, check all the connections inside the computer (sometimes the problem is as simple as a loose cable). If this turns out to be the problem, then once you have put your computer back together, you will need to start the installation, or reinstallation, process again from the start.

Note If you do not have experience exploring the inside of a computer, consult the manual that came with your computer or motherboard for information about safety precautions and the various connections for your computer.

---

5. If the problem still isn't resolved, then something slightly more serious might be wrong. You might want to consider switching off the computer and removing or replacing the hard drive. For example, the Windows Home Server Setup may have issues with a drive controller during the installation process but it might run perfectly once the installation has completed. You can easily add the drive and controllers later, which is explained in Chapter 8.

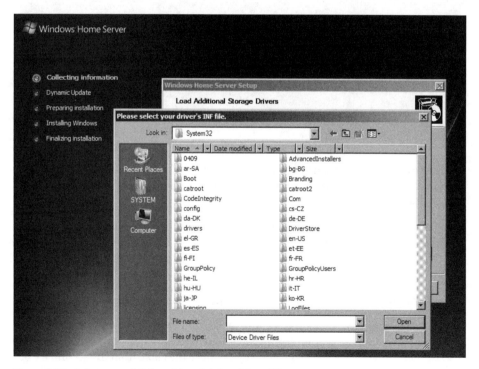

Figure 2-23. *Select an additional hard drive driver file.*

Hard Drive Problems

If you have a problem with your hard drive, you may see an error message similar to the one shown in Figure 2-24.

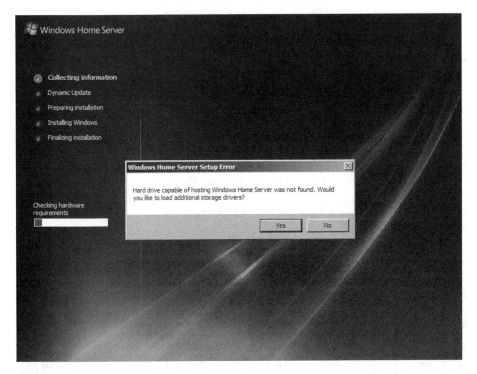

Figure 2-24. *Hard drive not found*

In the case of this particular error message, the error tells you that a hard drive capable of hosting Windows Home Server was not found. This could be for any number of reasons, although some of the more common would be the following:

- A hardware problem with the hard drive. Check to see whether it is spinning. You could do this by either listening to the drive when the computer powers up or by placing your hand on the drive and feeling the vibrations, although the latter action is not really recommended.

- The hard drive is not plugged in correctly. Check all the cables.

- You have plugged the hard drive into the secondary IDE port on your computer's motherboard and there is nothing plugged into the primary IDE port, and this configuration is not supported. If this is the case, just remove the cable from the secondary port and plug it into the primary. Most modern motherboards display which port is the primary and which is the secondary. If you are not sure, consult the manual that came with the computer or motherboard.

- A driver is needed in order for the hard drive to be used. If this is the case, click the Yes button to load an additional storage driver for your hard drive.

If none of the preceding solutions work, you should try another hard drive, if you have one available.

Another common error is the one shown in Figure 2-25.

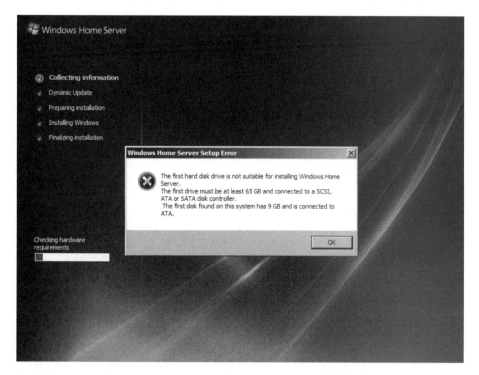

Figure 2-25. *Insufficient hard drive space available to perform the installation*

In the case of this example, the minimum required free hard drive space to perform the installation of Windows Home Server is 65 GB and the hard drive in this computer has only 9 GB available. The solution to this problem is to simply remove the hard drive and replace it with one that has a minimum of 65 GB.

■**Note** Sometimes the messages are not as useful as they may appear to be. For example, where the error is clearly the result of insufficient hard drive space, the recommended course of action might be to either change the BIOS settings or load additional storage drivers. So, while it is very important to read and understand the error messages that are displayed, you will also need to exercise a little judgment when it comes to the possible solutions.

Summary

This chapter explained how to install and reinstall Windows Home Server. It also examined some of the more common setup problems and offered possible solutions. The next chapter takes you through the steps that you need to perform to configure your Windows Home Server installation.

CHAPTER 3

■■■

Windows Home Server Post-Installation Configuration

Now that you have successfully installed Windows Home Server, the next step is to perform the post-installation configuration. This includes completing the setup process, logging into Windows Home Server, checking hardware and installing drivers, activating your copy of Windows Home Server, launching Windows Update, and installing additional software.

Completing the Setup Process

There are only a half dozen more steps to complete before you can start using Windows Home Server, so and it won't be long before you are ready to go.

1. If you successfully completed the installation steps in Chapter 2, at this point you should be viewing the Windows Home Server Welcome screen, shown in Figure 3-1. If so, click the arrow. If you did not reach this screen, then you might have encountered a problem with the installation and setup process. Try restarting your Windows Home Server computer and see if that helps. If it does not help, you need to restart the setup process—power off your computer and go back to Chapter 2.

2. The next screen is the Type a Password for Windows Home Server page, shown in Figure 3-2. You will use the password that you choose here when you need to configure the Windows Home Server from the Windows Home Server Console, and when you need to log into the Windows Home Server computer itself, although you will need to do that only very rarely. Enter the password you want to use, and then enter it again to confirm it (see the sidebar, "Creating a Strong Password"). You can also enter a password hint, which you can request to see if you forget the password. When you have entered these items, click the right arrow to continue.

■**Note** The password hint will be shown to anyone who clicks the link to display it. Therefore, you should create a password hint that has a unique meaning to you and won't enable anyone else to guess the Windows Home Server password.

Figure 3-1. *Click the arrow on the Windows Home Server Welcome screen.*

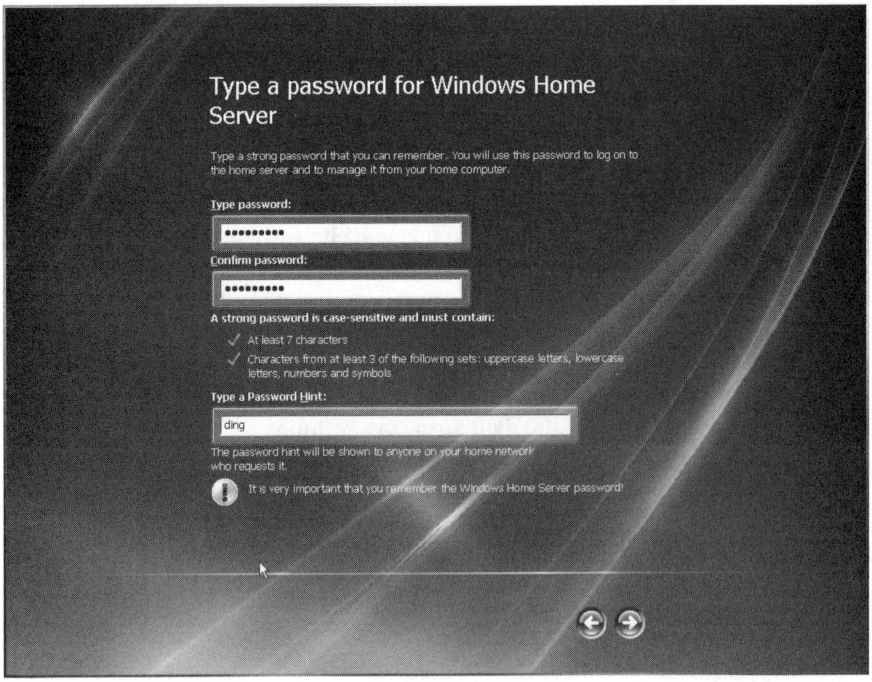

Figure 3-2. *Create a password for Windows Home Server.*

CREATING A STRONG PASSWORD

The password you enter in Step 2 must be a strong password, meaning that it must be at least seven characters in length and must contain at least three of the following four character sets:

- Uppercase letters

- Lowercase letters

- Numbers

- Symbols (such as !, *, %, etc.)

The password is also case-sensitive, so make sure that Caps Lock is not on, unless of course you want to use all capital letters.

You should choose a password that is not easy to guess. Steer clear of obvious passwords, such as the name of your child, pet, spouse, street, your birth date, and so on. Also, don't use passwords such as your favorite band or football team. And if you need to write down the password, make sure you keep it in a safe place and that you don't write "The Windows Home Server password is…" on the same piece of paper. This advice may sound obvious but it does happen.

■**Caution** If you forget the Windows Home Server password and the password hint is not enough to remind you what it is, you have no other option available than to completely reinstall Windows Home Server and create a new password.

3. The Help Protect Windows Home Server Automatically screen, shown in Figure 3-3, gives you the option to select On or Off. The recommended setting is On, which will configure Windows Update and keep Windows Home Server up to date with all relevant security patches and fixes, make your Internet browsing safer, and report any problems. If you choose the Off setting, you will need to manually update Windows Home Server with any relevant security patches and fixes—otherwise, your Windows Home Server will be susceptible to security vulnerabilities and other potential problems that could impact its smooth operation. For more information on how to manually launch Windows Update and check for patches and fixes, see "Launching Windows Update" later in this chapter. Make your selection by clicking the relevant radio button and then click the right arrow to continue.

■**Tip** Choosing the recommended setting of On is a very good idea so that you never miss an important security patch or fix. Yes, you check for updates manually, but why worry about having to remember to do it when Windows Home Server will happily do it for you?

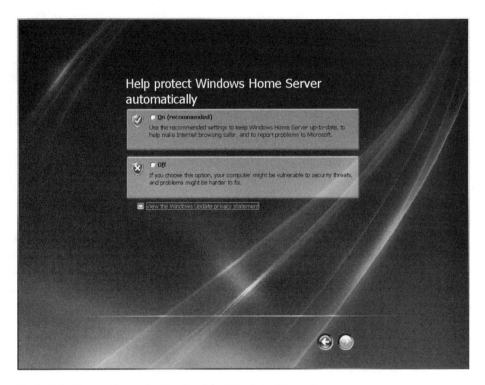

Figure 3-3. *Choose the protection level for Windows Home Server.*

4. On the Customer Experience Improvement Program screen, shown in Figure 3-4, click either the Yes or No radio button to specify whether you want to participate, and then click the right arrow to continue.

■**Note** The Customer Experience Improvement Program (CEIP) is designed to help Microsoft to improve the Windows Home Server product by allowing information about your Windows Home Server computer, its hardware, and how you actually use it to be sent to Microsoft for study. This information is collected in the background and does not affect anything that you are doing. This information is also sent anonymously, so there isn't information collected that could be used to identify you in any way. Whether or not to join is entirely your choice—just remember that the more information Microsoft has about the types of hardware in use and how its customers are using Windows Home Server, the better the improvements and enhancements that it can make to future versions of the product.

---

5. The Windows Error Reporting screen, shown in Figure 3-5, asks you to choose whether you want to enable automatic Windows Error Reporting. Make your selection by clicking the relevant radio button and then click the right arrow to continue.

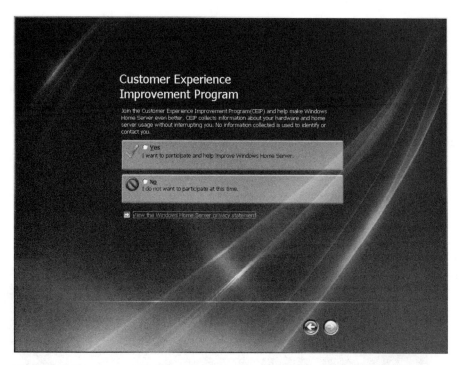

Figure 3-4. *Choose whether to join the Customer Experience Improvement Program.*

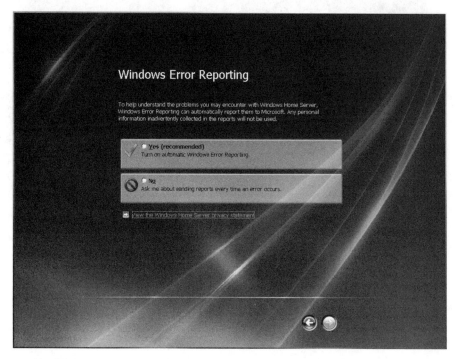

Figure 3-5. *Choose whether to enable automatic Windows Error Reporting.*

■**Note** Windows Error Reporting is used to send information to Microsoft about errors and problems you might encounter while using Windows Home Server. This information can be used to help identify common problems and bugs, which in turn means that Microsoft should release fixes or updates to resolve those problems. Again, agreeing to allow this feature is completely your choice. You should be aware that personal information about you could possibly be included in the reports, although Microsoft states that no personal information that it receives will ever be used. If the prospect of Microsoft having personal information about you makes you uncomfortable, then I suggest that you choose the No option.

---

6. The final screen is the Windows Home Server Setup Is Finished screen, shown in Figure 3-6. All you have to do here is click the arrow to finish. (You may see a slightly different screen from that shown in Figure 3-6, informing you that you need to install drivers for your network card. In that case, follow the steps in the section "Installing Drivers" later in the chapter.)

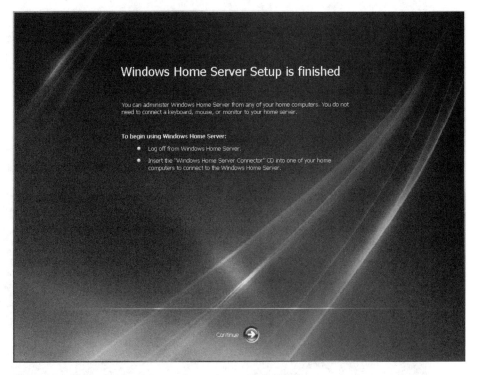

Figure 3-6. *Windows Home Server Setup is now finished.*

Congratulations! You have now successfully completed the installation and configuration of Windows Home Server. After you install the Windows Home Server Connector software (the subject of Chapter 4), you can perform all administrative functions from any other computer in your network.

Although you are advised at this point (see Figure 3-6) to log off from the Windows Home Server and insert the Windows Home Server Connector CD into one of your home computers to connect to the Windows Home Server, before you do that, it is a very good idea to check that all of the various pieces of hardware that are installed in your Windows Home Server computer are functioning correctly and that you don't have to manually install any drivers. The upcoming section "Installing Drivers" leads you through the process of installing drivers for hardware that isn't functioning. Also, there are a number of other tasks you should consider performing before you move on to Chapter 4, such as activating Windows Home Server, launching Windows Update (assuming that you didn't choose to turn on automatic updates in Step 3 during configuration), and installing any additional software. These tasks are also covered in this chapter.

If you do decide to log off at this point, perhaps for a break, and want to log back in to check your drivers, active Windows Home Server, or install additional software before you move on to Chapter 4, the following section explains how to do so.

Logging Into Windows Home Server

If you need to log into your Windows Home Server (which, as you've already read, is discouraged if you can do whatever you plan to do via the Windows Home Server Console instead), it is very simple, as explained in this section. There may be any number of reasons why you need to log in; for example, perhaps you have installed a new driver for some hardware that requires you to reboot your Windows Home Server, and now you want to check that it is functioning correctly (for more on installing drivers, see the next section).

■**Note** Depending on the type of hardware used for your Windows Home Server, to log into the Windows Home Server directly, you need to ensure that the mouse, monitor, and keyboard are connected. You can always remove them again when you have finished; in fact, it is a good idea to do so, if for no other reason than to deter you in the future from using the Windows Home Server for other functions that should be carried out on another computer on your home network. You may need to check the documentation that came with your Windows Home Server for more information.

---

1. Turn on the power to your Windows Home Server. When the Windows Home Server operating system has finished loading, you are presented with the Welcome to Windows login screen, shown in Figure 3-7. Log in by pressing Ctrl+Alt+Delete and entering the password for the Windows Home Server Administrator account.

2. Once you have logged in, you are presented with a warning screen (see Figure 3-8) advising you that there are many applications that can break Windows Home Server and that you should use the Windows Home Server Console installed on a separate computer instead.

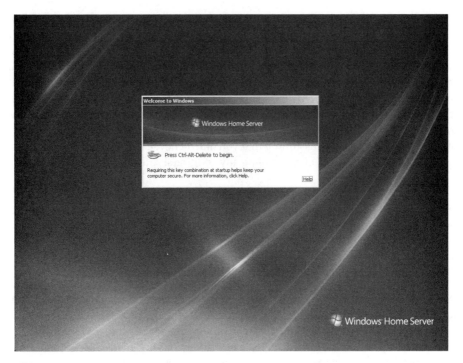

Figure 3-7. *Press Ctrl+Alt+Delete to log into Windows Home Server.*

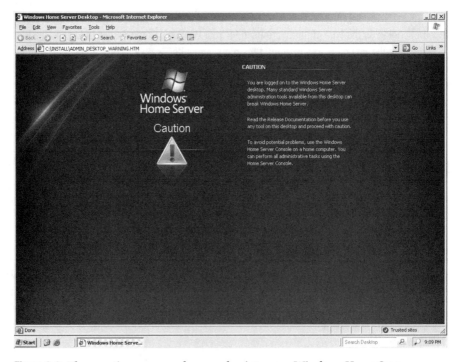

Figure 3-8. *The warning you see when you log into your Windows Home Server*

3. If you still feel that you need to be logged into your Windows Home Server, click the X in the upper-right corner of the caution screen to close the window, and proceed with your session. However, you should take Microsoft's advice and read the Release Documentation before you take any further action. If you decide to heed the caution and log out at this point, click the Start button and choose Shut Down, which displays the Shut Down Windows screen. Select Shut Down in the drop-down list and then click OK.

■**Caution** You really should heed this warning. Avoid the urge to install all of your favorite applications and tools onto the Windows Home Server. In fact, you won't actually be logging into the Windows Home Server as if it were a normal computer, so why install all of your favorite applications and tools on it? Of course, there are certain applications, such as antivirus, that you should in fact install on your Windows Home Server. Before you install any application, consider carefully whether you really need it on the Windows Home Server; if not, install it on one of your home computers.

Installing Drivers

Now that Windows Home Server is installed and effectively operational, you need to make sure that all of your hardware components are working, specifically that they have all the correct drivers installed.

For the most part, you likely will find that all of your hardware is functioning correctly. If you purchased a Windows Home Server computer and it has drivers that you need to install, you most likely have a driver CD or two that came in the box that the Windows Home Server computer came in.

If you do have some driver CDs or DVDs, then insert each in turn in the drive of your Windows Home Server and follow any instructions that came with it. The drivers are likely to be drivers for specific hardware related to that computer, so it is important that you follow the instructions and load all drivers for your computer.

After you have done this, and especially if you do not have any additional driver CDs, you can perform a quick check to see that all of your hardware is functioning correctly and that all drivers are installed. To do this, follow these simple steps:

1. Click the Start button.

2. Right-click the My Computer link on the Start menu and choose Manage, as shown in Figure 3-9. This launches the Computer Management Console, shown in Figure 3-10. This is also referred to as the Microsoft Management Console, or MMC.

■**Note** The Computer Management Console is where you can administer elements of your computer, including devices, and view the event logs, review services, and even perform disk management.

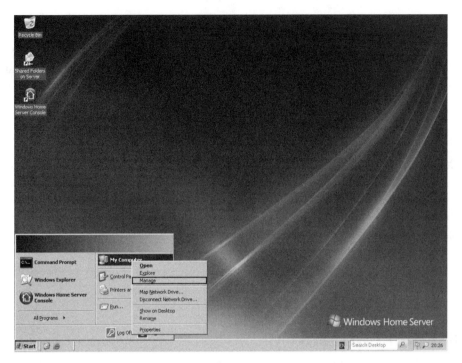

Figure 3-9. *Choose Manage to open the Computer Management Console.*

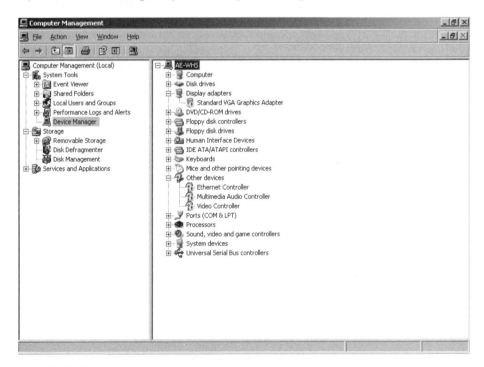

Figure 3-10. *Click Device Manager in the Computer Management Console to view hardware devices.*

3. In the left pane, select Device Manager. You might need to first click the plus sign to the left of System Tools to expand the System Tools node.

4. The right pane lists all of the various device classes that are part of your Windows Home Server computer, such as disk drives, network adaptors, and so on. Look for a device class called Other Devices. If it is listed, then your Windows Home Server computer has detected a device that it either cannot determine what it is, or can determine what it is but doesn't have the correct drivers for it. Expand the Other Devices category by clicking the plus sign. If you don't see a class called Other Devices, then all of your hardware should be correctly identified and have the necessary drivers installed, so you can safely close the Computer Management Console.

■**Note** The majority of any hardware that needs to be identified will appear in the Other Device class, although it is important that you check and confirm anything with an exclamation mark.

---

5. Double-click the device that has the exclamation mark (or the first device in the list if you have more than one) to open the Properties dialog box for that device. Figure 3-11 shows the Properties dialog box for the Ethernet Controller listed in Figure 3-10. This device will be used as an example so that you can follow the process.

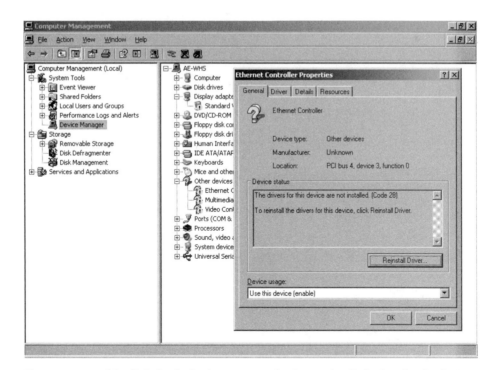

Figure 3-11. *Double-click the device icon to open the Properties dialog box for the device.*

■Note The exclamation mark indicates a possible problem, which could be that the driver is not working or is missing, or that the device itself is nonfunctioning.

6. Click the Driver tab to list the driver details of that device, as shown in the example in Figure 3-12. In this example, the key driver information is not there: the driver provider is unknown, the driver date and version are not available, and there is no digital signature. For a fully functioning device, you would expect to see all of that information, as shown in the example in Figure 3-13.

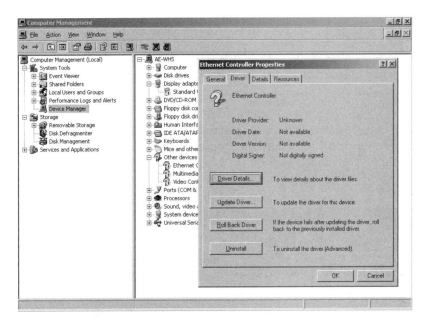

Figure 3-12. *Click the Driver tab of the device's Properties dialog box.*

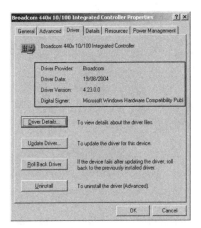

Figure 3-13. *A device driver list for a working device driver*

■**Note** In this example, because you know that the device in question is an Ethernet controller, you should have enough information to be able to find the correct driver CD or at least connect to the Internet to download the latest version from a computer with a working connection. Sometimes, however, the device is listed as Unknown, which can make that task even harder. Often, the simplest way of solving that problem is to systematically eliminate all of the working devices from a list of all the devices you think, or know, are installed in your Windows Home Server and then just try a driver CD and hope for the best. Nine times out of ten this approach will work.

7. Click the Update Driver button to begin the process of installing the driver. You are presented with the Welcome to the Hardware Update Wizard dialog box, shown in Figure 3-14, which offers you two options:

   - *Install the software automatically (Recommended)*: Attempts to locate the driver automatically for you by searching all available drives on your computer, including the CD/DVD drive

   - *Install from a list or specific location (Advanced)*: Allows you to select a specific location where you know the correct driver is located

■**Tip** The best and easiest way to install or update a device driver is to do so from the driver CD, which usually involves just running the setup program on the CD.

   If you are not 100 percent certain about the driver's location, the first option is the best (which is why it is the default and recommended). Ensure that this option is selected and click Next to continue.

8. You may be presented with an option to connect to the Internet and search for the relevant drivers online, as shown in Figure 3-15. If you want to search the Internet for the driver, choose the Yes, Connect and Search for the Software on the Internet radio button and click Next. Otherwise, go to Step 9.

■**Note** Searching on the Internet is always a good option, unless of course, as in the example, the driver you are looking for happens to be for the Ethernet controller, which probably means that you don't have a working connection to the Internet at the moment!

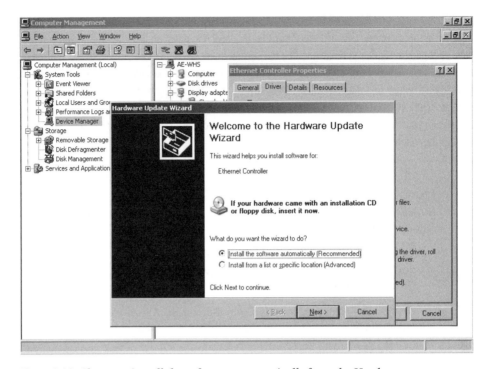

Figure 3-14. *Choose to install the software automatically from the Hardware Update Wizard.*

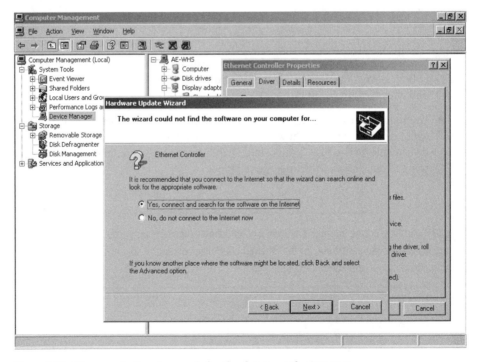

Figure 3-15. *Choose whether to search for the driver on the Internet.*

If the online search fails to find the driver, or you have no connection to the Internet, you will see the Cannot Install This Hardware message, as shown in Figure 3-16. Don't worry, there is still another method you could try, described in Step 9. If the online search is successful, the driver is installed automatically and you are presented with the Completing the Hardware Update Wizard screen—skip to Step 13.

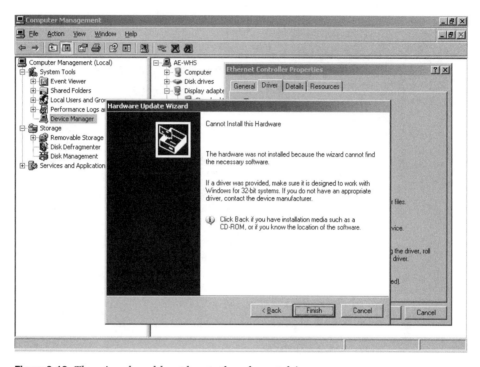

Figure 3-16. *The wizard could not locate the relevant drivers.*

9. Click the Back button repeatedly until you return to the Welcome to the Hardware Update Wizard screen (see Figure 3-14). This time select the Install from a List or Specific Location (Advanced) radio button and click Next to continue.

10. You now have the option of where to search for the drivers, as shown in Figure 3-17. The default option is Search for the Best Driver in These Locations. The check boxes allow you to limit or expand the default search:

   - *Search removable media (floppy, CD-ROM)*: If you choose this option, if the driver is located anywhere on any removable media, it should be located and installed for you automatically.

   - *Include this location in the search*: Choose this option if you know exactly where the driver is (for example, if you have already copied it to a folder on your computer ready to be installed).

If you choose the first check box, click Next. If the driver is located, it is installed automatically and you are presented with the Completing the Hardware Update Wizard screen; skip to Step 13. If you choose only the second check box, go to Step 11. You can of course choose both boxes if you wish, which just means that all removable media, along with the location you specified, will be checked.

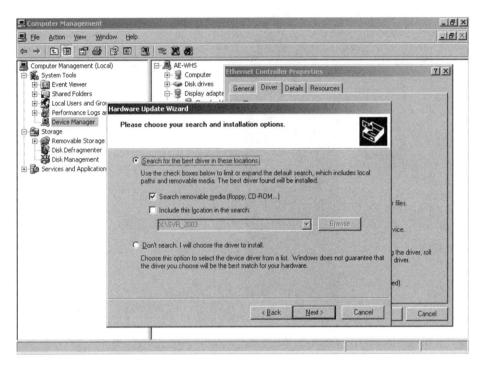

Figure 3-17. *Choose where to search for the drivers.*

11. After checking Include This Location in the Search, click the Browse button.

12. In the Browse for Folder dialog box, shown in Figure 3-18, expand the relevant drives and folders until you find the folder where the driver is located. Select that folder and then click the OK button.

   The driver should be automatically installed for you, assuming that it is compatible. You will know that it has worked when you see the Completing the Hardware Update Wizard screen, shown in Figure 3-19.

13. Click the Finish button to complete the installation process.

14. Repeat all the steps for every device that is listed as needing a driver.

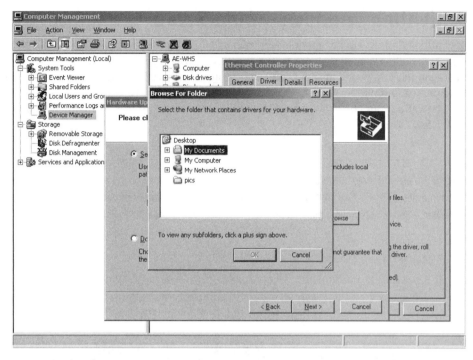

Figure 3-18. *Search a specific folder for the driver.*

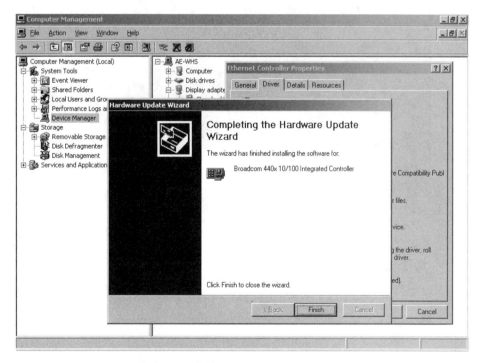

Figure 3-19. *Driver installed successfully*

Activating Windows Home Server

Activating Windows Home Server is very important—if you don't activate your copy within 30 days of installing Windows Home Server, it will stop working. Windows Home Server will then no longer back up your computers and share your folders. You can still activate it after 30 days have passed, but Windows Home Server will not function until you do activate it.

Activating your copy of Windows Home Server is very simple and should take no longer than a few moments:

■**Note** Before you try to activate your copy of Windows Home Server, you must have a working connection to the Internet, so make sure you have confirmed that your network interface card is working, that your Windows Home Server computer is plugged into your home network, and that you can browse the Internet.

---

1. Click the Start button and choose All Programs ➤ Activate Windows, as shown in Figure 3-20. You can also start the activation process by double-clicking the activation icon in the task tray (the one that looks like a pair of keys).

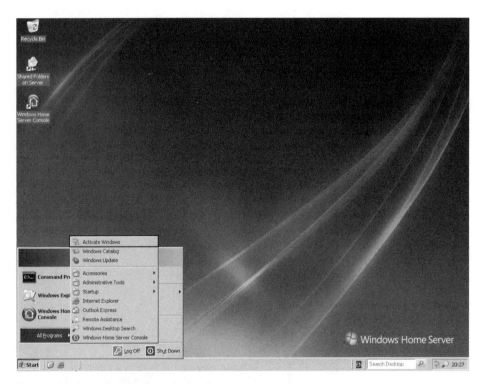

Figure 3-20. *Start the Windows Activation sequence.*

2. On the Let's Activate Windows screen, shown in Figure 3-21, select whichever method you want to use to activate Windows and then click the Next button to continue.

■**Tip** The most common, and easiest, method is to activate Windows over the Internet. For this option, you must be connected to the Internet already.

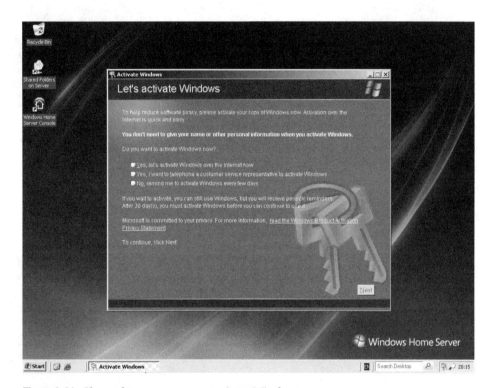

Figure 3-21. *Choose how you want to activate Windows.*

3. You are presented with the option to register your copy of Windows Home Server with Microsoft, as shown in Figure 3-22. This is purely optional and doesn't affect the activation process. Choose whether or not to register and then click the Next button to continue.

4. If all is successful, you should see the Thank You screen, shown in Figure 3-23 (and the activation icon should disappear). This means that your copy of Windows Home Server is now activated and you don't need to worry that it will stop working after 30 days. Click OK to complete the activation process.

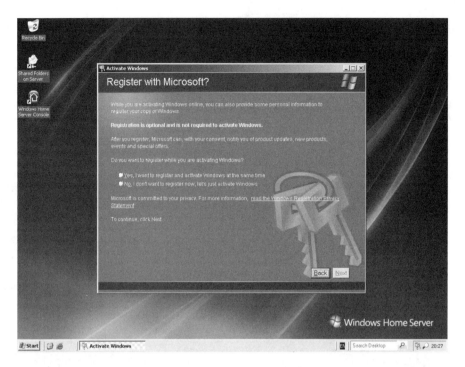

Figure 3-22. *Do you want to register your copy of Windows?*

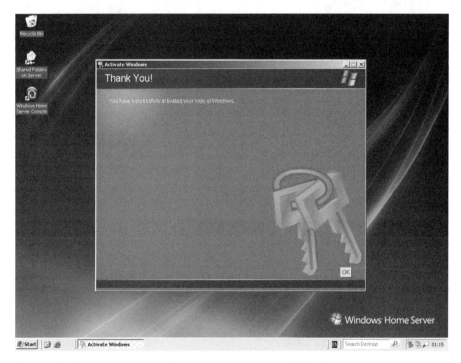

Figure 3-23. *You have successfully activated your copy of Windows Home Server.*

■**Tip** Don't worry if you don't activate your copy of Windows Home Server immediately. You can always activate it later by using the Windows Home Server Console, as long as you do it within the 30 days. For more information on doing this, see Chapter 5.

Launching Windows Update

As anyone who has ever used Windows knows, Microsoft releases a large number of patches for its software. These patches might include software updates, but much more importantly, they include security patches. When new vulnerabilities are discovered in its software, Microsoft releases a patch as soon as possible.

■**Tip** It would be worth subscribing to Microsoft's Security Notification Service to find out about issues and vulnerabilities when they are exposed. You can subscribe by going to `http://www.microsoft.com/technet/security/bulletin/notify.mspx`.

It is a very good idea to keep your machine up to date with security patches, which is why it was a good idea to allow automatic updates in Step 3 of the "Completing the Setup Process" section. If you didn't then, you can active Windows Update now.

Before Windows Update was available, you had to visit the Microsoft Windows Update web site and download whatever patches and fixes you needed. For most people, this worked fine. But some people either did not know about the site or just did not have the time to continually check for updates, so they would miss important patches. It is for those people especially that Windows Update comes in extremely handy.

To launch Windows Update, click the Start button and choose All Programs ➤ Windows Update, as shown in Figure 3-24.

Follow the various steps that appear, including the notification of the Information Bar, the required installation of any Active X controls needed to run Windows Update, and any requests to install newer versions of the software. Once you have completed all of these many steps (and there may even be a couple of reboots involved), you should be presented with a list of available updates. You can then choose and download whichever updates you want to install.

■**Tip** All Windows updates can and should be installed via the Windows Home Server Console, which is covered in Chapter 5.

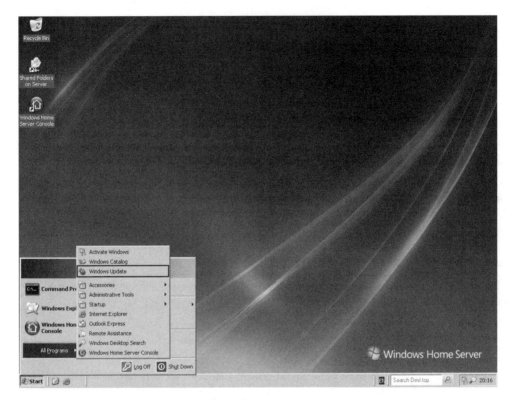

Figure 3-24. *Launch Windows Update from the Start menu.*

Installing Additional Software

When all of the device drivers are installed and working, and you have activated your copy of Windows Home Server (assuming you decided to do so at this stage), you should install any other software that you might need, such as antivirus software. The reason for doing this now is that you may need direct access to your Windows Home Server for whatever software you want or need to install, and it's a lot easier to do it now while everything is connected than later when you have removed the keyboard, monitor, and mouse and have moved your Windows Home Server to its permanent home.

Tip Installing and running antivirus software is extremely important, because you do not want to leave your computer unprotected!

For more information on additional software you could install for your Windows Home Server, take a look at Chapter 13.

Shutting Down

Once you have checked everything and are completely happy with the Windows Home Server installation, including any additional software you may have installed, such as antivirus software, you can safely shut down Windows Home Server and remove the monitor, keyboard, and mouse. Before you reboot the Windows Home Server, you may want to put it in a different location, so that it is out of the way; after all, you won't be accessing it again directly unless you really need to because of a problem or a major change.

To shut down Windows Home Server, click the Start button and choose Shut Down, which displays the Shut Down Windows screen, shown in Figure 3-25. Make sure Shut Down is selected in the drop-down list box and then click OK to shut down.

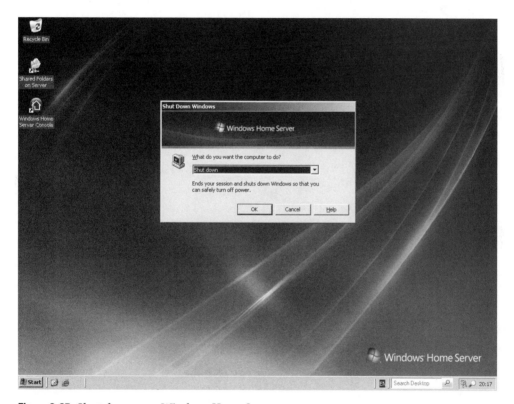

Figure 3-25. *Shut down your Windows Home Server.*

■**Note** If your Windows Home Server will not boot without an attached keyboard or monitor, you may need to make some minor settings changes to the BIOS of your computer to enable booting to take place without these devices attached. Before you make any changes in the BIOS, you should consult the documentation that came with the computer.

Summary

This chapter guided you though the post-installation tasks to configure your Windows Home Server. You learned how to create your Windows Home Server Administrator account, check that the hardware has all the correct drivers installed, and install any missing drivers. You also learned how to activate your copy of Windows Home Server. In the next chapter, you will learn all about the Windows Home Server Connector and how to install it.

CHAPTER 4

■■■

Windows Home Server Connector Installation and Configuration

Now that your Windows Home Server is installed and up and running, you next need to start installing and configuring the Windows Home Server Connector on each of your computers that you want to connect to your Windows Home Server.

The Windows Home Server Connector performs the following functions:

- Connects your computer to your Windows Home Server

- Automatically backs up your home computer on a daily basis

- Monitors the health of your home computer

- Enables you to manage your Windows Home Server from your computer

This chapter first identifies the operating systems on which you can install the Windows Home Server Connector, and then explains how to install the Windows Home Server Connector. It also explains how to remove the Windows Home Server Connector and reinstall it. Finally, for those of you who have multiple network subnets, this chapter describes how to make changes to Windows Firewall to enable computers located on different subnets to connect to your Windows Home Server.

Identifying Supported Operating Systems

You can install the Windows Home Server Connector on any of the following Windows operating systems and their variants:

Windows Vista Operating System

- Windows Vista Home Basic

- Windows Vista Home N (European Union only)

- Windows Vista Home Premium

- Windows Vista Business

- Windows Vista Business N (European Union only)

- Windows Vista Enterprise

- Windows Vista Ultimate

■**Note** Windows Vista Home N and Windows Vista Business N are editions of Windows Vista that do not come preinstalled with Windows Media Player and other related software, including Windows Movie Maker. You can install Windows Media Player on these versions or you can choose to install a third-party media application. These editions are available only in the European Union.

Windows XP Operating System

- Windows XP Home with Service Pack 2 (SP2)

- Windows XP Professional with SP2

- Windows XP Media Center Edition 2005 with SP2 and Rollup 2

- Windows XP Media Center Edition 2005 with SP2

- Windows XP Media Center Edition 2004 with SP2

- Windows XP Tablet Edition with SP2

■**Note** If you have one of the supported operating systems, you can easily add the Connector; if you don't have one of the supported operating systems and you want to gain the benefits of connecting to Windows Home Server, you need to upgrade to a supported operating system, which could be as easy as updating the version of the Service Pack if you are using Windows XP.

Installing the Windows Home Server Connector

This section shows you how to install the Windows Home Server Connector on each computer (the screenshots shown are from a Windows Vista computer, but the steps are identical for a Windows XP computer). If you have the Windows Home Server Connector CD available, start at Step 1 and then skip to Step 9. If you don't have the Windows Home Server Connector CD available, you can connect to the Software share on your Windows Home Server, because a copy of the Windows Home Server Connector software is placed there automatically during the installation of Windows Home Server. Start at Step 2 to connect to the Software share on your Windows Home Server and run the Setup program.

1. Insert the Windows Home Server Connector CD into the drive. In the AutoPlay dialog box, shown in Figure 4-1, click the Run setup.exe option. (If you do not see this dialog box, then locate the CD drive folder manually and double-click Setup.exe.) You may then also be asked to confirm your permission to run the program, in which case click Continue. Next, skip to Step 9.

Figure 4-1. *Run the setup.exe file to begin installation.*

2. Click the Start button and then click Network to view all of the available computers and devices on your home network, as shown in Figure 4-2.

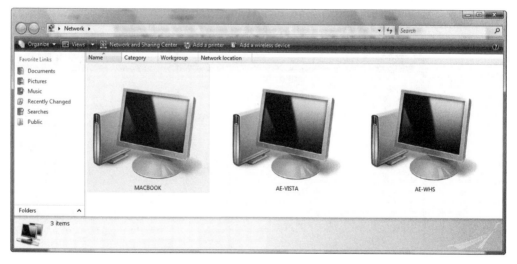

Figure 4-2. *View the available shared computers on your network.*

3. Double-click the computer that represents your Windows Home Server (AE-WHS in the example shown in Figure 4-2).

4. Enter the username and password to access your Windows Home Server, as shown in Figure 4-3, and then click OK to continue.

Figure 4-3. *Enter the username and password to access the Windows Home Server share.*

Note Don't forget that the username is "administrator" and the password is the one you created during the post-configuration steps in Chapter 3.

5. You are presented with all the shared folders that are available on your Windows Home Server, including Music, Photos, and Videos, as shown in the example in Figure 4-4. Double-click the Software shared folder to continue.

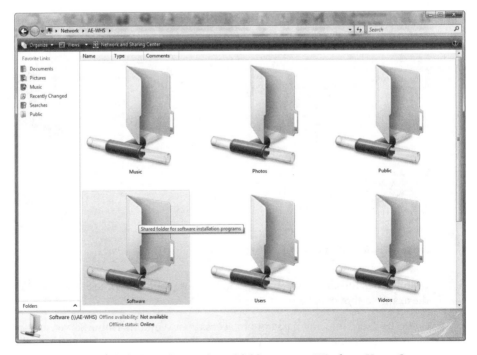

Figure 4-4. *Double-click the Software shared folder on your Windows Home Server.*

6. You are presented with the contents of the Software shared folder, as shown in the example in Figure 4-5. Double-click the Home Server Connector Software folder to continue.

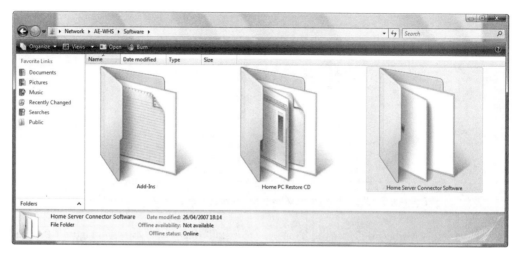

Figure 4-5. *Double-click the Home Server Connector Software folder.*

7. You are presented with the contents of the Home Server Connector Software folder, as shown in the example in Figure 4-6. Double-click the Setup icon to start the installation process.

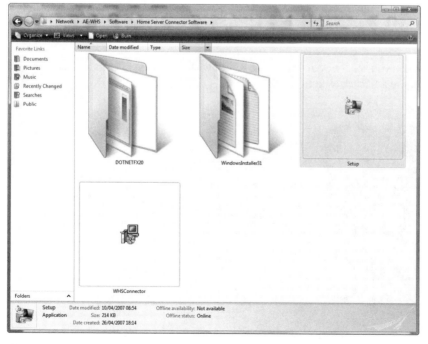

Figure 4-6. *Double-click the Setup icon in the Home Server Connector Software folder.*

8. You may be presented with an Open File – Security Warning dialog box, as shown in Figure 4-7. This dialog box advises you that a file is attempting to run and asks you to confirm that you want to run it. Click the Run button to continue.

Figure 4-7. *Click Run in the Open File – Security Warning dialog box.*

You may briefly see the "Preparing to install" dialog box, shown in Figure 4-8. (You can cancel the installation by clicking the Cancel button if you wish to do so for some reason.)

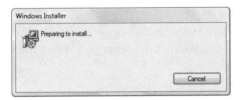

Figure 4-8. *Windows Installer is preparing to install the Windows Home Server Connector.*

9. When you see the Welcome to the Windows Home Server Connector screen, shown in Figure 4-9, click Next to continue.

Figure 4-9. *Read the Welcome screen and then click Next.*

10. Read the End-User License Agreement, shown in Figure 4-10. Click the I Accept the Terms of the License Agreement radio button and then click Next to continue. (Of course, if you don't accept the terms, you can't continue the installation.)

Figure 4-10. *Read and accept the End-User License Agreement.*

11. The installation commences and you can monitor the progress, as shown in Figure 4-11.

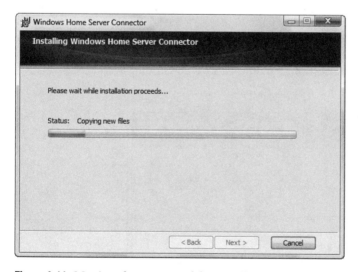

Figure 4-11. *Monitor the progress of the installation, if you care to.*

This completes the installation phase of the Windows Home Server Connector. You next need to configure it, as described in the following section.

Configuring the Windows Home Server Connector

After the Windows Home Server Connector installation has completed, the wizard automatically tries to locate your Windows Home Server, as shown in Figure 4-12. This process can be quick or it can take a few minutes—it all depends on your home network.

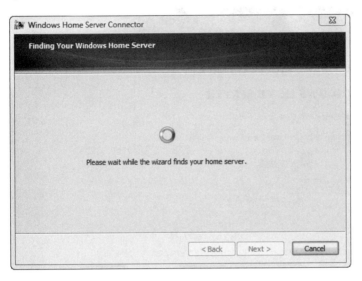

Figure 4-12. *Finding your Windows Home Server*

If the wizard successfully locates your Windows Home Server, then skip to the subsection "Completing the Windows Home Server Connector Configuration." If the wizard cannot locate your Windows Home Server, you are presented with the screen shown in Figure 4-13, in which case read the following subsection, "Finding Your Windows Home Server."

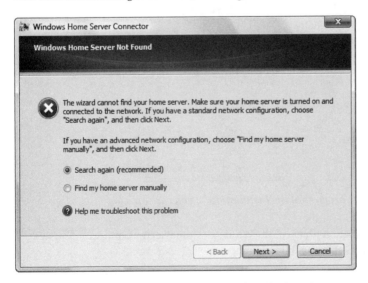

Figure 4-13. *Your Windows Home Server could not be found.*

Finding Your Windows Home Server

As indicated in Figure 4-13, before you continue with the wizard, it is a good idea to make sure that your Windows Home Server is switched on and connected to your network and that the computer on which you are installing the Windows Home Server Connector is also connected to your network.

To ensure that your Windows Home Server can be seen by other computers on your home network, you can check a number of different things.

- If you are using a wired connection on your Windows Home Server, check that it is connected and that you have flashing activity lights on the network card (if your network card has them).

- If you are using a wireless connection on your Windows Home Server, check that the wireless connection is working and that nothing is interfering with the signal, such as a microwave oven, baby monitor, or wireless telephone.

- Check that all the computers on your network are using the same Workgroup name (in particular, that the Windows Home Server computer has the correct Workgroup name). To do this, right-click My Computer, choose Properties, and then click the Computer Name tab, shown in Figure 4-14. If you need to change the Workgroup name to match the rest of your network, click the Change button and enter the new name, as shown in the example in Figure 4-15. You will need to reboot the computer for the changes to take effect.

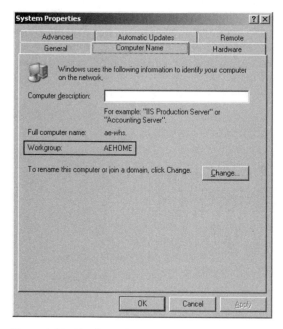

Figure 4-14. *Checking the Workgroup name*

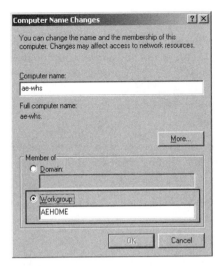

Figure 4-15. *Changing the Workgroup name*

- Perform a ping against the server name. In Windows XP, click the Start button, click Run, type **cmd** in the Run dialog box, and click OK to open a command prompt. In Windows Vista, click the Start button, type **cmd** in the Start Search box, and press Enter to open a command prompt. Type **ping** *servername*, where *servername* is the name that you have given your Windows Home Server (remember, the default server name is SERVER). If you receive a response similar to the one shown in Figure 4-16, then your computer can locate your Windows Home Server by its name. If you do not get a similar response, you might have network-related problems. Check that all the network cables are properly connected and that there are flashing network connectivity lights on the network card, if you can see them.

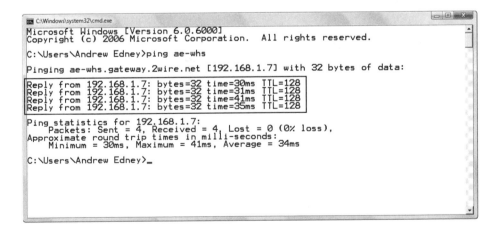

Figure 4-16. *Performing a ping against the server name*

- Perform a ping against the server IP address. Open a command prompt (as described in the preceding bullet) and type **ping *ipaddress***, where *ipaddress* is the actual IP address assigned to your Windows Home Server. (You can get the IP address from your Windows Home Server by either checking the results of the server name ping or checking the Support tab of the Local Area Connection Status dialog box on the Windows Home Server itself, as shown in Figure 4-17.) If you receive a response similar to the one shown in Figure 4-18, then your computer can locate your Windows Home Server by its name. If you don't receive a similar response, then you might have networking or routing problems and you should investigate that.

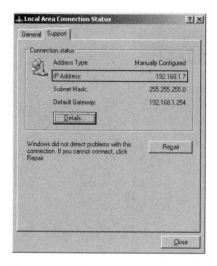

Figure 4-17. *Obtaining the server IP address*

■**Tip** To open the Local Area Connection Status dialog box, click the Start button, choose Control Panel ➤ Network Connections, and then right-click Local Area Connection and choose Status.

```
C:\Windows\system32\cmd.exe

Microsoft Windows [Version 6.0.6000]
Copyright (c) 2006 Microsoft Corporation.  All rights reserved.

C:\Users\Andrew Edney>ping 192.168.1.7

Pinging 192.168.1.7 with 32 bytes of data:

Reply from 192.168.1.7: bytes=32 time=32ms TTL=128
Reply from 192.168.1.7: bytes=32 time=49ms TTL=128
Reply from 192.168.1.7: bytes=32 time=107ms TTL=128
Reply from 192.168.1.7: bytes=32 time=133ms TTL=128

Ping statistics for 192.168.1.7:
    Packets: Sent = 4, Received = 4, Lost = 0 (0% loss),
Approximate round trip times in milli-seconds:
    Minimum = 32ms, Maximum = 133ms, Average = 80ms

C:\Users\Andrew Edney>_
```

Figure 4-18. *Performing a ping against the server IP address*

After you have performed the preceding recommended checks, click the Search Again (Recommended) radio button (refer to Figure 4-13) and then click Next to have the Windows Home Server Connector wizard search again for you.

If this still does not find your Windows Home Server, then you can find the server manually by clicking the Find My Home Server Manually radio button and then clicking Next. On the Find the Windows Home Server Manually screen, shown in Figure 4-19, enter the name for your Windows Home Server or enter the IP address and click Next to perform the manual search. Remember that the name for your server will be SERVER if you left it as the default name.

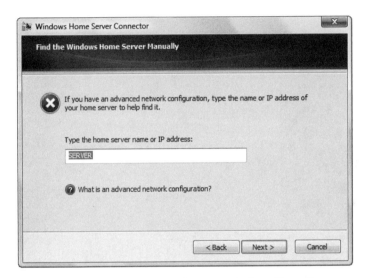

Figure 4-19. *Manually searching for your Windows Home Server*

■Note An *advanced network configuration*, as referenced in Figure 4-19, is defined by the Windows Home Server documentation as "a home network that has been logically divided into two or more networks (subnets)." If this definition describes your home network setup, then you need to perform a few tasks to be able to connect to your Windows Home Server—see the "Connecting from a Different Subnet" section later in this chapter. The majority of home users likely have only a single subnet; only more advanced users are likely to have this configuration.

Completing the Windows Home Server Connector Configuration

Once your Windows Home Server has been located, you are asked to enter your Windows Home Server password, as shown in Figure 4-20. Enter the password and click Next to continue.

Figure 4-20. *Enter your Windows Home Server password and click Next.*

Don't worry if you have forgotten the password; if you click the Password Hint button, you will see the password hint that you entered in Chapter 2, similar to the example shown in Figure 4-21. Click the OK button to return to the Log On screen.

Figure 4-21. *Access your password hint to recall your password.*

The Windows Home Server Connector wizard will now complete the configuration of your computer by performing two steps, as shown in Figure 4-22 and described next.

- *Joining Windows Home Server:* The computer will connect to Windows Home Server and then will be added to the list of computers being monitored.

- *Configuring computer backup:* A backup schedule is created for the computer, which you can change at a later stage.

When those two steps have completed successfully, click the Next button to complete the installation and configuration process. You should then see the screen shown in Figure 4-23. As you can see, the automatic backup for this computer has been set to be performed between the hours of midnight and 6 a.m. You can change this later if you want to set a different time, as described in Chapter 7. Just click Finish to close this screen.

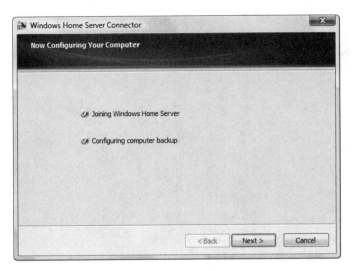

Figure 4-22. *Automatic configuration of your computer*

Figure 4-23. *The Windows Home Server Connector installation and configuration is complete.*

You may then notice a message bubble appear on the screen telling you that Windows Home Server does not recognize your user account, as shown in Figure 4-24. Don't worry if you see this message, because it is likely at this stage that you have not yet created your account, so the Windows Home Server Connector is trying to use the account you are currently signed into your computer as. Creating accounts is covered in Chapter 6. Click the X button to dismiss the message bubble.

Figure 4-24. *Don't be concerned if you see this Windows Home Server message bubble.*

Don't forget to repeat all of the preceding installation and configuration steps for each computer that you want to connect to Windows Home Server.

Removing the Windows Home Server Connector

You may decide that you no longer want to use the Windows Home Server Connector software on a particular computer. You can easily remove the Windows Home Server Connector from a computer by following these simple steps:

1. On the computer you want to remove the Windows Home Server Connector from, click the Start button and open the Control Panel, shown in Figure 4-25.

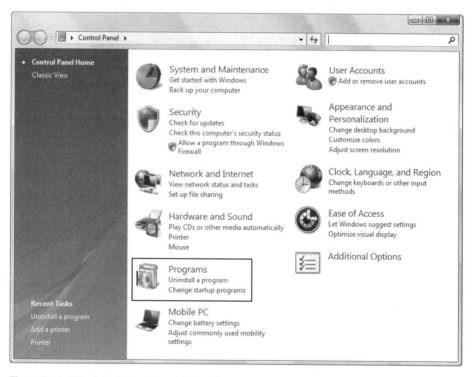

Figure 4-25. *Windows Vista Control Panel*

2. Select Uninstall a Program from the Programs group.

3. Highlight the Windows Home Server Connector in the list of programs and click Uninstall, as shown in Figure 4-26.

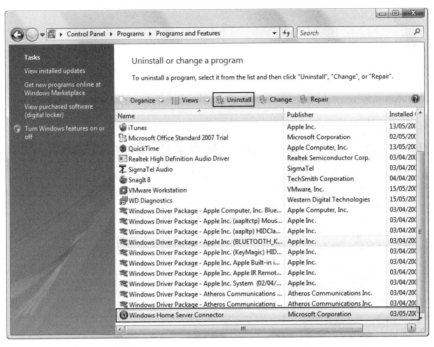

Figure 4-26. *Uninstalling the Windows Home Server Connector*

4. When prompted, as shown in Figure 4-27, click Yes to start the uninstall process.

Figure 4-27. *Confirming the uninstall of the Windows Home Server Connector*

You may then see the information box shown in Figure 4-28, which is just an advisory message—chances are you will miss it because it can flash on the screen and be gone again in a matter of seconds.

Figure 4-28. *Gathering the required information*

Reinstalling the Windows Home Server Connector

If you need to reinstall the Windows Home Server Connector (for example, because the software has become corrupt or appears not to be working correctly), you don't need to uninstall the Connector software and then reinstall it—there is a slightly quicker way. If you run the Windows Home Server Connector installation program again while the Windows Home Server Connector is already installed, you are presented with the screen shown in Figure 4-29, advising you that the Windows Home Server Connector is already installed and giving you the option to reinstall it.

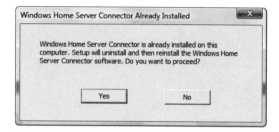

Figure 4-29. *The Windows Home Server Connector is already installed.*

All you have to do is click the Yes button and then, after it has been removed, follow the steps to perform the installation, starting at Step 9 in the "Installing the Windows Home Server Connector" section in this chapter.

Cancelling an Installation

You can choose to cancel the installation of the Windows Home Server Connector at any time. If you click the Cancel button on any of the wizard screens, you are presented with a dialog box asking you to confirm that you want to cancel the installation, as shown in Figure 4-30.

Figure 4-30. *Confirm that you want to cancel the installation.*

Simply click the Yes button to cancel the installation and remove any files that have already been copied or installed to your computer. You then are presented with a screen advising you that the installation has been cancelled before it had time to finish, as shown in Figure 4-31. Click the Finish button to complete the process.

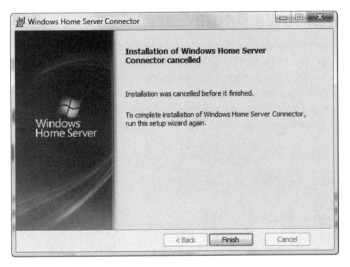

Figure 4-31. *Installation was cancelled.*

Note You will need to restart the whole installation process if you later decide to install the Windows Home Server Connector on that computer.

Connecting from a Different Subnet

As mentioned earlier in the chapter, by default, any computers that you want to connect to your Windows Home Server computer must be located on the same subnet. This is primarily because your Windows Home Server's built-in firewall (Windows Firewall) is configured to allow connections only from computers that are located on the same subnet as itself. For most users, this works fine, because they will use the same subnet and probably the same hub to connect all of their computers and other network devices together.

Although this is the default setting, you can make a few changes to the Windows Home Server firewall to allow connections from other subnets to take place. You need to change the scopes of the following services:

- Remote Desktop Connection

- Windows Home Server Computer Backup

- Windows Home Server Transport Service

Note For more information on firewalls and scopes, take a look at Appendix A.

If you know for sure that you are on a different subnet, then you need to follow these steps to enable the firewall to allow your computers on the other subnets to connect to your Windows Home Server computer:

■**Caution** Be very careful when altering the rules and exceptions on your firewall—one mistake could leave your computer and your network vulnerable to attack. Make sure you know what you are changing and the desired effect the changes will have, that you have the correct details available to you, and that you have triple-checked everything before continuing. If you are in any doubt whatsoever, then don't make any changes.

---

1. Log on directly to your Windows Home Server using the Administrator account (yes, this is one of those rare occasions when you actually need to perform a task on the Windows Home Server itself, so you may need to plug the mouse, keyboard, and monitor back into the Windows Home Server before continuing).

2. Click the Start button and select Control Panel ➤ Windows Firewall, as shown in Figure 4-32.

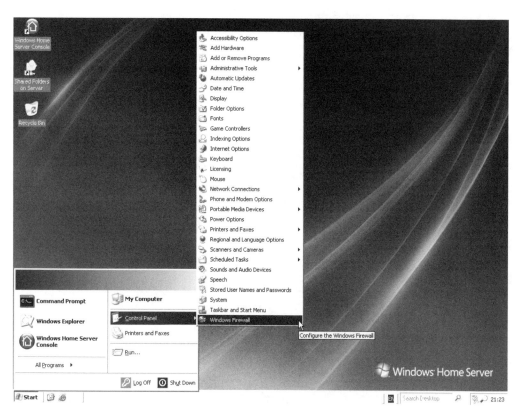

Figure 4-32. *Select Windows Firewall from the Windows Home Server itself.*

3. You are presented with the Windows Firewall window, shown in Figure 4-33. From here, you can confirm that the Firewall is On. Click the Exceptions tab, which is where you change the scopes on the previously mentioned services.

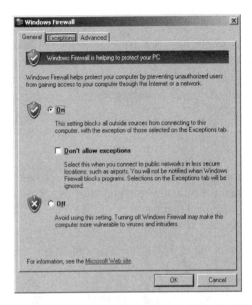

Figure 4-33. *Select the Exceptions tab in the Windows Firewall window.*

4. Scroll down through the Programs and Services list on the Exceptions tab until you see Remote Desktop, Windows Home Server Computer Backup, and Windows Home Server Transport Service, as shown in Figure 4-34.

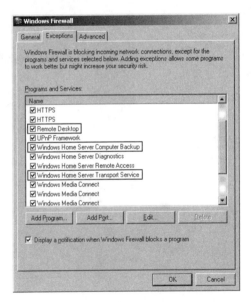

Figure 4-34. *Locate and select the correct services and programs on the Exceptions tab.*

5. Select each one in turn and then click the Edit button. The Remote Desktop service is shown in Figure 4-35, the Windows Home Server Computer Backup program is shown in Figure 4-36, and the Windows Home Server Transport Service is shown in Figure 4-37.

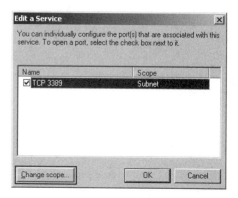

Figure 4-35. *Click Change Scope to change the scope for the Remote Desktop service.*

Figure 4-36. *Click Change Scope to change the scope for the Windows Home Server Computer Backup program.*

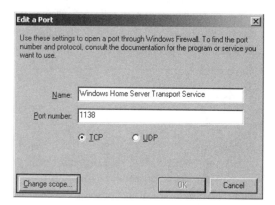

Figure 4-37. *Click Change Scope to change the scope for the Windows Home Server Transport Service.*

6. For each service, click the Change Scope button to launch the Change Scope dialog box, shown in Figure 4-38.

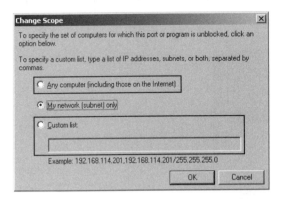

Figure 4-38. *Change the scope for each of the required services and programs.*

7. In the Change Scope dialog box, you can change the scope from My Network (Subnet) Only, the default, to either Any Computer, which also includes computers that are located on the Internet, or Custom List, which enables you to limit the scope to a custom list of computers. Choose the Custom List option and enter the IP addresses of the computers on the other subnets, in the format 192.168.114.201/255.255.255.0, where the 192.168.114.201 part is the IP address and the 255.255.255.0 part is the subnet. You can get the IP address of each machine by typing **ipconfig** at a command prompt on each machine.

8. After you have changed the scope, click the OK button to save the changes.

■ Note The most secure option other than using the My Network (Subnet) Only option is the Custom List option because you can very specifically identify which computers and which subnets to allow to connect. Resist the urge to take the easiest and riskiest configuration option, Any Computer, because this potentially allows any computer anywhere to connect to your Windows Home Server and take control of it!

Summary

In this chapter, you learned how to install the Windows Home Server Connector onto each of your computers. This installation enables you to join each computer to the Windows Home Server and to control the Windows Home Server from those computers. You also learned how to uninstall the Windows Home Server Connector and how to quickly perform a reinstallation. Finally, you learned how to make changes to Windows Firewall to enable computers located on different subnets to connect to your Windows Home Server. The next chapter shows you how to interact with Windows Home Server from the Windows Home Server Console.

■ ■ ■

CHAPTER 5

Windows Home Server Console and Settings

Now that you have installed the Windows Home Server Connector, you will be able to use the Windows Home Server Console to connect to and control Windows Home Server, including making changes that affect how Windows Home Server functions. In this chapter, you will learn how to connect to Windows Home Server and adjust settings to suit your personal preferences and requirements.

Connecting to Windows Home Server

The main way that you will be connected to Windows Home Server is through the Windows Home Server Console on any of your home computers. These are the computers you just installed using the Windows Home Server Connector software (and if you haven't done so yet, then go back to Chapter 4 to learn all about it—go on, you know you want to).

Starting the Windows Home Server Console

You can start the Windows Home Server Console in a few different ways, as described in the following sections. Use whichever method you prefer.

Launching from the Task Tray

An icon for Windows Home Server now appears in your task tray, as shown in Figure 5-1. If you right-click this icon, you will be presented with a menu, which is often referred to as a *context menu,* as shown in Figure 5-2.

■**Note** A context menu (or a shortcut menu) is a menu of commands and functions that appears (or pops up) when you right-click an item, such as an icon on the screen. Context menus are provided to help you perform certain tasks or give you certain options, depending on what you were doing or selecting at that time.

Figure 5-1. *The Windows Home Server icon on the task tray*

Figure 5-2. *The Windows Home Server context menu*

Because you are not yet signed in to Windows Home Server, some context menu options, such as Backup Now and Update Password, are currently unavailable. These options will become available when they are applicable, hence the context nature of the menu. The task you want to perform is launching the Windows Home Server Console, so just click Windows Home Server Console in the context menu.

Launching from the Start Menu

Another way to launch the Windows Home Server Console is from the Windows Start menu. Just click the Windows Start button and select Windows Home Server Console, as shown in Figure 5-3. If you don't see that option on the main Start menu, click All Programs and select Windows Home Server Console from the submenu.

Figure 5-3. *Selecting Windows Home Server Console from the Windows Start menu*

Creating a Desktop Shortcut

You can also create a shortcut on your desktop for the Windows Home Server Console. To do this, highlight the Windows Home Server Console icon (don't click it) on the Start menu, right-click, and choose Copy from the context menu, as shown in Figure 5-4.

Figure 5-4. *Selecting Copy to create a desktop shortcut*

Next, move your mouse pointer to anywhere on the desktop that is empty, right-click, and choose Paste from the context menu, as shown in Figure 5-5.

Figure 5-5. *Choosing Paste to add your desktop shortcut*

This simple sequence will add a Windows Home Server Console icon to your desktop, as shown in Figure 5-6. Now you can quickly launch the Windows Home Server Console by double-clicking this icon.

Figure 5-6. *The Windows Home Server Console desktop shortcut*

If you want to remove the desktop shortcut at any time, either drag it to the Recycle Bin or click it once to highlight it, and then press the Delete key on your keyboard. You will be asked to confirm your action, as shown in Figure 5-7. Clicking Yes here will not remove the actual Windows Home Server Console application; it will just remove the icon from your desktop.

Figure 5-7. *Moving the shortcut to the Recycle Bin*

Logging In to Windows Home Server

When you launch the Windows Home Server Console, you will be presented with the Windows Home Server login screen, as shown in Figure 5-8. Here, you must type in the password that you created for your Windows Home Server account.

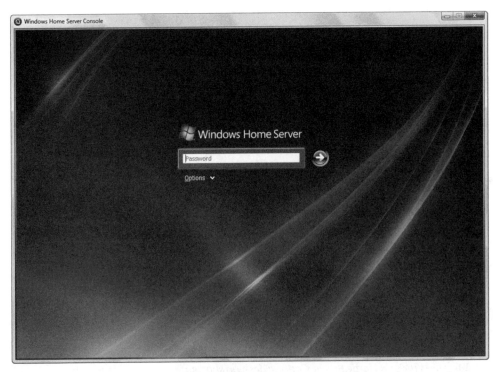

Figure 5-8. *Logging in to Windows Home Server from the Windows Home Server Console*

But what if you forgot your password? As you may remember, you had the option of creating a password hint, and this is where it can come in handy. Just click the Options button, and then click Password Hint, as shown in Figure 5-9.

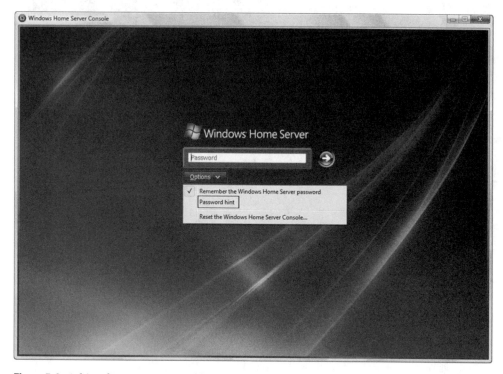

Figure 5-9. *Asking for your password hint*

Your password hint will be displayed, as shown in Figure 5-10. With any luck, this will be enough of a hint, and you can now enter your password and continue. If it is not, then you have a bit of a problem, and the only way to resolve it is to completely reinstall your Windows Home Server—so try not to forget the password!

Figure 5-10. *Viewing your password hint*

After you have typed in your password, click the arrow to continue. You will see a progress bar indicating that a connection is in progress, as shown in Figure 5-11. This process should take only a few seconds; anything longer than that could indicate a problem of some kind. If you have problems connecting, take a look at the "Troubleshooting Windows Home Server Connections" section towards the end of this chapter for some possible assistance.

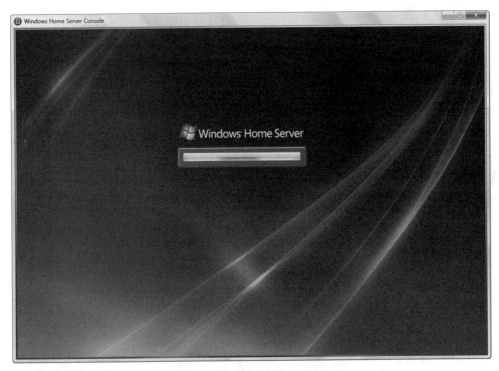

Figure 5-11. *Windows Home Server connection in progress*

You may also have spotted the first item in the login screen's Options menu: Remember the Windows Home Server Password, as shown in Figure 5-12.

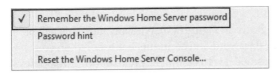

Figure 5-12. *Remember the Windows Home Server password is the default.*

With this option checked, as it is by default, you need to enter your password only the first time you log in to the Windows Home Server Console. After that, it is already typed in for you. If you don't want your password entered automatically, now is your chance to turn off this option. Just click it to switch it off. To switch it back on, click it again.

■**Caution** Although it can be quite convenient to have your password already entered for you on the login screen, it is also a potential security risk. Anyone with access to this computer will now be able to control Windows Home Server via the console, and there will be nothing you can do to stop it. Needing to enter the password each time should deter some people from gaining unauthorized access—assuming that your password hint is not so obvious that it gives away your password without much effort.

Viewing the Windows Home Server Console

After you log in, you should see the Windows Home Server Console screen, as shown in Figure 5-13. The icons across the top of the Windows Home Server Console give you access to different functions:

- *Computers & Backup*: Allows you to view your computers and perform backup and restore operations

- *User Accounts*: Allows you to manage Windows Home Server accounts

- *Shared Folders*: Allows you to manage shared folders on your Windows Home Server

- *Server Storage*: Allows you to view the storage usage on your Windows Home Server

- *Network*: Shows you the status of the computers on your network

On the top-right side of the screen are two smaller buttons: Settings (which will be covered shortly) and Help.

When you start the Windows Home Server Console for the first time, you will see the Computers & Backup window, which displays a list of your computers that have the Windows Home Server Connector software installed, along with any description you have entered, the operating system version, and its current backup status (you'll learn more about the backup status in Chapter 7). After the initial startup, whenever you open the Windows Home Server Console, you will see whatever view appeared the last time you closed the console.

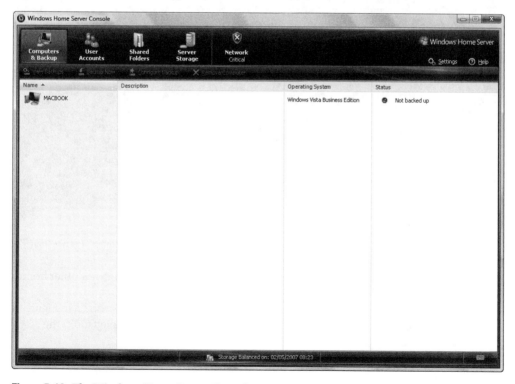

Figure 5-13. *The Windows Home Server Console*

Most functions you will need to perform can be done from the Windows Home Server Console. This chapter covers configuring Windows Home Server settings. The other elements within the Windows Home Server Console will be covered in upcoming chapters.

Launching the Windows Home Server Console on the Server

You can also launch the Windows Home Server Console directly on your Windows Home Server. But to be honest, this is not a very good idea, as the whole purpose behind having your server as a headless unit (without a keyboard, mouse, or monitor) was so that you didn't need to do anything, or at least very much, directly on that computer itself. But, if you do need to do it, just click the Start button and select Windows Home Server Console from the menu, as shown in Figure 5-14.

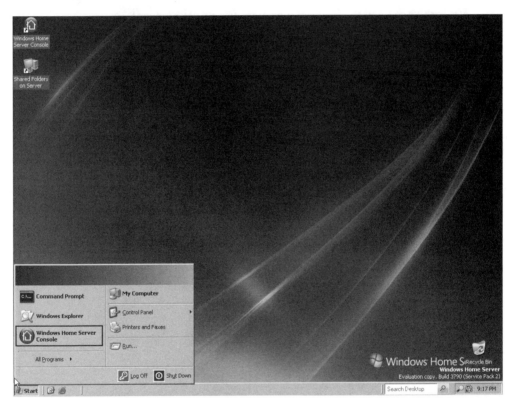

Figure 5-14. *Selecting the Windows Home Server Console on the Windows Home Server computer*

You will notice that this menu has fewer options than you saw earlier on your other home computer.

You will then be presented with the Windows Home Server Console, as shown in Figure 5-15. As you can see, the console running on your Windows Home Server itself looks the same as it does when running on your other computers.

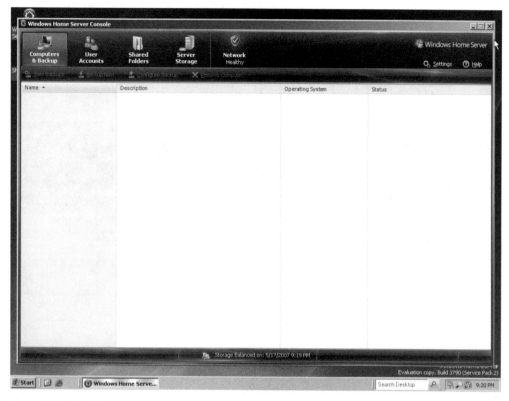

Figure 5-15. *The Windows Home Server Console running on the Windows Home Server*

Configuring Windows Home Server Settings

Through the Windows Home Server Console, you can configure a number of settings that control how Windows Home Server works in your home environment. To access these settings,
click the Settings button on the Windows Home Server Console. You will see the Windows
Home Server Settings window, as shown in Figure 5-16.

As you can see, the window is split into three areas. On the left is a list of settings
categories:

- *General*: Provides access to general settings, such as the date and time, regional settings, Windows Update settings, and so on.

- *Backup*: Provides access to backup-related settings. You can configure the backup time,
  configure automatic backup management, and run Backup Cleanup.

- *Passwords*: Allows you to change the Windows Home Server password and configure
  the user accounts password policy.

- *Media Sharing*: Allows you to configure Media Library Sharing for the Music, Photos,
  and Videos shared folders, so that you can stream digital media from your Windows
  Home Server to a device that supports Windows Media Connect.

- *Remote Access*: Provides access to remote-access-related settings, such as those for your Windows Home Server web site and broadband router.

- *Add-ins*: Allows you to install and uninstall Windows Home Server add-ins.

- *Resources*: Provides access to server activation, information, and resources for Windows Home Server.

Figure 5-16. *Windows Home Server Settings window*

To the right of the categories list, the main window pane displays the settings for the selected category.

Below the categories list is a Shut Down button. Let's look at what that button does first, and then review the settings in each category.

Shutting Down or Restarting Your Home Server

You can use the Shut Down button to do exactly what it says: shut down your Windows Home Server. It can also be used to restart your Windows Home Server, if you need to do that for whatever reason. Having this functionality available to you from the Windows Home Server Console means that you don't need to actually visit the computer to perform the restart manually. This can be very useful if your server is hidden away or hard to reach.

When you click the Shut Down button, you are presented with the choice to shut down or restart, as shown in Figure 5-17.

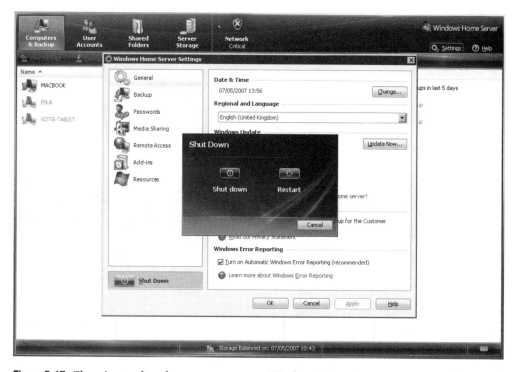

Figure 5-17. *Choosing to shut down or restart your Windows Home Server*

After you click the Shut Down button, your connection to your Windows Home Server will be terminated. You will see a message about the lost connection, as shown in Figure 5-18.

Figure 5-18. *The Windows Home Server Console reports when your computer loses its connection to your Windows Home Server.*

If you want to restart your Windows Home Server, you will need to do it the old-fashioned way: press the power button on the computer!

If you clicked the Restart button, your connection to your Windows Home Server will also be terminated; however, you will be able to reconnect after it has restarted.

Configuring General Settings

The General settings enable you to perform a number of simple functions, as shown in Figure 5-19, including the following:

- Change the date and time

- Change the regional and language settings

- Turn Windows Update on or off, and perform a manual update

- Enable or disable Customer Experience Improvement

- Turn Windows Error Reporting on or off

Figure 5-19. *General settings*

Date and Time

You can change the date and time on your Windows Home Server by clicking the Change button, which will bring up the Date and Time Properties dialog box, as shown in Figure 5-20. From here, you can change the day, month, and year, and also set the time.

On the Time Zone tab of the Date and Time Properties dialog box, you can change the Time Zone setting, if it is set incorrectly or if you move to a different time zone.

Use the Internet Time tab to ensure that you automatically synchronize your Windows Home Server time with an Internet time server such as time.windows.com, as shown in

Figure 5-21. Make sure the Automatically Synchronize with an Internet Time Server check box is checked, and select a suitable Internet time server from the drop-down list. You can also force a synchronization by clicking the Update Now button.

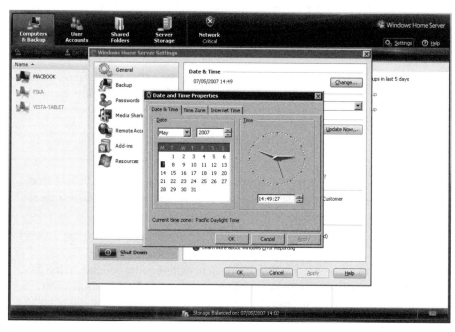

Figure 5-20. *Changing the date and time*

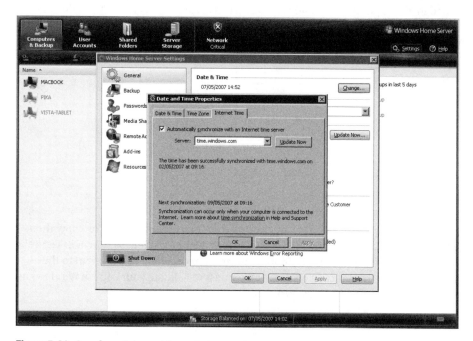

Figure 5-21. *Synchronizing with an Internet time server*

Regional and Language

If your regional language settings are incorrect, you can choose a new setting from the Regional and Language drop-down list. This setting is used to display information such as dates, times, currency, and measurements in the format of your preferred language and region.

Windows Update

As anyone who has ever used Windows knows, Microsoft releases many patches for its software. These patches can include software updates, but the most frequent and important updates are security patches. When new vulnerabilities are discovered in its software, Microsoft releases a patch as soon as possible.

Tip It would be worth subscribing to Microsoft's Security Notification Service in order to find out about issues and vulnerabilities when they are exposed. You can subscribe by going to `http://www.microsoft.com/technet/security/bulletin/notify.mspx`.

It is a very good idea to keep your machine up-to-date with security patches. In the past, you would need to visit the Microsoft Windows Update web site and download whatever patches and fixes you needed. Some people did not know about this site or just did not take the time to keep checking for updates, so important patches would be missed. This is where Windows Update is extremely handy.

The recommended setting for Windows Update is On, as shown in Figure 5-22, which downloads and installs updates automatically. Leave this setting to ensure that you don't ever miss an important update. It's all too easy to forget about updating your home server when it's tucked away somewhere!

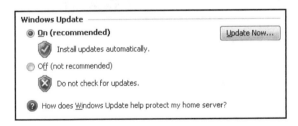

Figure 5-22. *Windows Update options*

You can also perform a manual check by clicking the Update Now button. You may then see a screen showing which updates are being downloaded and installed, as shown in Figure 5-23. This screen will also display any additional information that may be pertinent to the update, such as a request to confirm a change or a request to validate your copy of Windows as part of the Windows Genuine Advantage program.

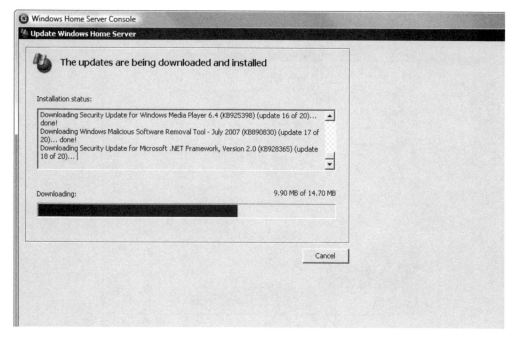

Figure 5-23. *Updating Windows Home Server*

Note Windows Genuine Advantage is Microsoft's way of ensuring that you are using genuine legal software and not a pirated copy of Mircrosoft software. If you are using legal software, and it has been verified by the Windows Genuine Advantage program, you will be able to receive support from Microsoft, including such things as being able to update your software. To read more about Windows Genuine Advantage, point your web browser to http://www.microsoft.com/genuine/downloads/WhyValidate. aspx?displaylang=en.

Configuring Backup Settings

The Backup settings, shown in Figure 5-24, relate to the backup functions of Windows Home Server, including the following:

- Change the backup times
- Change the automatic backup management profile.
- Perform backup cleanups.

We'll look at each of these settings here. Chapter 7 covers backup and restore operations in detail.

Figure 5-24. *Backup settings*

Backup Time

The backup time is when Windows Home Server performs the daily backups of all of your connected computers and also performs any maintenance tasks. The following tasks occur during the available time period:

- Back up all connected home computers on your network.

- Install any Windows updates and restart your Windows Home Server if one of the updates requires it.

- Run Backup Cleanup every Sunday.

The minimum time period is 1 hour, and the maximum is 23 hours. The default setting is a start time of 00:00 (midnight) and an end time of 06:00 (6 a.m.), as shown in Figure 5-25. The idea behind this default is that the computers you want to back up will not be used at this time. Obviously, this won't be the same for everyone, which is why you can set the time periods.

■**Caution** Don't forget that your computer must be switched on in order for the backups to be performed. If a computer is not switched on or is unavailable for any other reason, it will be skipped (this will be recorded in the logs).

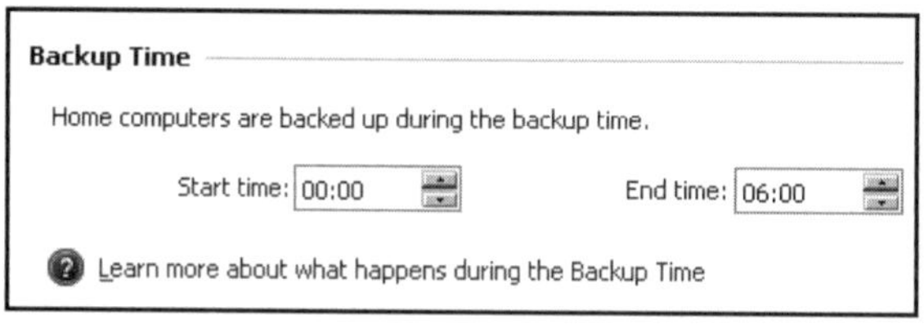

Figure 5-25. *Setting the backup time*

Set the backup start time and end time, remembering that the times are in a 24-hour format. Keep in mind that each computer is backed up one after another, so you must set enough time for this to happen. The time required depends on the number of connected computers you want to back up. Don't forget to click Apply after you have made the changes.

Automatic Backup Management

Because daily backups of all of your computers are run, the number of backups and the amount of disk space used accumulates over time. To take the pressure off of you to perform some sort of backup management, Windows Home Server provides automatic backup management. All you need to do is make a few simple choices:

- How many months do you want to keep the first backup of the month? The minimum number is 0 and maximum number is 120.

- How many weeks do you want to keep the first backup of the week? The minimum number is 0 and maximum number is 52.

- How many days do you want to keep the first backup of the day? The minimum number is 0 and maximum number is 90.

■**Note** Remember that these settings affect all of the backups for your computers, so each computer backup will be kept for the same amount of time. You cannot set a different number of backups to be kept for a computer you might consider to be more important than other computers on your network.

The default settings for days, weeks, and months are all 3, as you can see in Figure 5-26. This may be perfectly sufficient for your needs.

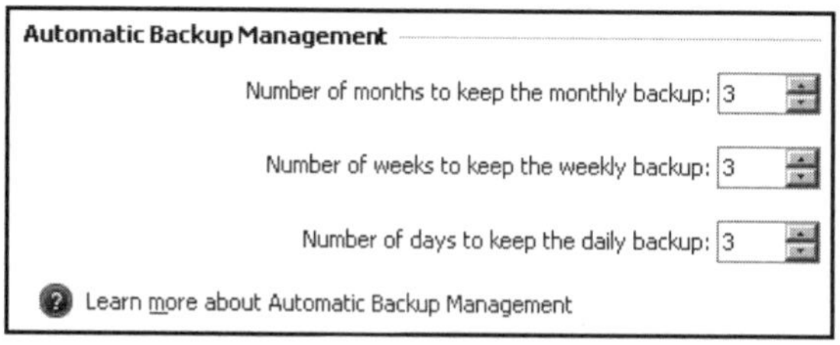

Figure 5-26. *Setting automatic backup options*

■**Note** If you decide to stop backing up one or more of your computers, or you miss a backup for whatever reason, Windows Home Server will continue to apply the automatic backup management settings. For more information about backups, including how to stop and start backups, see Chapter 7.

After you've entered the numbers for the automatic backup management settings, click the Apply button.

Backup Cleanup

Backup Cleanup is a utiltity that works in conjunction with automatic backup management to remove old backups that fall outside the set number of kept backups. You can also run Backup Cleanup manually to remove backups that you want to delete.

Backup Cleanup runs automatically every Sunday during the hours you have set for the backup time.

■**Note** Depending on the number and size of the backups to be removed, the Backup Cleanup process can take some time.

If you want to run a manual cleanup for whatever reason, such as you have decided to remove some old backups now and you don't want to wait until Sunday, all you need to do is click the Cleanup Now button, as shown in Figure 5-27.

Figure 5-27. *Clicking the Cleanup Now button starts Backup Cleanup.*

You will then be asked to confirm that you are sure you want to perform a cleanup, as shown in Figure 5-28. Click Yes if you are sure that is what you want to do.

You can now monitor the progress of Backup Cleanup, as shown in Figure 5-29.

■**Caution** Don't forget that once the Backup Cleanup process has completed, those backups that have been removed are gone forever.

Figure 5-28. *Performing a manual cleanup*

Figure 5-29. *Monitoring the progress of a manual cleanup*

Managing Passwords

The Passwords settings, shown in Figure 5-30, let you change the Windows Home Server password and set a password policy.

Figure 5-30. *Passwords settings*

Windows Home Server Password

If you want to change the password that you use to access Windows Home Server, click the Change Password button. You will be presented with the dialog box shown in Figure 5-31.

Figure 5-31. *Changing the Windows Home Server password*

Type in the new password, and then type it in again to confirm it. You can also add a password hint. Click OK to finish.

▌Note Don't forget that your password must be at least seven characters in length. It must also be a complex password. And keep in mind that the password hint can be seen by anyone on your home network, so don't make the hint so easy that anyone can guess it. Try to make the password as long and complex as you can. And don't forget that it never expires, so changing your password on a regular basis is a good idea!

User Accounts Password Policy

You can create a user account password policy that ensures that all user passwords meet certain requirements. Changing the policy affects only new user accounts; existing user accounts will remain unchanged.

You can set the account password policy to one of the following levels of security:

Weak: Passwords of any length can be created, which means a user would not need to have a password at all. This setting is extremely risky, as it offers little or no protection against someone else gaining access to that user's account.

Medium: Passwords must be at least five characters. This is the recommended setting, but it offers only a minimal amount of protection. If users can have a password with a minimum of five characters, then they will usually go for just five characters, making the password easier to discover.

Strong: Passwords must be a minimum of seven characters, and complex passwords are required. Complex passwords must contain at least three of the following:

- Uppercase letters
- Lowercase letters
- Numbers
- Symbols (such as $, @, and so on)

▌Note Regardless which user account password policy you set, all user accounts that are enabled for remote access require the use of strong passwords. This cannot be changed (and to be honest, you wouldn't want to change it anyway). For more information about remote access, see Chapter 11.

To change the user accounts password policy, move the slide bar to your desired setting (you can set it to only Weak, Medium, or Strong—there is no middle ground), as shown in Figure 5-32.

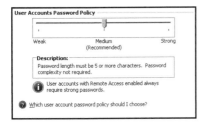

Figure 5-32. *Setting the user accounts password policy*

Tip Even though the recommended setting is Medium, it is a good idea to set the password policy to Strong in order to increase the protection that stronger passwords can give you.

Media Sharing

You can control the streaming of media content— music, photos, and videos—from your home server to other devices on your home network, such as an Xbox 360 or other supported digital media receivers (DMRs). For more information about DMRs and streaming media, see Chapter 10.

The Media Sharing settings allow you to switch on or off sharing of each of the three media types, as shown in Figure 5-33. The default setting for all three shared folders is Off.

Figure 5-33. *Media Sharing settings*

■**Caution** When you enable sharing for any or all of the media types, any device on your home network will be able to access the shared content, so make sure that you are happy sharing these files among everyone before you continue. Content can be accessed even by users without a Windows Home Server user account, so be very careful. If you have media content you want to be able to stream to only certain users, you should put it into a folder that only those users can access.

Configuring Remote Access

The Remote Access settings, shown in Figure 5-34, allow you to set up and configure remote access to your Windows Home Server and network from other locations, such as the Internet or your work office.

Figure 5-34. *Remote Access settings*

Remote access is a large topic, and even has its own chapter in this book. For more information about how to set up and configure remote access, take a look at Chapter 11.

Managing Add-Ins

The Add-in settings, shown in Figure 5-35, allow you to manage your Windows Home Server add-ins. *Add-ins* are additional features or functionality that can be easily added to Windows

Home Server. Like remote access, add-ins have their own chapter in this book. For information about adding and removing add-ins, along with some of the add-ins that should be available, take a look at Chapter 13.

If you are interested in developing your own add-ins for Windows Home Server, you can use the Windows Home Server software development kit (SDK). See Appendix C for more information.

Figure 5-35. *Add-ins settings*

Accessing Resources

The Resources window shows information about Windows Home Server, such as version information, and provides links to various support options, as shown in Figure 5-36.

Figure 5-36. *Resources window*

Microsoft Windows

The Microsoft Windows area lists information about your Windows Home Server operating system, including the product ID. If you are running an evaluation copy, you can see when it expires, as shown in Figure 5-37.

Figure 5-37. *Windows Home Server operating system information*

If you have not yet activated your copy of Windows Home Server, you can click the Activate Windows button in order to start that process. (Remember that if you don't activate it within the available time period, it will stop working.) You will then see the Let's Activate Windows screen, as shown in Figure 5-38.

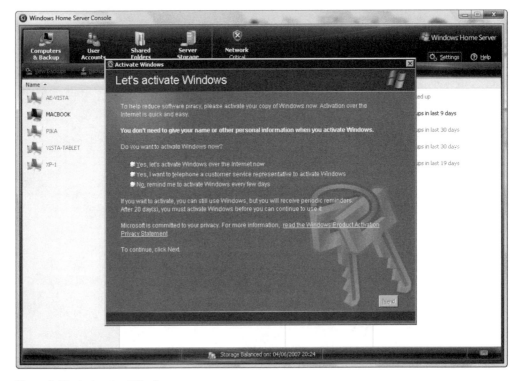

Figure 5-38. *Activating Windows*

Select whichever method you want to use to activate Windows, and then click the Next button to continue. The most common and easiest method is to activate Windows over the Internet. You must be connected to the Internet before you select this option. You will then be presented with the option to register your copy of Windows Home Server with Microsoft, as shown in Figure 5-39. This is purely optional and doesn't affect the activation process. Choose whether or not to register, and then click the Next button to continue.

If all is successful, you should then see the Thank You screen, as shown in Figure 5-40. This means that your copy of Windows Home Server is now activated, and you don't need to worry about it stopping working after 30 days! You will also notice that the Activate Windows button has now disappeared from the Resources window.

You can also view the Microsoft Software License Terms (which are sometimes referred to as the End User License Agreement) by clicking the link. This will open the document for you to read. You should read the license terms at least once, just so you know what terms you need to follow in order to use the software.

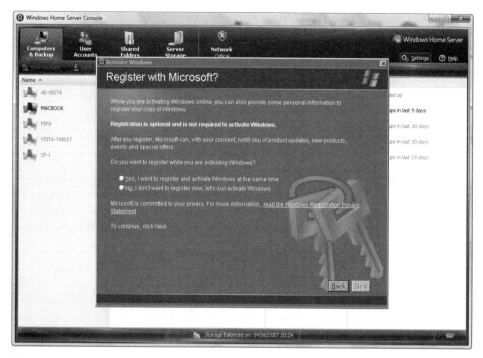

Figure 5-39. *Do you want to register your copy of Windows?*

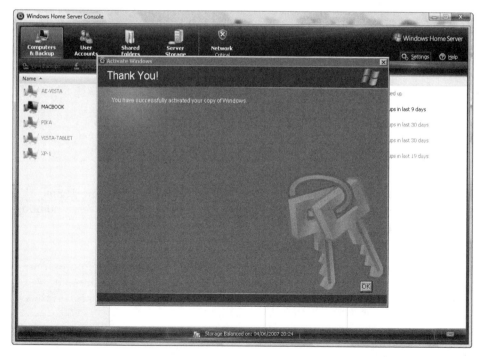

Figure 5-40. *You have successfully activated your copy of Windows Home Server.*

Home Server

The Home Server area lists specific information about your server hardware, as shown in Figure 5-41.

Figure 5-41. *Windows Home Server hardware information*

Here, you can see the make and model of your Windows Home Server, along with information about the processor speed and how much RAM you have. This information can be useful if you want to determine if you might need to upgrade any of your hardware in the future. Take a look at the latest hardware, in your local computer store or online, and compare it to the hardware shown here.

Version Information

The Version Information area lists all of the Windows Home Server services that are currently running on your home server, along with the version numbers, as shown in Figure 5-42. This information can be very useful for determining which services are running and whether you are running the latest versions. Check out the Microsoft Windows Home Server web site for information about the latest version of Windows Home Server.

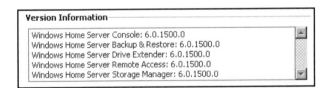

Figure 5-42. *Windows Home Server version information*

Learn More

The Learn More area has two choices, as shown in Figure 5-43:

Learn more about Windows Home Server. Takes you to the Microsoft Windows Home Server web site. You can also visit the product page for Windows Home Server by pointing your web browser to `http://www.microsoft.com/windows/products/winfamily/windowshomeserver/default.mspx`.

Windows Home Server Community. Takes you to the Window Home Server forums. You can also manually visit the forum for Windows Home Server by pointing your web browser to `http://forums.microsoft.com/windowshomeserver/default.aspx?siteid=50`.

Figure 5-43. *Windows Home Server Learn More options*

Support

The Support area displays a link to the Windows Home Server Product Support page, as shown in Figure 5-44. To contact product support, just click this link.

Figure 5-44. *Windows Home Server product support link*

Troubleshooting Windows Home Server Connections

Sometimes things can go wrong. Here, you'll learn about dealing with the problems of connecting to the Windows Home Server Console and staying connected to your Windows Home Server.

A Nonresponsive Windows Home Server Console

The most common problem you may experience is the Windows Home Server Console timing out when you are trying to connect to it. If you do experience this, don't panic. Just close the Windows Home Server Console login screen and then fire it up again—but this time, click Options and select Reset the Windows Home Server Console, as shown in Figure 5-45.

You will then be presented with the screen shown in Figure 5-46, which advises you that this action should be performed only if the console appears to be nonresponsive. As this is the the case, or at least appears to be the case, click OK to reset the console.

If this action does not resolve the problem, reboot your home server itself, and then try to connect again.

If this still does not resolve the problem, it might be time to reconnect that keyboard, mouse, and monitor and see if you can connect "the old-fashioned way."

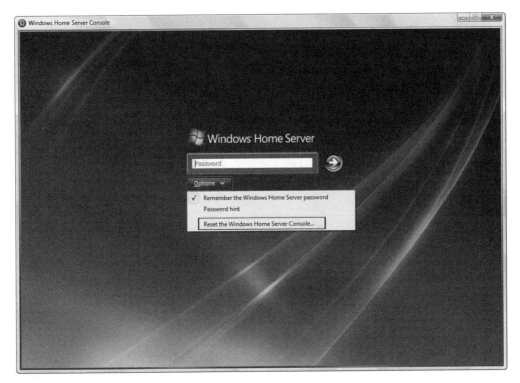

Figure 5-45. *Select Reset the Windows Home Server Console from the Options menu.*

Figure 5-46. *Resetting the Windows Home Server Console*

Losing Your Connection

You might lose your connection to your Windows Home Server for any number of reasons, including a problem with the server itself or issues with your network.

The Windows Home Server Console will advise you that the connection has been lost, as shown in Figure 5-47, and it will automatically try to reconnect your session for you. You will notice that something is wrong as the whole screen, with the exception of the Reconnecting box, will be in black and white.

Figure 5-47. *Attempting to reconnect to your Windows Home Server*

The reconnection attempt will happen up to 20 times before it effectively gives up trying. Now 20 times might seem like quite a lot, but those attempts happen pretty quickly, so that may not actually be enough time for the problem to be resolved.

If the Windows Home Server Console does not reconnect to your server in that time, try closing down the console and launching it again.

If this still does not work, see if you can track down the problem, as follows:

- On the computer you are using, can you access the Internet? If you cannot, but you could before, then it is a network problem.

- Can you ping your Windows Home Server? If the ping fails, it might be a problem with the server itself. (See Chapter 4 if you need a refresher on pinging the server.)

- Is your Windows Home Server still powered up?

- Did you just perform any updates to Windows Home Server? Could your server be rebooting following a critical update?

Investigating these areas should give you an idea of the source of the problem.

Summary

In this chapter, you learned how to start the Windows Home Server Console. Then we focused on the different settings that you can change using the Windows Home Server Console, including password policies and backup schedules. It is very important to spend some time going through each of the settings, ensuring that you have configured them specifically for your environment. For example, it is of no use to have your backups performed at 1 a.m. if the computer you want to back up is never switched on at that time.

The final section presented some steps for troubleshooting problems connecting to the Windows Home Server Console and to your Windows Home Server.

CHAPTER 6

■■■

User Accounts

To benefit from all the features and capabilities that Windows Home Server has to offer, you must create a user account for each user in your household. For example, if there are four people in your household, then you need to create four separate Windows Home Server user accounts, one for each person.

In this chapter you will learn how to create a user account, set permissions on that account, delete an account if necessary, and synchronize the passwords on your Windows Home Server user account and your normal Windows logon account.

Note To perform all of the user account tasks requires that you use the Windows Home Server Console, which means you will be connected using the Windows Home Server Administrator account, as discussed in Chapter 5.

As you may remember from Chapter 4, when you finished installing the Windows Home Server Connector, you saw the message shown in Figure 6-1, warning you that your Windows Home Server does not recognize your user account.

> ⓘ Windows Home Server does not recognize your user account. ✕
> Create a Windows Home Server user account for easy access to your home server.
> Click on this message to find out more.

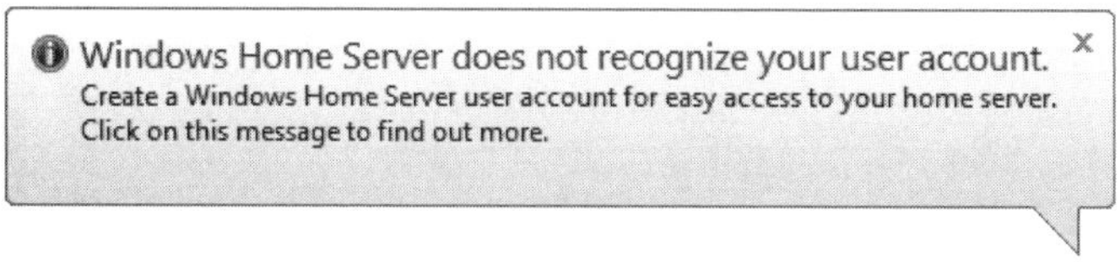

Figure 6-1. *Windows Home Server does not recognize your user account.*

If you click the message, the dialog box shown in Figure 6-2 appears, telling you that a user account with the logon name of whatever account you are currently logged into your Windows computer as (in my case, andrew edney) does not exist on Windows Home Server.

What this essentially means is that, although Windows Home Server can safely back up your computer for you, you cannot use some of the other features, such as certain shared folders, until you create an account.

By now you should be familiar with logging into the Windows Home Server Console, so go ahead and log in so that you can add an account.

Figure 6-2. *A user account for your current logon name does not exist on Windows Home Server.*

Adding a User Account

As mentioned earlier, a user account must be created for each person who will have access to your Windows Home Server. Once the Windows Home Server Console is up and running, click the User Accounts tab to display the list of user accounts, as shown in Figure 6-3.

Figure 6-3. *The User Accounts list*

As you can see, there is only one account at the moment, the Guest account. The Guest account is not configured for remote access and is also disabled.

The User Accounts tab has four columns:

- *Name*: Lists the name of the person that the user account belongs to

- *Logon Name*: Lists the user account name, which is what is used to log on with

- *Remote Access*: Lists whether the account is allowed to use the remote access features

- *Status*: Lists whether the account is enabled or disabled

You will also notice three buttons available above the Name column:

- *Add*: Used to add a user account

- *Properties*: Used to view and change the properties of a user account, including the password, among other things

- *Remove*: Used to remove the user account

To add a new Windows Home Server user account, perform the following steps:

1. Click the Add button to open the Add a New User to Your Home Server screen, shown in Figure 6-4.

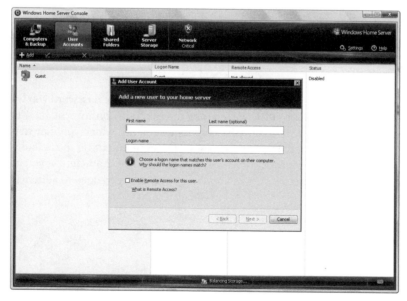

Figure 6-4. *Enter the first, last, and logon names for the new user account.*

2. Enter a first name, which is mandatory and can be up to 31 characters in length. Entering a last name is optional. It can also be up to 31 characters in length. You must also enter a logon name. It can contain both letters and numbers and should match the user's account on their computer. For example, if my Windows user account on my laptop is Andrew, then my Windows Home Server user account logon name should also be Andrew.

Note The logon names need to match in order to make it easier for you to access shared folders on the Windows Home Server computer. When you log on to your Windows computer, your account details are passed through to Windows Home Server automatically, so you don't have to log on twice. This is sometimes referred to as single sign-on (SSO). You don't *have* to have user accounts that match, but accessing shared folders is much easier if you do; otherwise, you have to enter your username and password each time you want to access a shared resource, which can become very tedious! For more information on how to ensure that your passwords are the same, take a look at the "Matching Passwords" section later in this chapter.

---

3. If you want to enable Remote Access for this user, check the Enable Remote Access for This User check box. Enabling Remote Access for a user enables that user to access their shared folder, and any other shared folders they have access to, via the Internet. By default, this option is unchecked, so if you want to enable the account for Remote Access, check the box. For more information about remote access, take a look at Chapter 11. Click Next to continue.

Note Each logon name must be unique, so if you want to create accounts for two users named Andrew, they both cannot have accounts called Andrew.

---

4. On the Type a Password screen, shown in Figure 6-5, enter the password you want to use for the account you are creating, and then re-enter it to confirm you have typed it correctly. You will also see here the password requirements, which you may remember from the previous chapter. If you left the password requirements at the default setting, then you have to create a password with a minimum of five characters. If you have changed these requirements, they will be shown here and you need to adhere to them. Click Next.

Figure 6-5. *Set your password.*

5. On the Set Access to Shared Folders screen, shown in Figure 6-6, set access privileges to all of the available shared folders: Music, Photos, Public, Software, and Videos, along with any other shared folders that may appear, depending on when you perform this step. The following are the three permissions that you can set:

- *Full*: Enables the user to create, change, and delete any files within the shared folder. This is the default setting.

- *Read*: Enables the user only to read files that are within the shared folder.

- *None*: Gives the user no privileges to any files that are in the shared folder.

If this is not the first user account you are adding, you have the option to set permissions on other users' shared folders, as shown in Figure 6-7. A user's personal shared folder is available only to that user by default, so everyone else has the None privilege assigned for that folder, unless you choose otherwise.

■**Note** Once you have created a user account, or when you have created any other shared folders, it will be listed here as well so that you can set access privileges when you create any new account. But don't worry if you don't want to set any access privileges just yet; you can easily set the access privileges later, as described later in the chapter, in the section "Changing Account Properties."

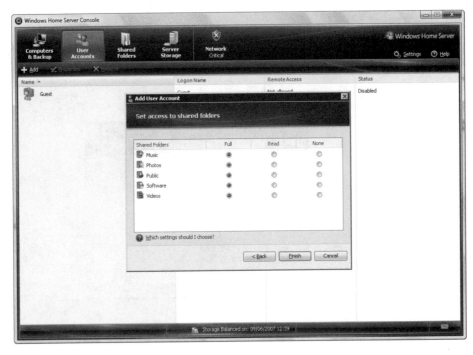

Figure 6-6. *Set shared folder access.*

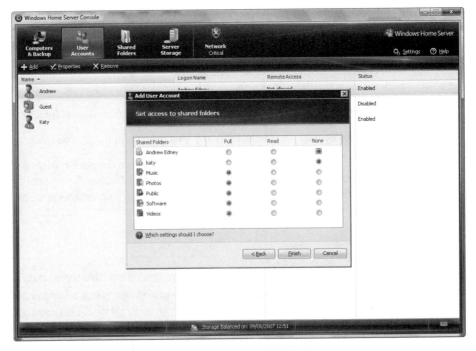

Figure 6-7. *Set access to other user accounts' shared folders.*

6. After you have set all the shared folder privileges, click Finish.

7. The user account is created, access to the existing shared folders are set in line with whatever options you selected, and a new shared folder specific to that user is created on Windows Home Server. When the new user account has successfully been created, you see the Adding the New User Account screen, as shown in Figure 6-8. Click Done to complete the process.

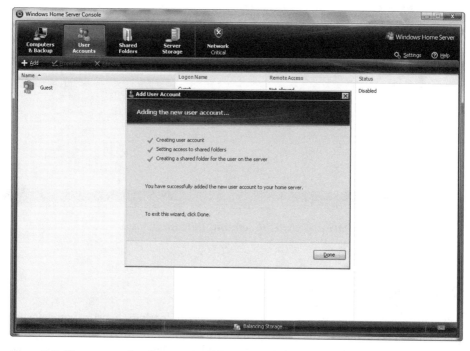

Figure 6-8. *The account has been created for you.*

You should now repeat the entire process to create a user account for every person who will need access to your Windows Home Server, although you are limited to ten accounts, not including the Guest account. If you try to create more than ten accounts, you will receive a warning telling you that you have reached the maximum number of user accounts, as shown in Figure 6-9.

■Note The Guest account is not included in the maximum ten user accounts, and you cannot remove the Guest account.

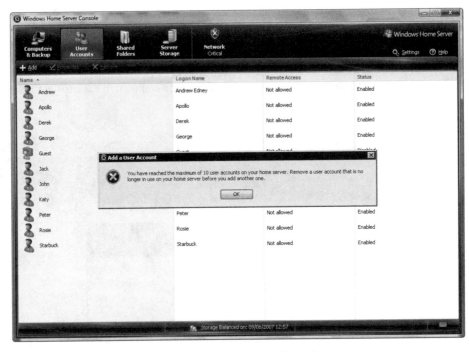

Figure 6-9. *You have added all the accounts that are allowed.*

Removing a User Account

You may decide at some point to remove a user account, perhaps because you have used all of
your ten user accounts. It is very easy to remove a user account, and you can also choose
whether or not to remove the personal shared folder for that user. If you decide not to remove
the folder, you can give someone else access to it.

To remove a user account, follow these simple steps:

1. On the User Accounts tab, click the user account that you want to remove.

2. Click the Remove button.

3. You are asked whether you want to keep or remove the selected user's shared folder, as
   shown in Figure 6-10. If you want to remove the user's shared folder, click the Remove
   the Shared Folder radio button and click Next to continue. If you want to keep the
   user's shared folder, skip to Step 6.

■Caution If you decide to remove the shared folder, the contents of that folder will be gone forever, so
make sure that you copy any files stored in that shared folder if you want to keep them.

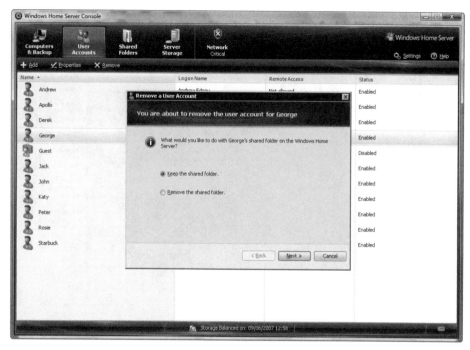

Figure 6-10. *Decide whether to remove the user's shared folder.*

4. You are advised that you are about to remove the selected user account from your Windows Home Server and that you are also about to delete the shared folder for that user, as shown in Figure 6-11. Click Finish to remove the account and delete the shared folder.

5. The process then removes any access that the selected user had to any of the other shared folders, deletes the user's shared folder, and then removes the user account. You can observe this process taking place, as shown in Figure 6-12. When the process has completed, click Done to close the wizard.

6. If you want to keep the user's shared folder, click the Keep the Shared Folder radio button and click Next to continue.

7. You then can assign access rights to another user, or choose not to let any other user account access that shared folder and have the Windows Home Server administrator modify access at a later time, as shown in Figure 6-13. If you want to reassign access rights to another user, choose that user from the drop-down list and click Next. If you want to assign rights to that shared folder at a later time, click the Do Not Let Any Other User Account Access the Shared Folder radio button and click Next.

Note For more information on shared folders, take a look at Chapter 9.

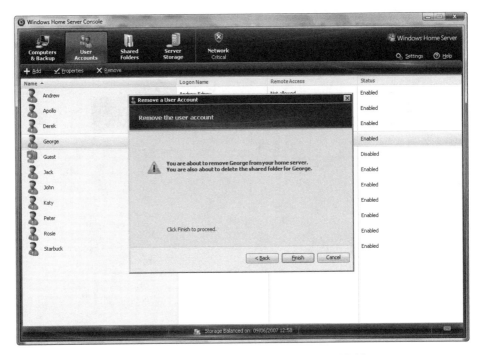

Figure 6-11. *Confirm the removal of the user account and shared folder.*

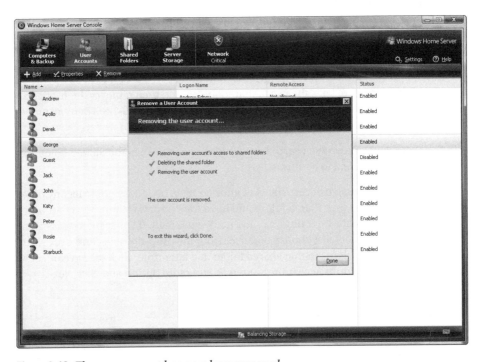

Figure 6-12. *The user account has now been removed.*

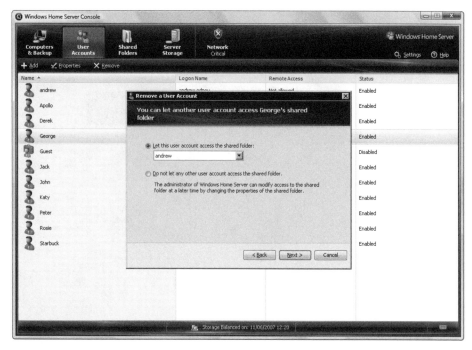

Figure 6-13. *Decide whether to reassign the access rights to the user's shared folder.*

8. You are advised that you are about to remove the selected user account from your Windows Home Server. You are also advised that you are about to reassign rights to the shared folder for that user to a different user, as shown in Figure 6-14, unless you chose the option to not let any other user account access the shared folder, in which case you see that no user account will have access to the shared folder. Click Finish to remove the account and reassign access rights to the shared folder.

9. The process then removes any access that the selected user had to any of the other shared folders, reassigns access to the user's shared folder to the chosen user (if any), and removes the user account, as shown in Figure 6-15. When the process has completed, click Done to close the wizard.

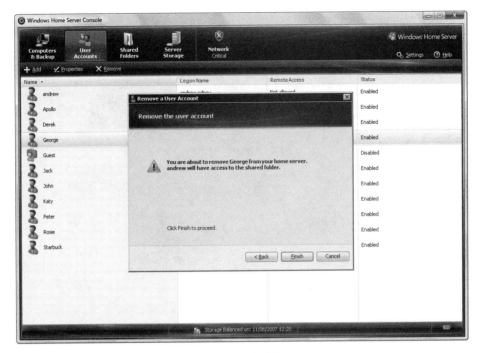

Figure 6-14. *Click Finish to confirm the removal of the user account.*

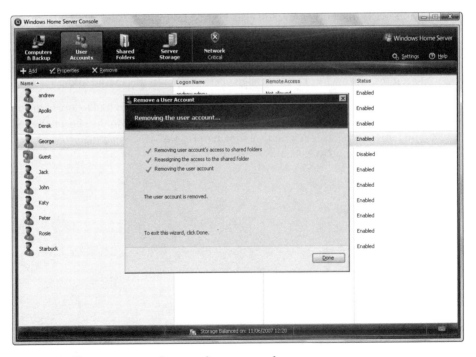

Figure 6-15. *The user account has now been removed.*

Disabling and Enabling a User Account

Instead of deleting a user account completely, you have the option to disable it. This is useful if you only want to temporarily prevent a user from accessing shared folders on Windows Home Server. There could be many reasons for doing this. For example, you might want to have accounts available for relatives who stay with you on a regular basis, and you don't want to continually create and delete accounts for them. When a user account is disabled, all of the user's shared folders and files remain on the Windows Home Server but that user is unable to access them.

■**Note** Any other user with access to that user's shared folders will still be able to access the files stored within. If you want to stop everyone from accessing the contents of the shared folder, then you need to remove everyone's access to the folder. For more information on how to do this, take a look at Chapter 9.

To disable a user account, perform the following steps:

1. On the User Accounts tab, right-click the user account that you wish to disable.

2. Click Disable Account on the context menu, as shown in Figure 6-16.

Figure 6-16. *Choose Disable Account to disable a user account.*

3. You are asked to confirm you want to disable the user account, as shown in Figure 6-17. Click Yes to disable it.

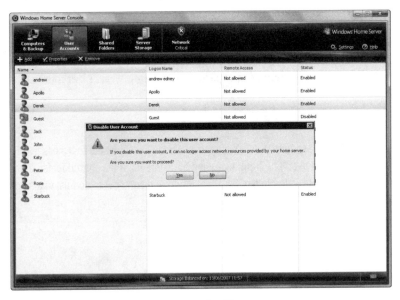

Figure 6-17. *Confirm that you want to disable a user account.*

To re-enable a user account, perform the following steps:

1. Right-click the user account that you wish to enable.

2. Click Enable Account on the context menu, as shown in Figure 6-18.

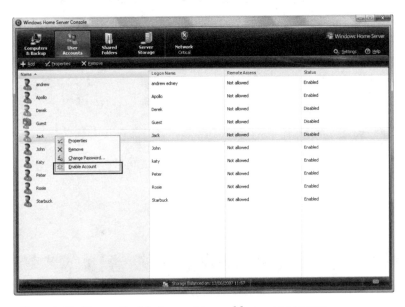

Figure 6-18. *Choose Enable Account to enable a user account.*

Changing Account Properties

Once the user account has been created, you can easily change any of the account properties, such as the actual name, the logon name, the password, and even the shared folder access privileges.

To open the properties of a particular user account, either double-click that user account or select the user account and then click Properties. You then see the Properties dialog box for the selected user account, as shown in Figure 6-19.

Figure 6-19. *User account properties*

The Properties dialog box has two tabs, General and Shared Folder Access. The General tab has two sections:

- *Properties*: You can change the first name, last name, and logon name for the selected account, as well as enable remote access for the user by placing a check in the box.

- *Account Status*: You can view the current status of the user account and click a button to change the password or disable the account.

If you want to change the user account password, click the Change Password button to open the Change Password dialog box, shown in Figure 6-20. Enter the new password (conforming to whatever password requirements are set up), enter it again to confirm, and then click the OK button.

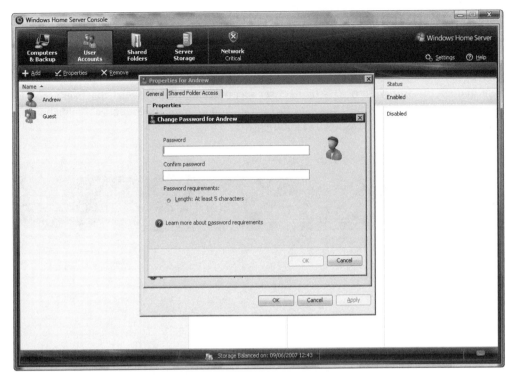

Figure 6-20. *Changing the password for the selected user account*

■**Tip** You can also access the dialog box to change the password for a user by right-clicking the user account on the User Accounts tab and clicking Change Password from the context menu.

The other Properties dialog box tab is the Shared Folder Access tab, shown in Figure 6-21, which lists all of the shared folders and their current access rights.

On this tab, you can easily change the access privileges to any of the shared folders. You can choose between Full, Read, and None, just as before. Notice that the user account you are looking at is shown in bold.

Figure 6-21. *Shared Folder Access tab for the selected user account*

Matching Passwords

To make life easier for users, if the passwords for their Windows user account (the one they use on their computer) and their Windows Home Server user account match, they won't be prompted to enter their username and password every time they access a shared folder on the Windows Home Server. Entering both might not seem like a big deal, but if that user accesses a lot of shared folders on a regular basis, then it can become a real pain and waste a lot of time.

■**Note** Each user can change their own passwords so that they match—this is not something that you as the "administrator" are expected to do. All they need is the Windows Home Server Console installed on their computer.

If the passwords do not match, then you will see the Passwords Do Not Match warning message, as shown in Figure 6-22. This message will appear when your computer detects the Windows Home Server on your home network.

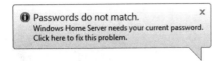

Figure 6-22. *Your passwords do not match.*

Ensuring that the passwords match certainly makes more sense from an ease-of-use perspective, but if you are concerned about security and would prefer a different password, you can ignore this message and leave things as they are.

■**Tip** If you are concerned about password security, you can also change the password complexity rules to make sure you have a very strong password.

If you want to update the password, you have the choice either to keep your password on the Windows computer and change your password on your Windows Home Server user account or to keep your password on your Windows Home Server user account and change your password on the Windows computer. (This example is worded as if you are changing your own password, not another user's; the process is the same either way.)

To keep your Windows computer password and change your Windows Home Server user account password, follow these steps:

1. Right-click the Windows Home Server Console icon in the task tray and click Update Password in the context menu, as shown in Figure 6-23.

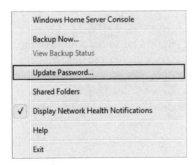

Figure 6-23. *Choose Update Password from the context menu.*

2. In the Update Password dialog box, shown in Figure 6-24, click the Keep My Password on This Computer radio button.

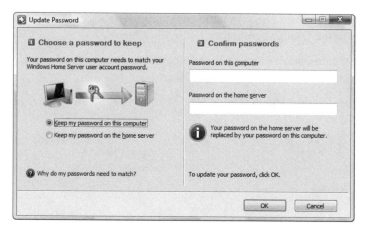

Figure 6-24. *Choosing to keep the password on the Windows computer*

3. Enter your password for the Windows computer in the first box.

4. Enter your password for the Windows Home Server user account in the second box.

5. Click OK to continue.

Note If you enter an incorrect password, or you don't enter a password in the two boxes, you receive an error stating that "the parameter is incorrect." Don't worry; enter the passwords again in the relevant boxes and click Retry.

---

6. The password on your Windows Home Server user account will then be changed for you, and you should see a confirmation of this event, as shown in Figure 6-25. Click Close to finish.

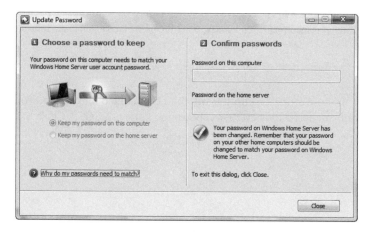

Figure 6-25. *Your password has been updated.*

If you want to keep the password on your Windows Home Server user account and change the password on your Windows computer, follow these steps:

1. Right-click the Windows Home Server Console icon in the task tray and click Update Password in the context menu (see Figure 6-23).

2. Click the Keep My Password on the Home Server radio button, as shown in Figure 6-26.

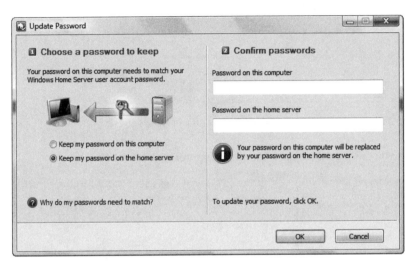

Figure 6-26. *Choose to keep your Windows Home Server user account password.*

3. Enter your password for the Windows computer in the first box.

4. Enter your password for the Windows Home Server user account in the second box.

5. Click OK to continue.

▄**Note** If you enter an incorrect password, or you don't enter a password in the two boxes, you receive an error stating that "the parameter is incorrect." Don't worry; enter the passwords again in the relevant boxes and click Retry.

---

6. Your password on the Windows computer will then be changed for you, and you should see a confirmation of this event, as shown in Figure 6-27. Click Close to finish.

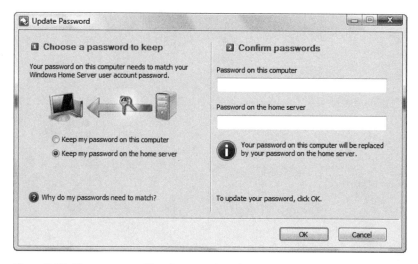

Figure 6-27. *Your password has been updated.*

Summary

In this chapter, you learned how to create a user account for access to shared resources on your Windows Home Server. You learned why it is useful for the logon name and password to match, and how to ensure that they do match. You have also seen how to disable and delete accounts when necessary and how to use the password wizard to set your passwords for you.

CHAPTER 7

Home Computer Backups and Restores

Backing up your data and computers is crucial to ensure that you don't lose anything important. As long as you have recent backups, you know that you can easily and quickly recover in the event of a major problem. This chapter explains how to back up and restore data using Windows Home Server.

How Do Backups Work?

It might be quite useful, or at least fairly interesting, to understand how the Windows Home Server backups actually work. Would you believe by magic? No, I didn't think so. I will try to explain how they work as simply as possible. If you really don't care how they work—just that they *do* work—feel free to skip ahead to the next section.

Let's say that you have three computers in your home that you connect to Windows Home Server, and you want to back up those computers on a nightly basis. Those three computers combined use a total of around 250GB of disk space. Well, it's easy to do the math and realize that if you backed up 250GB of data a night even for a week, your backup storage requirements would be well over 1.5 terabytes (TB), which is a lot of data and is possibly more storage than you have on your Windows Home Server!

The good news is that Windows Home Server backups don't actually work like that. Most backup software operates at the file level, backing up each individual file. In contrast, Windows Home Server operates with *clusters*. Clusters are the lower-level constructs of the file system and are usually very small—around 4KB.

Windows Home Server examines each cluster on each computer that you want to back up and stores only *one copy* of that cluster, even if it is on all three of those computers. For example, if the Windows Vista operating system files are on all three computers, Windows Home Server stores one copy of that cluster. Along with the cluster, the backup stores information about that cluster, including on which computer(s) it is found. This fantastic technology is known as *single-instance storage*.

But that's not all! Each time a backup takes place, Windows Home Server checks the data for that machine against the data in the existing backups and will back up only the data that has changed since that last backup. That is why you may have noticed that once the initial backup has taken place, subsequent backups seem to complete a lot quicker (or maybe you haven't noticed, if the backups are taking place while you are asleep).

There is a much more technical explanation of what takes place during backups, but I don't want to give you, or me, a headache trying to explain it.

Working with Backups

The Windows Home Server Console's Computers & Backup tab allows you to manage your backups. As shown in Figure 7-1, this tab displays a list of all of your home computers that have the Windows Home Server Connector installed, with four columns of information.

- *Name*: This is the name of the computer.

- *Description*: This will be populated only if you have entered something in the Computer Description box on the Computer Name tab of the System Properties dialog box for that computer, as shown in Figure 7-2.

■**Tip** Checking the backup status may be easier if you ensure that each computer has something in the Computer Description box, such as "Andrew's PC in Study," especially if the computer names you use are not very specific. To view the Computer Name tab of the System Properties dialog box, right-click the Computer icon on the desktop and click Properties. Then on the System page, find the Computer Name, Domain, and Workgroup Settings area, and click the Change Settings button.

- *Operating System*: This is the version of the operating system that is on that computer, such as Windows Vista Ultimate Edition.

- *Status*: This is the backup status and can show status messages including Not backed up, No backups in last *x* days, Backed up, or even Off if you decide that you don't want to back up that machine. Those messages are accompanied by colored status lights: gray for off, green for backed up, yellow for no backup in last *x* days, and red for not backed up or no backup performed after a longer period than the previous *x* days used for yellow.

Figure 7-1. *The Computers & Backup tab in the Windows Home Server Console*

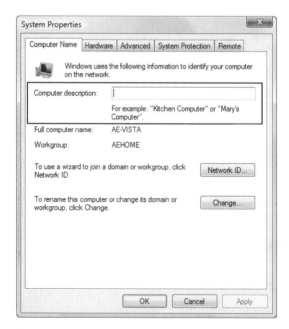

Figure 7-2. *Entering a computer description*

Any computer that is not switched on will be grayed out in the Computers & Backup tab's list.

Managing Backups

From the Computers & Backup tab of the Windows Home Server Console, you can select a computer and click View Backups to display a list of all backups that are available for that computer, as shown in Figure 7-3. All backups—whether they completed successfully or failed—will be listed here. The padlock shown next to the date in the example indicates that the backup will be kept until you choose to have it deleted.

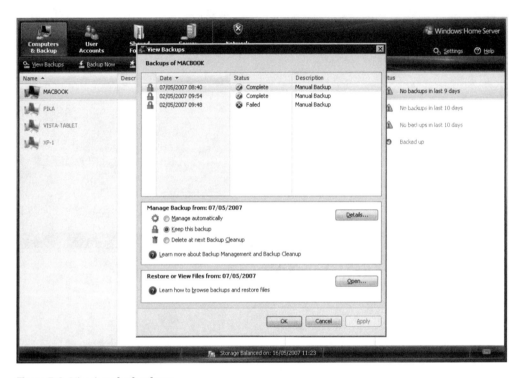

Figure 7-3. *Viewing the backups*

Three options are available for managing backups:

- *Manage automatically*: Keeps the backup until the time specified in the backup settings.

- *Keep this backup*: Does exactly what it says—keeps the backup until such time as you decide to delete it.

- *Delete at next Backup Cleanup*: Allows Windows Home Server to delete the backup during the next scheduled backup cleanup, as you defined in the backup settings (as described in Chapter 5).

You can go through each of the backups in the list and select any one of those options.

Note The default option for manual backups is to keep the backup so you don't need to worry about losing a backup by mistake. The default option for normal automated backups is to manage automatically, which is accordance with the settings you have defined for keeping backups.

You can also choose to view the details of any of the backups by clicking the Details button. This will open the Backup Details dialog box, as shown in Figure 7-4. The Backup Details dialog box displays various useful pieces of information, such as the status, the description (Manual Backup in the example), which volumes were backed up, and which files were excluded from the backup.

Figure 7-4. *Viewing the details of a particular backup*

You can also easily turn off backups from the main Computers & Backups tab. Right-click the computer for which you want to turn off backups and select Turn Off Backups. If you select this option, backups will be switched off for that computer. You can easily switch backups back on by right-clicking the computer again and selecting Turn On Backups.

Note Even though the option to Backup Now is available when you have turned off backups, it will fail. If you want to perform a manual backup on a computer, you must first turn on backups for that computer.

Finally, you can completely remove a computer from the set of computers that are being backed up and monitored by Windows Home Server. This could be for any number of reasons, including that you no longer have that computer or you have used all ten of your computer licenses. To remove a computer, click it, and then click the Remove Computer button above the list. You will then be warned that all backups will be deleted from the Windows Home Server, as shown in Figure 7-5. Place a check in the box next to "I am sure I want to remove this computer," and then click Remove. The computer will then be removed from the backup set.

■**Caution** When you delete a computer from the Computers & Backup tab, all backups for that computer are also deleted.

Figure 7-5. *Stating that you are sure you want to remove the computer*

Creating or Changing a Backup Configuration

As you may remember from Chapter 4, when you installed the Windows Home Server Connector software onto your computer, part of the installation and configuration process included creating a backup configuration that was set to back up your computer between midnight and 6 a.m. each day.

You can easily change the backup configuration or create a new backup configuration from the Windows Home Server Console. This includes adding or excluding volumes and excluding specific folders. However, if you want to change the backup window, you must do this through the Settings option within the Windows Home Server Console, as described in Chapter 5.

Follow these steps to create or change a backup configuration:

1. Start the Windows Home Server Console. You can create or change the backup configuration for another computer other than the one you are currently using, as long as it is switched on and connected to the network. You can easily tell if this is the case because any computer not switched on and connected is grayed out.

2. On the Computers & Backup tab, click the computer for which you want to create or change the backup configuration.

3. Click the Configure Backup button to launch the Backup Configuration Wizard, as shown in Figure 7-6.

Figure 7-6. *Launching the Backup Configuration Wizard*

4. Click the Next button to continue. The wizard will collect some information about the chosen computer. This could take a few moments, so be patient. You will then see a list of all of the available volumes that can be backed up, as shown in Figure 7-7. You will also see the capacity of each volume, how much space has been used, whether or not it is an internal or external drive, and its status.

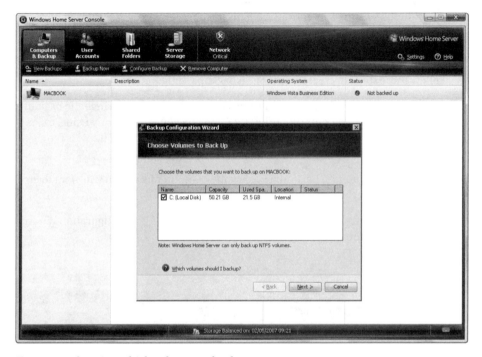

Figure 7-7. *Choosing which volumes to back up*

5. Ensure there is a check in the box for each volume you want to back up. If you don't want to back up a volume for whatever reason, just remove the check.

Note Windows Home Server can back up only NTFS volumes. If you have a drive that is configured as FAT or FAT32, it won't be backed up. If you want that drive backed up, you should consider converting it to NTFS. For more information about how to convert a drive to NTFS, see the Windows help files.

---

6. Click Next to continue. You will see a list of folders that are automatically excluded from the backup, as shown in Figure 7-8. As you can see, certain folders are excluded because they are not really important and can safely be ignored. These folders can include the following:

- Client-side cache folders

- User temporary files

- System page file

- Hibernation file

- Windows Media Center temporary files

At this point, you have the opportunity to exclude other folders that you don't want to back up. For example, you may have a folder full of music that you don't want to back up because you already have a copy elsewhere. If you don't want to exclude any other folders, you can skip to step 9.

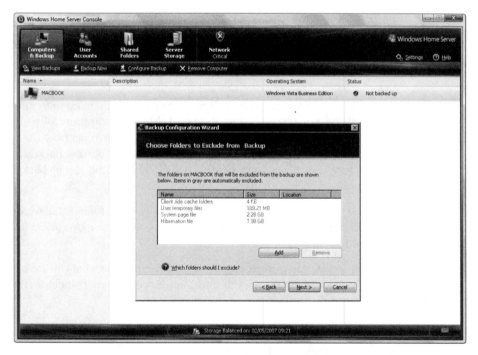

Figure 7-8. *Folders that are automatically excluded from the backup process*

7. Click the Add button in order to specify other folders to be excluded from the backup. A list of all folders on that volume will appear, as shown in the example in Figure 7-9.

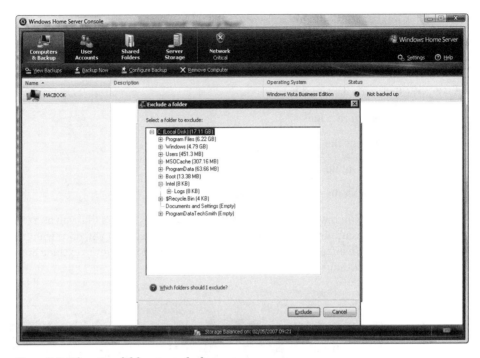

Figure 7-9. *Choosing folders to exclude*

8. Work through the list of folders and highlight the ones you want to exclude, and then click the Exclude button. If you change your mind about excluding any folders, just click the Cancel button. Note that you cannot exclude the root folder from the backup. If you try, you will see a warning advising you to cancel the whole disk backup instead, as shown in Figure 7-10. If you don't want to back up that volume, just go back to the volume selection screen and uncheck the volume.

9. Any folders you have selected will be displayed along with the folders that were automatically selected for you. Make sure you are happy with the excluded folder list, and then click Next to continue.

10. You will see the final wizard screen, which shows a summary of what you are backing up, as shown in Figure 7-11. Review this information. The summary includes the following important information:

- The number of volumes that are being backed up

- The number of folders that are being excluded from the backup

- The estimated backup size

- The time frame in which the backup will take place

11. Click the Done button to finish.

Figure 7-10. *Warning telling you that you cannot exclude the root folder*

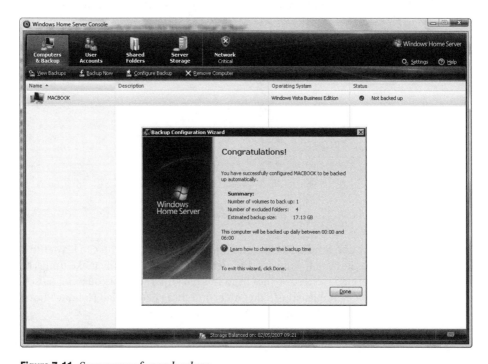

Figure 7-11. *Summary of your backup*

■**Caution** Automatic backups of laptops will take place only if the laptop is connected to AC power. This is to avoid a power drain on the laptop during the backup process. Make sure your laptop is plugged into the power outlet before leaving it to be backed up automatically.

Performing a Manual Backup

Now that your automatic backups are configured and you have set a time frame that you are happy with, you can rest easy knowing that your computers will be backed up regularly.

But wait—what if you want to perform a backup before the usual backup window? Suppose that you just created a load of new files or imported some new digital camera pictures, and you want to back up those files immediately. Well, you are in luck, because you can run a manual backup at any time. This will have no effect on your automatic backups—they will still take place as scheduled.

You can start a manual backup from within the Windows Home Server Console or from the task tray.

Starting a Backup from the Task Tray

You can start a manual backup without needing to have the Windows Home Server Console open. To do this, follow these simple steps:

1. Right-click the Windows Home Server task tray icon and click Backup Now, as shown in Figure 7-12.

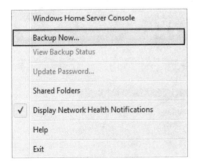

Figure 7-12. *Choosing to start a manual backup from the task tray*

2. Enter a description for this backup, as shown in Figure 7-13. You can leave the description as Manual Backup if you wish, but replacing it will certainly make things easier for you if you later need to restore files from this backup. I suggest you enter a useful description; for example, you could enter something like "Added Holiday Photos" for the backup that contains your new digital pictures.

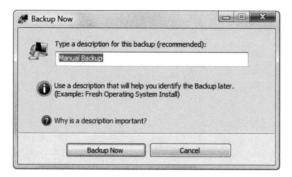

Figure 7-13. *Entering a description for the manual backup*

3. Click Backup Now to start the backup. You will see a message informing you that the backup is starting, as shown in Figure 7-14.

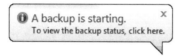

Figure 7-14. *Message balloon telling you that the backup is starting*

You can click the message balloon to view the backup status. If you missed the chance to click it here, you can right-click the Windows Home Server task tray icon (which has now turned blue) and choose View Backup Status, as shown in Figure 7-15.

Figure 7-15. *Choosing to view the backup status from the task tray*

Next, five backup status windows are displayed in sequence, as shown in Figures 7-16 through 7-20. You will see the backup starting, Windows Home Server determining which files and clusters have changed since the last backup took place, the backup data being sent to the Windows Home Server, and finally that the backup has completed.

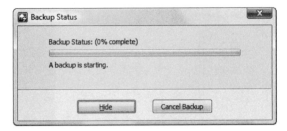

Figure 7-16. *The backup is starting*

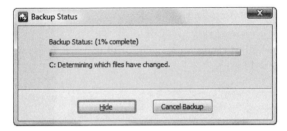

Figure 7-17. *Determining which files have changed*

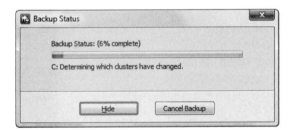

Figure 7-18. *Determining which clusters have changed*

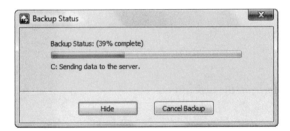

Figure 7-19. *Sending backup data to the server*

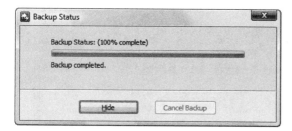

Figure 7-20. *The backup has completed.*

You will also see a message balloon telling you that the backup is complete, as shown in Figure 7-21, regardless of whether or not you are viewing the backup status.

Figure 7-21. *The Backup Is Complete message balloon*

Starting a Backup from the Windows Home Server Console

You can also start a manual backup from the Windows Home Server Console. The advantage of starting a backup from the console is that you can choose to back up any of your computers, as long as they are currently switched on and connected to your home network.

From the Windows Home Server Console, click the computer you want to back up, and then click the Backup Now button above the list. You will be asked to enter a backup description, just as when you start a backup from the task tray, as shown in Figure 7-22.

Everything that follows is the same as if you started the manual backup from the task tray, rather than from the Windows Home Server Console. The only difference is that you can also view the status of the backup from within the Windows Home Server Console, as shown in Figure 7-23.

At any point during a backup, you can choose to stop it by right-clicking the computer name and choosing Cancel Backup, or by clicking the Cancel Backup button in the Backup Status dialog box. If you do choose to cancel the backup, you will see a message balloon telling you that the backup was canceled, as shown in Figure 7-24.

You are also given the option to run the backup again by clicking the message balloon. You can do that if you wish, or you can just run a manual backup again later when you are ready.

Figure 7-22. *Starting a manual backup from within the Windows Home Server Console*

Figure 7-23. *Viewing the backup status from within the Windows Home Server Console*

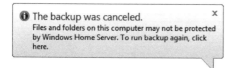

Figure 7-24. *The Backup Was Canceled message balloon*

Troubleshooting Backup Failures

Backups can fail. Fortunately, this is a rare occurrence and is usually accompanied by some additional information that will help you to diagnose the problem and correct it before trying to perform another backup.

I won't go into all the possible reasons for a failed backup, but I will show you where to get additional information to help you find the source of the problem.

During the course of a manual backup, the backup on the computer I was using failed. A message balloon appeared with a message saying that the backup failed because of an error reading data from my hard drive, as shown in Figure 7-25.

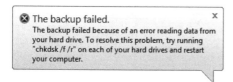

Figure 7-25. *A message balloon advising of a failed backup*

The same error message appeared in the Backup Status dialog box, as shown in Figure 7-26. It is useful to view the backup status messages, as you may not see the message balloon. It will appear and disappear again in only a few seconds, so if you happen to be away from your computer at the time, you could miss it.

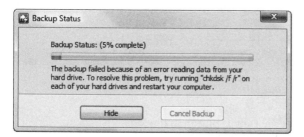

Figure 7-26. *The Backup Status dialog box also advising of the failed backup*

As you can see from both of the error messages I received, in this case, a possible resolution is provided: to run chkdsk /f /r on each of the hard drives on that computer.

Another message balloon will appear, telling you that the most recent backup for that computer was not successful, as shown in Figure 7-27. This message advises you to look at the details of the backup to try to determine the problem.

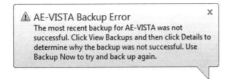

Figure 7-27. *Another message balloon advising you to investigate further*

To see the backup details, open the Windows Home Server Console, and on the Computers & Backup tab, double-click the computer in question. Look through the list of backups until you find the failed backup, or latest failed backup if you have more than one, as shown in Figure 7-28.

Figure 7-28. *Viewing all the backups for the computer*

Click the failed backup, and then click the Details button in the Manage Backup section of the dialog box. This will display the details of the failed backup, as shown in Figure 7-29. You can see that, in this case, the backup failed because "an error occurred reading or writing from the computer's hard drive. C:."

As you can see from this example, the Backup Details dialog box doesn't suggest any steps for resolving the error. You can try the suggestions that appeared earlier when the backup failed. You may also want to investigate the problem further, which could mean looking at Windows event logs.

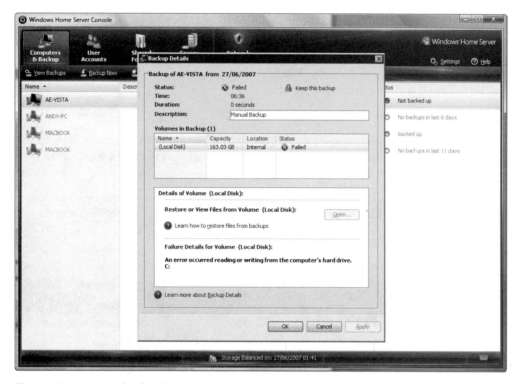

Figure 7-29. *Viewing the details of the failed backup*

■Note To find out more about event logs and Event Viewer, click the Help and Support button on the Start menu and type **event logs**. You will see a list of helpful topics on this subject.

Just to wrap up this section, I performed the chkdsk /f /r as suggested, and it found and corrected a problem on the hard drive. When I ran the manual backup again, it was successful.

Restoring Files and Computers

We have now covered backing up your computers, and you should be quite comfortable with both manual and automatic backups. So what happens if you need to actually restore a file or a number of files because you accidentally deleted something you needed or because some files have become corrupted? Or how about if you need to restore your entire home computer? As long as you have your backups, you can do both types of restore operations through the Windows Home Server Console.

Restoring Selected Files

The easiest place to restore a file or selected files is on the computer where you want the files restored. However, you can use the Windows Home Server Console from any of your home computers, and then just copy the files over to the computer where you want the files.

Follow these steps to restore selected files:

1. Start the Windows Home Server Console.

2. On the Computers & Backup tab, double-click the computer for which you want to retrieve the backup, or click to highlight the computer, and then click the View Backups button above the list.

3. Work through the list of backups until you find the one you want to restore, and then click it. Next, click the Open button in the Restore or View Files section of the dialog box, as shown in Figure 7-30.

Figure 7-30. *Selecting the backup from the list of available backups*

4. If the backup contains more than one volume, you will be asked to select which volume you wish to open from a drop-down list, as shown in Figure 7-31.

■**Note** If you are running Windows Vista and have User Account Control running, you will be asked to give your permission for the program to be run.

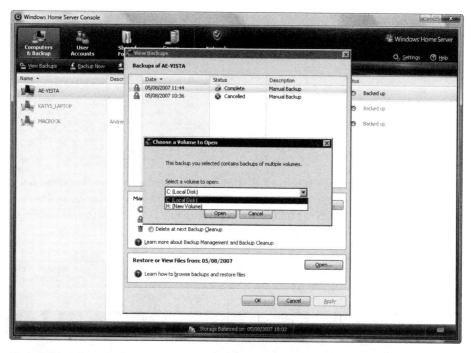

Figure 7-31. *Selecting the volume from the list of available volumes*

5. If this is the first time you have tried to open a backup file, you might be asked to install some device software from Microsoft, as shown in Figure 7-32. You will only need to install this once per computer. It is used to open the backup file and display it as though it were another drive on your computer.

Figure 7-32. *You need to install some device software to open a backup file.*

6. It may take a few minutes for the backup to be displayed on your computer. You can monitor the progress while you are waiting, as shown in Figure 7-33.

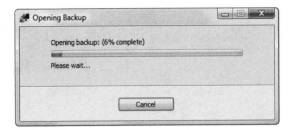

Figure 7-33. *Monitoring the progress of opening the backup file*

7. When the backup file has opened, it will be displayed in Windows as though it were a normal drive (in this example, as a local disk with the drive letter Z), as shown in Figure 7-34. Search through the folders in the backup until you locate the file or files you want to restore.

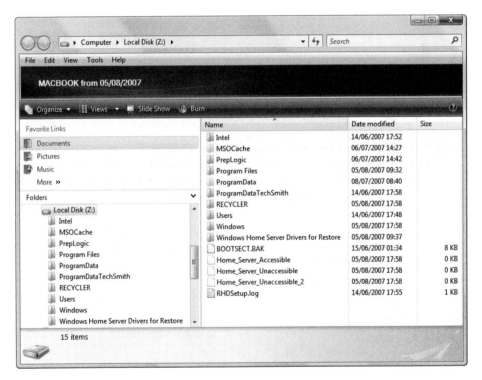

Figure 7-34. *Viewing the contents of the backup file*

8. Drag and drop the file or files you want to restore anywhere on your computer, or copy them to a USB flash drive or other device if that's easier for you.

9. When you have copied all of the files you want, click the X in the top-right corner to close the window.

10. Click OK or Cancel in the View Backups dialog box.

You should find that your backup has been restored to the location you specified.

Restoring a Home Computer

A time may come when you need to do more than just restore a few files. You may need to restore your entire computer, just the system volume, or even just a data drive. Performing a restore could be for any number of reasons, including a failed hard drive or a serious virus infection on your computer.

Note The system volume contains, among other things, hardware-specific files that Windows requires to start up. You can restore a system volume only back to the original computer where it was backed up.

Usually, the process of restoring a computer can be quite painful and time-consuming. It can mean starting from scratch—reinstalling the operating system, installing drivers, performing updates, applying security patches, reinstalling applications, reconfiguring applications, and then getting your data back. As you can imagine, or even remember, this can be quite painful. Well, that's no longer the case.

If you have backed up your computer to your Windows Home Server, restoring it is quite a simple process that requires only the Windows Home Server Home Computer Restore CD and any specific drivers you might need.

Caution You can restore your computer only up to the last successful backup that was taken. Any changes that were made to your computer, including any files that may have been created, will not be part of the recovery. This is why you should back up each of your computers on a daily or other regular basis.

Starting the Restore Process

The home computer on which you want to perform the restore must be connected to your home network with an Ethernet cable; a wireless connection will not work. Make sure you have connected an Ethernet cable to your computer before you continue with the following steps.

1. Ensure the Windows Home Server is switched on and connected to your home network (chances are you will never switch it off!).

2. Place the Windows Home Server Home Computer Restore CD into the drive of the computer you want to restore.

■**Note** Don't worry if you don't have a copy of the Windows Home Server Home Computer Restore CD handy. A copy of the ISO image is stored in the Software shared folder on the Windows Home Server, so you can easily create one if necessary. An ISO image is a file that contains everything needed to perfectly duplicate the contents of a disc. Windows itself cannot write an ISO image to a CD, but most CD and DVD writing software can do this easily. If you don't have the software to create a CD from an ISO image, just do a search on the Internet for a program that has this capability.

3. Restart your computer and boot from the CD/DVD drive. It can be set to boot from the CD/DVD drive, or you can press the appropriate key on your keyboard during the initial boot sequence to choose where to boot from, and select the CD/DVD drive. When your computer starts to boot from the CD, after a few minutes, you will be presented with the screen shown in Figure 7-35. (This process may take a few minutes; essentially, your computer is being prepared for the restore process.)

■**Note** If you are not sure how to change the boot sequence or which key on your computer keyboard allows you to select which device to boot from, consult the manual that came with your computer.

Figure 7-35. *Initializing the Restore CD*

4. Eventually, you will be asked to select your regional and keyboard settings, as shown in Figure 7-36. Select the time and currency format from the drop-down list. Select the keyboard or input method from the drop-down list. When you are happy with your selections, click the Continue button.

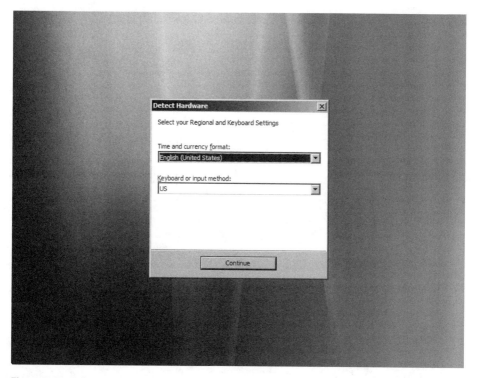

Figure 7-36. *Selecting your regional and keyboard settings*

5. The restore process will now detect your network connection and hard drives attached to the computer, as shown in Figure 7-37. In order to check that all the hardware has been detected properly, click the Show Details button.

■**Note** It is very important that your network connection be functioning so that your computer can communicate with and connect to your Windows Home Server in order to access the computer backup. It is also equally important that your hard drives are functioning correctly in order to recover the backup.

---

6. You will see all of the detected network devices and storage devices, as in the example shown in Figure 7-38. Check that your devices have been detected correctly. If they have all been detected, just click the Continue button, and skip to the "Running the Restore Computer Wizard" section. If some devices are missing, continue to the next section.

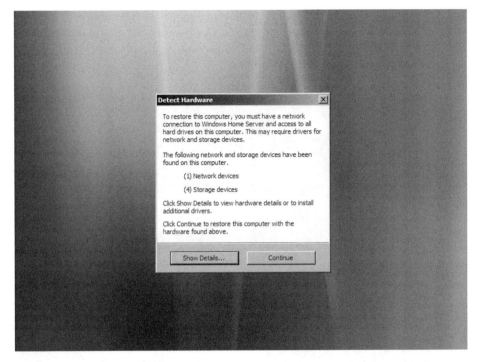

Figure 7-37. *Detecting your hardware*

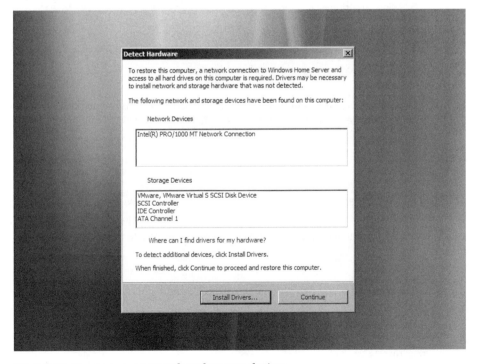

Figure 7-38. *Viewing your network and storage devices*

Loading Missing Drivers

If some hardware was not detected, this may be because a driver needs to be installed. If you are missing any drivers, they are most likely the network drivers or the storage-device drivers.

Note You could also be missing some hardware because of an actual hardware fault. After all, you could be recovering your computer because of a hardware failure. In that case, after you have replaced the faulty piece of hardware, start the restore process again. It is also a good idea to check all of the connections to the hardware; it is very easy for a cable to become loose.

From the Detect Hardware dialog box, click the Install Drivers button. You will then be asked to insert a USB flash drive or a floppy disk that contains the drivers for your missing hardware, as shown in Figure 7-39.

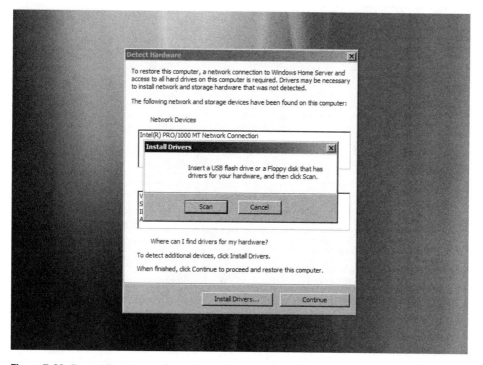

Figure 7-39. *Preparing to scan for missing drivers*

Caution You will need to ensure the driver is on either a USB flash drive or a floppy disk, as there is no other way to install the driver. You cannot take the Windows Home Server Home Computer Restore CD out of the drive and replace it with a driver CD.

If you are missing drivers, you can easily copy them to a USB flash drive or floppy disk and be certain that they are the correct ones. This is because, during the backup process, Windows Home Server creates a folder called Windows Home Server Drivers for Restore and places all relevant drivers into that folder. In order to copy those files to either a USB flash drive or a floppy disk, you need to be at one of your computers that has the Windows Home Server Console running on it. Open the Computers & Backup tab and double-click the computer that you are planning on restoring. Then click the specific backup you are going to use and click the Open button in the Restore or View Files area of the dialog box (in the same way as when you recover single or multiple files). The backup file will then be opened and the files displayed, as shown in Figure 7-40.

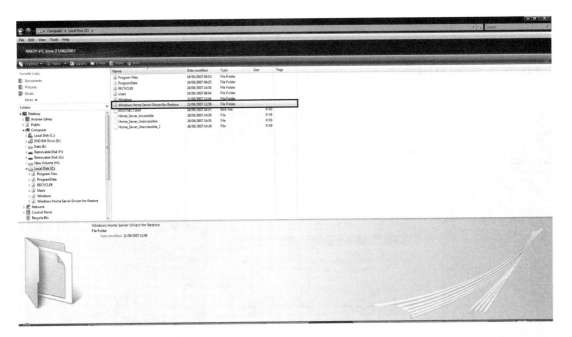

Figure 7-40. *The contents of the backup file*

Now copy the Windows Home Server Drivers for Restore folder to either the USB flash drive or the floppy drive. If you open the Windows Home Server Drivers for Restore folder, you should see a number of folders similar to those shown in Figure 7-41. This is just a quick check to ensure they are there and have been copied over.

After you have inserted either the USB flash drive or a floppy disk, click the Scan button to begin the scanning process to locate the missing drivers. If the drivers are located and installed, you can continue the restore process.

If the drivers cannot be found, you will see a message to that effect, as shown in Figure 7-42. Click OK to close the message box. Now you can either try again using a different USB flash drive or floppy disk, or recopy the drivers and attempt to load them again.

When you have loaded all of the correct drivers, you are ready to continue, so just click the Continue button in the Detect Hardware dialog box.

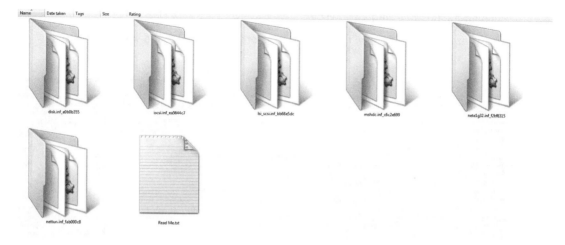

Figure 7-41. *The contents of the Windows Home Server Drivers for Restore folder*

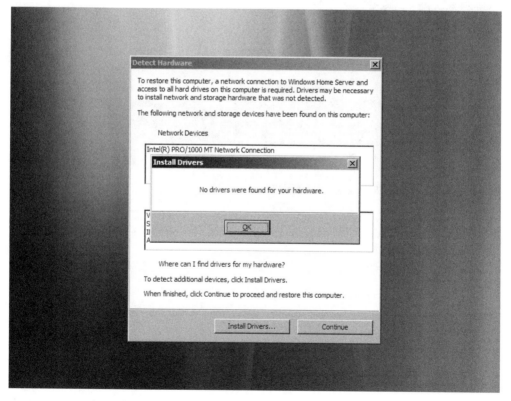

Figure 7-42. *Unfortunately, no drivers could be found.*

Running the Restore Computer Wizard

After your hardware has been detected, the Restore Computer Wizard starts, as shown in Figure 7-43.

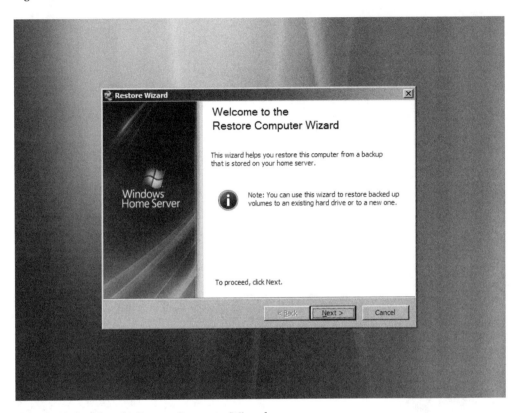

Figure 7-43. *Starting the Restore Computer Wizard*

1. Click the Next button to continue. You will be asked to enter the Windows Home Server password, as shown in Figure 7-44.

■Note If you have forgotten the password (shame on you), you can click the Password Hint button to get a reminder.

---

2. Type in the Windows Home Server password and click Next to continue.

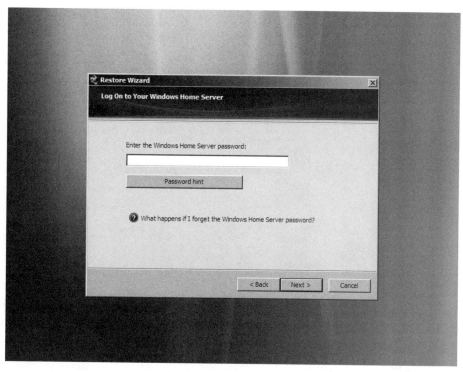

Figure 7-44. *Type in the Windows Home Server password.*

3. The wizard will now attempt to connect to your Windows Home Server in order to check which backups are available. When that process is complete (it shouldn't take more than a few seconds), you will be presented with a list of computers for which backups are available, as shown in Figure 7-45. Select the computer that you want to perform a recovery on from the drop-down list, and then click Next to continue.

■**Caution** Make sure you select the correct computer from the list. Otherwise, who knows what strange things might happen!

---

4. You will then be presented with a list of all of the available backups for the computer you selected, as in the example in Figure 7-46. Select the backup to restore. Chances are that you will want to restore the latest available backup, so just make sure you select that before continuing.

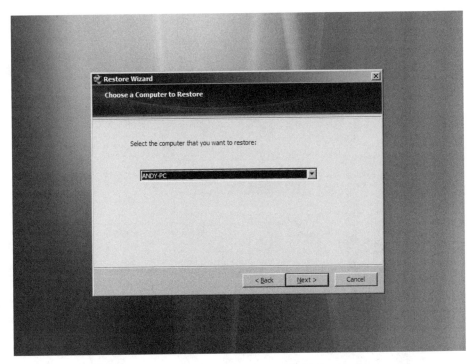

Figure 7-45. *Selecting the computer from the list of available backups*

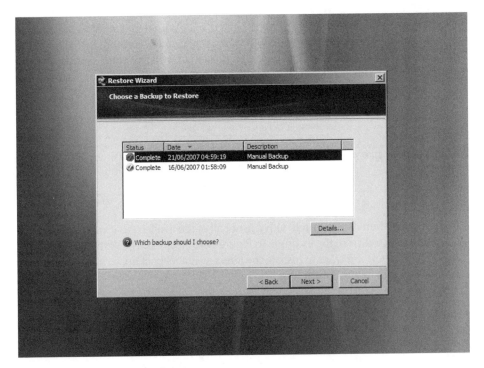

Figure 7-46. *Selecting the backup to restore*

5. If you want to see additional details about any of the available backups, just click the backup, and then click the Details button. This will bring up additional information about the backup, including when the backup took place and which files were excluded from the backup, as shown in Figure 7-47. Click OK after you have reviewed the backup details to return to the backup selection screen.

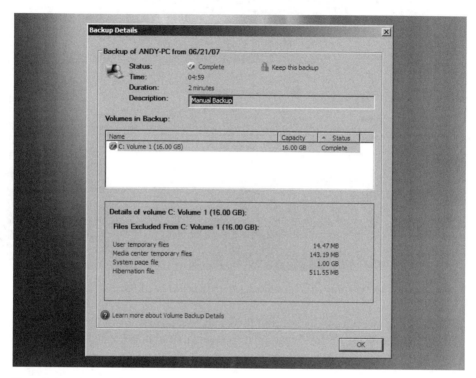

Figure 7-47. *Viewing details on a specific backup*

6. Click Next to continue. If you have not configured your disks yet—for example, you have added a brand-new hard disk to replace a failed one—you will be presented with a warning advising you that there were no initialized disks found, as shown in Figure 7-48. Click OK to clear the warning message. You will then be presented with the volume selection screen.

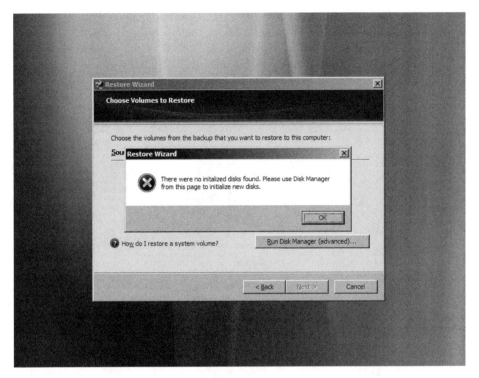

Figure 7-48. *Warning that no initialized disks could be found*

If you have already configured your disks or are using existing disks, you can skip ahead to the "Completing the Restore" section. If you need to initialize the disks before continuing, follow the instructions in the next section.

Initializing Disks

If no initialized disks were found, your volume selection screen will look like Figure 7-49. So, you need to initialize the disks before you can continue, which you can do through Disk Manager.

In the volume selection screen, click the Run Disk Manager (Advanced) button. Disk Manager will launch, and you will be presented with the Initialize Disk dialog box, as shown in Figure 7-50.

In this example, only one new disk drive is in the computer. It is shown as Disk 0, and the box is already checked. You can also select the partition style for each of the available disks. The choices are MBR (Master Boot Record) or GPT (GUID Partition Table). Make sure the disks you want to initialize are checked, and ensure you have selected the partition style you want to use, and then click OK.

Right-click anywhere in the white space next to the new disk marked Unallocated and select New Simple Volume from the context menu to launch the New Simple Volume Wizard, as shown in Figure 7-51.

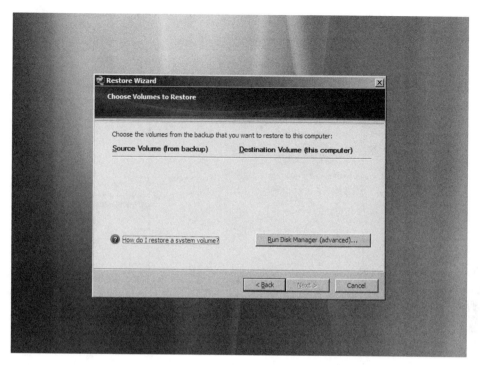

Figure 7-49. *The volume selection screen when no initialized disks could be found*

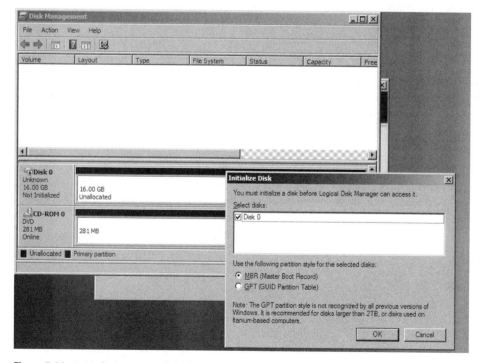

Figure 7-50. *Initializing your disks*

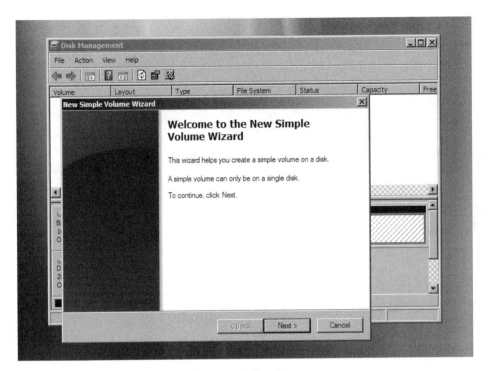

Figure 7-51. *Starting the New Simple Volume Wizard*

Click Next to continue. Select the volume size you wish to use in megabytes, a shown in Figure 7-52, and then click Next to continue.

■**Caution** You will see from the Specify Volume Size screen that you can specify any figure between the minimum disk space and the maximum disk space. You must ensure that the disk space at least equals the size of the backup you have; otherwise, it won't work!

You will then be asked to assign a drive letter to the newly created partition, as shown in Figure 7-53. This is most likely to be the C drive, but only you will know if you have changed the drive letter! Make sure the drive letter is what you want it to be, and then click Next to continue.

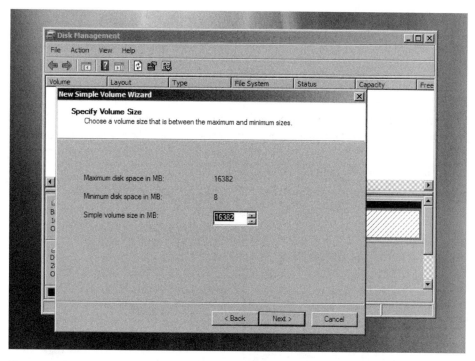

Figure 7-52. *Selecting a volume size for the new disk*

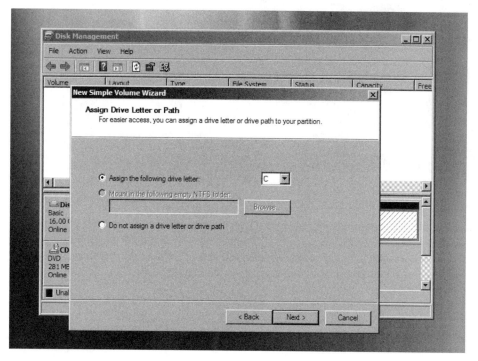

Figure 7-53. *Assigning a drive letter to the new drive*

You will then be given the option to format the partition, as shown in Figure 7-54. Obviously, you need to format the partition—otherwise, the restore process cannot continue—so the wizard has already reselected the Format option. Make any changes you wish and click Next to continue.

Note If you want to speed up the formatting process, you can check the Perform a Quick Format box. However, it is important to note that performing a quick format does not check the disk first; it just assumes there are no problems with the disk. Unless you are in a desperate rush to complete your restore, I strongly suggest not checking this box.

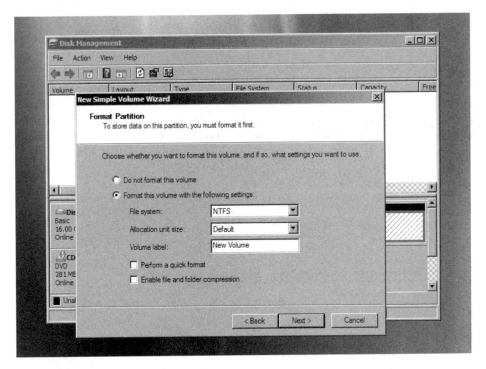

Figure 7-54. *Selecting formatting options*

Now you will see a summary listing of your chosen selections. Click Finish to complete the New Simple Volume Wizard. The process will take a few moments. When it has completed, you will again be presented with the volume selection screen, only this time you can select a source volume from the backup to restore to your newly created destination volume on the computer.

Completing the Restore

The volume selection screen allows you select a source and destination volume, as shown in Figure 7-55. If you have more than one volume in the backup set, you can select each volume and each destination.

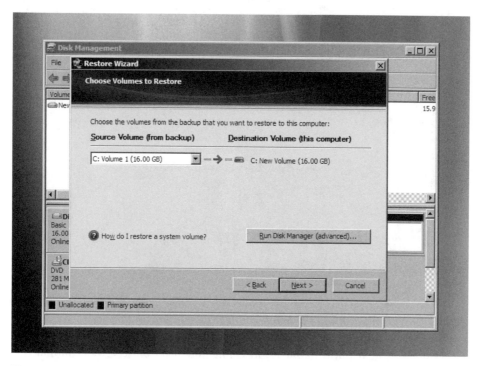

Figure 7-55. *Selecting the source volume from the backup to restore*

1. Make sure your have selected your source volumes from the backup and that you are happy with the selections, and then click Next to continue.

2. You will be prompted to confirm the restore configuration, as shown in Figure 7-56.

■**Caution** It is important to note the warning that if you proceed, all data on the destination drive will be deleted. This is not a problem if you are using a brand-new drive, as in this example. However if you are using an existing drive, you should make sure you have backed up any important files you want to keep, especially any files that have changed or been created since the last successful backup took place.

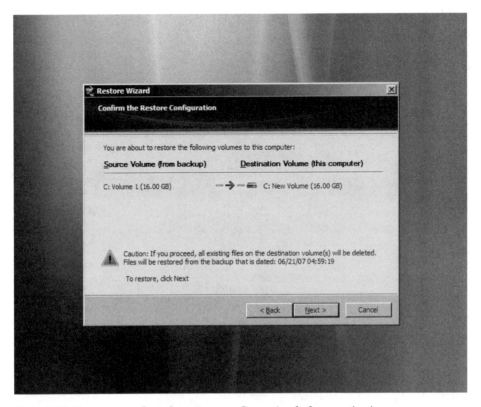

Figure 7-56. *You must confirm the restore configuration before continuing.*

3. Check that you are happy with the restore configuration and click Next to continue. The restore process will now begin. You can watch the progress of the restoration, including a very rough estimate of how long it will take, as shown in Figure 7-57.

Note This process can take a considerable amount of time, depending on the amount of data and number of volumes to be restored, so be patient.

---

4. When the restoration process has completed, you will see the Restore Successfully Completed screen, as shown in Figure 7-58. This screen will also display a summary of the restored volumes. Click the Finish button to complete the restoration process, which will reboot your computer.

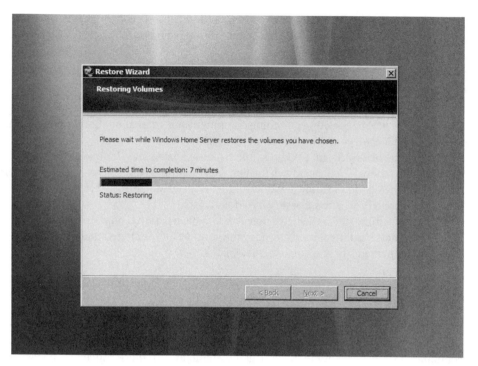

Figure 7-57. *Checking the progress of the restore*

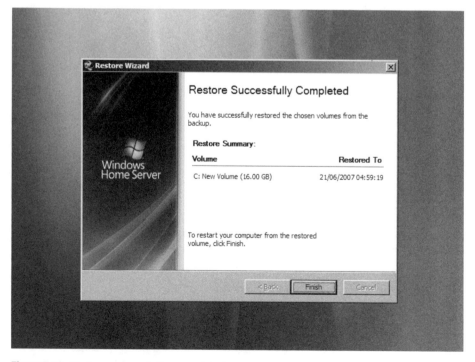

Figure 7-58. *Restore successfully completed*

And that's it! It may seem like a lot of steps and screens to go through, but the process itself is very simple, and you should be up and running in no time—well, as long as it takes to successfully restore from backup.

Backing Up Your Windows Home Server

You have seen how to back up your home computers, but what about backing up the data in the shared folders on your Windows Home Server?

At the time of writing, no backup solutions are available for Windows Home Server, but this is likely to change. You can check the current situation by doing a search on the Internet or checking the Windows Home Server web site (`http://www.microsoft.com/windows/products/winfamily/windowshomeserver/default.mspx`).

In the meantime, the best suggestion is to attach an external hard drive to one of your home computers, and then manually copy the contents of the shared folders to that drive. You should repeat this process on a regular basis.

Summary

In this chapter, you learned about the different ways you can perform backups and the differences between restoring a single file or a number of files versus restoring an entire home computer. It is worth spending the time getting familiar with these concepts—believe me, you will be glad you did if you have a problem and need to go through the restoration process.

■■■

CHAPTER 8

Windows Home Server Storage

One of the key elements of Windows Home Server revolves around server storage. Basically, the more storage you have available, the more digital files you can share, the more backups you can store, and so on. Unlike other operating systems and computers, adding and removing storage on a Windows Home Server is very simple. This chapter explains how to add, remove, and repair hard drives on your Windows Home Server.

How Does Server Storage Work?

The magic surrounding Windows Home Server storage is known as Drive Extender. This technology enables you to easily add and remove internal and external hard drives of varying sizes.

To add a hard drive, all you need to do is connect the new hard drive, start up the Windows Home Server Console, run a wizard, and make a few mouse clicks—it really is as simple as that. Windows Home Server will take care of everything else for you. You don't need to worry about formatting the drive, assigning it a drive letter, adding file permissions, or anything else that you might be used to if you've added a hard drive to a computer in the past. The same is true if you want to remove a hard drive from Windows Home Server—everything is handled for you, including moving any data that may be stored on that drive to another drive (assuming you have enough free space).

Unlike a normal computer operating system, such as Windows XP or Windows Vista, the storage that is available to a user in Windows Home Server does not use drive letters. That means you don't need to remember on which drive you stored a certain document or a song. Instead, each user just sees a single storage area divided by folders. Now all you have to do is double-click the Shared Folders on Server icon on your computer desktop, and away you go. We'll get to the details of shared folders in the next chapter. In this chapter, you'll learn how to manage your server storage.

Managing Server Storage

As you've seen, the Windows Home Server Console has a tab called Server Storage. Click this tab to view information about any of the hard drives you currently have available in your Windows Home Server, as shown in Figure 8-1.

Figure 8-1. *The Server Storage tab of the Windows Home Server Console*

The following information is displayed for each hard drive on your Windows Home Server:

- *Name*: This is the name of the hard drive, which will also contain the name of the manufacturer.

- *Capacity*: This is the total amount of space *available* on the hard drive, as though it were brand new. This is not to be confused with the amount of space that is left on the hard drive to be used.

- *Location*: This displays if the hard drive is internal or external, as well as the type of hard drive (ATA, USB, and so on).

- *Status*: This displays the health and status of the hard drive, which may be one of the following:

  - *Healthy* means that the hard drive is functioning correctly. This is what you would expect to see normally.

  - *Not Added* means that the hard drive is connected to your Windows Home Server but is not currently part of the server storage pool.

  - *Initializing* means that the hard drive has been added to the server storage pool, and Windows Home Server is in the process of formatting the hard drive so that it can be used.

- *Removing* means that the hard drive is being removed by Windows Home Server.

- *Missing* means that the hard drive has been added to the server storage pool but Windows Home Server is unable to detect it. Figure 8-2 shows an example.

- *Unhealthy* means that one or more volumes on the hard drive are corrupt and the hard drive needs to be repaired.

Figure 8-2. *A hard drive is missing.*

On the Server Storage tab, you can also easily see how much space has been used, and for what purpose, as well as how much space is available by looking at the pie chart on the right side of the screen. As you can see in Figure 8-1, I currently have around 434 GB of free space, so I can store and share a few more files if I wish.

Adding a New Hard Drive

You can easily add a new hard drive to your server storage pool by literally just plugging it in and making a few clicks with your mouse.

■**Caution** Make sure that you have enough spare ports on your Windows Home Server for the new hard drives. For example, if you want to add a new internal hard drive, you will need a spare power cable and the relevant cable for attaching to the motherboard, along with a spare port on the motherboard to connect the cable. If you want to connect an external hard drive, you will need spare USB or FireWire ports.

Here's the procedure for adding a hard drive:

1. Connect the new hard drive to your Windows Home Server. If you are connecting an internal hard drive, you will need to first power off your Windows Home Server.

2. When the Windows Home Server has been powered back on, using one of your home computers, launch the Windows Home Server Console.

3. Click the Server Storage icon to display your available server storage. Your new drive will be listed in the Non Storage Hard Drives area, with a status of Not Added. Figure 8-3 shows an example where a Maxtor 6V250F0 internal (ATA) drive with a capacity of 233.76 GB is being added.

Figure 8-3. *The newly added hard drive appears.*

■**Note** There might be situations, such as an application or Windows Home Server add-in needing its own hard drive, where you don't want to add the new hard drive to the server storage pool. In these instances, you can just leave the new hard drive in the Non Storage Hard Drives area. This just means that the hard drive is not used as part of the Windows Home Server storage pool, even though it can be used for "other" storage outside the storage pool.

4. Click the newly added hard drive, and then click the Add button above the list, or right-click the hard drive and select Add from the context menu. This will start the Add a Hard Drive Wizard, as shown in Figure 8-4.

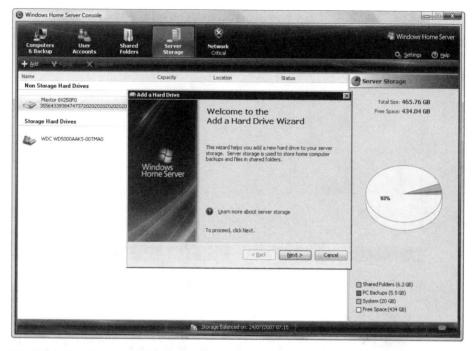

Figure 8-4. *Starting the Add a Hard Drive Wizard*

5. Click Next to start the Add a Hard Drive wizard. The next screen in the wizard warns you that if you click Finish, the hard drive will be formatted, and any files stored on that drive will be deleted, as shown in Figure 8-5. You can also see information about the drive on this screen.

■**Caution** If this newly added drive contains any data that you want to keep, stop the process now! Remove the drive from the Windows Home Server, connect it to one of your other home computers, and copy the data.

---

6. If you are sure that you want to format the drive, and that you have copied any data you want to keep to another storage location, click Finish. The hard drive will be formatted, and then it will be added to the storage pool. When those two things have taken place, you will see the screen that tells you that the new hard drive was successfully added, as shown in Figure 8-6.

7. Click Done to finish. Your new hard drive has become part of your available storage pool.

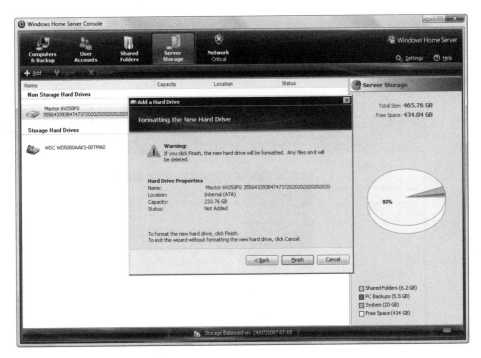

Figure 8-5. *Preparing to format the new hard drive*

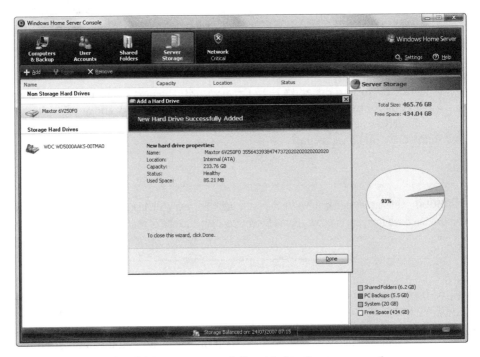

Figure 8-6. *The new hard drive was successfully added to the storage pool.*

■**Note** Depending on the size of the hard drive you are adding, the formatting process may take a few minutes, so be patient.

You will now be able to see the new drive, along with any other drives you already had as part of your storage pool. As you can see in the example in Figure 8-7, the status of my new drive is healthy, and my server storage pool total is 699.52 GB.

Figure 8-7. *The updated list of storage hard drives*

You will notice that the total server storage size may not be a rounded-off number. This is because you can add all different size drives to your server storage pool. You can add any drives you have lying around at home to increase your server storage—and believe me, you will soon want to do this!

The procedure for adding a USB or FireWire hard drive is the same as just described. I also added a USB hard drive to the pool, as shown in Figure 8-8. You will notice that the icon of the USB drive is slightly different, in that it shows a cable attached to the drive to indicate it is an external drive. You can also see that the Location column indicates that it is External (USB).

Note You should consider using only USB 2.0 or FireWire external drives. Do not use USB 1.1 external drives, as they are slow and will cause your Windows Home Server to perform slowly, which you really don't want to happen.

Figure 8-8. *Adding an external USB hard drive to the pool*

After you've added the new hard drive to your Windows Home Server, it becomes part of the total amount of shared server storage. Under no circumstances should you just disconnect it and use it for something else, as this will cause major problems to your storage. If you need to remove it, follow the instructions in the next section.

Removing a Hard Drive

A time may come when you want to remove a hard drive from your Windows Home Server, either because you suspect that there might be a problem with it or because you want to replace it with a larger and possibly faster hard drive.

Note You cannot remove the primary hard drive, which is the one with the Windows Home Server program files stored on it. If you want to replace the primary hard drive, you will need to reinstall Windows Home Server.

To remove a hard drive, just perform the following simple steps:

1. In the Windows Home Server Console, click the Server Storage tab.

2. Click the hard drive that you want to remove, and then click the Remove button above the list, or right-click the hard drive and select Remove from the context menu. This will launch the Remove a Hard Drive Wizard, as shown in Figure 8-9.

■**Caution** Because the removal process moves the files that are stored on that hard drive to another hard drive, you must ensure that you have sufficient space available in the storage pool before continuing. Otherwise, you may lose files or some shared folder duplication may stop.

Figure 8-9. *Starting the Remove a Hard Drive Wizard*

3. Click Next. The wizard will check that there is enough storage available to move the files to before continuing, as shown in Figure 8-10.

■**Note** Depending on how many hard drives you have in your server storage pool and how much data is stored within the pool, the process of calculating the available space could take a few minutes. As usual, be patient!

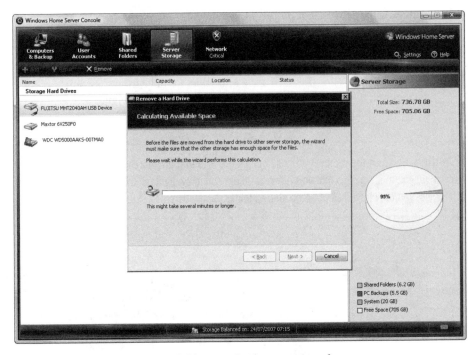

Figure 8-10. *Calculating the available space in the storage pool*

4. Once the calculation has completed, you will be presented with a Hard Drive Removal Consequences page, as shown in Figure 8-11. Review this information. There are two major areas of possible consequence, plus a reminder if you're removing an external drive.

   - Files and Folders is where you will be informed if files that are stored in duplicated folders will continue to be duplicated.

   - Computer Backups is where you will be informed if any computer backups will be lost.

   - Do Not Disconnect will appear if the drive being removed is an external hard drive. The wizard is reminding you that this drive must be connected and powered on until the wizard has completed.

5. Click Finish. The hard drive is removed from the server storage pool, and the data is moved to other hard drives within the pool. You can monitor the progress while this is taking place, as shown in Figure 8-12.

■**Note** Depending on how much data needs to be moved from the hard drive, the removal process can take a long time. The wizard even advises that this process could take several hours to complete. Do I need to say that you should be patient?

Figure 8-11. *Hard Drive Removal Consequences summary*

Figure 8-12. *Monitoring the progress of the hard drive removal*

6. Once the removal process has completed, you will be presented with a Hard Drive Successfully Removed screen, as shown in Figure 8-13. Click Done to complete the removal process.

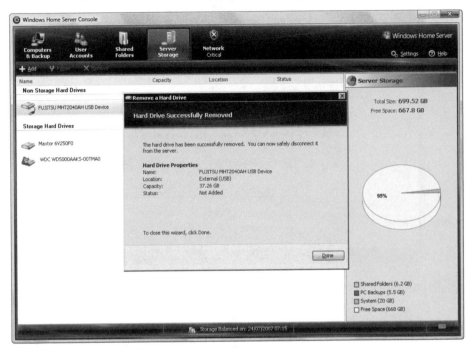

Figure 8-13. *The hard drive has been successfully removed.*

If the hard drive is an external hard drive, you can now safely unplug it from the Windows Home Server. If the hard drive is an internal hard drive, you will need to power off your Windows Home Server and remove the hard drive before restarting the Windows Home Server.

If you have only two hard drives in your Windows Home Server and decide to remove one of them, the biggest consequence is that shared folder replication (discussed in Chapter 9) cannot continue, because a minimum of two hard drives are required for replication. You will be warned of this on the Hard Drive Removal Consequences screen, as shown in Figure 8-14.

Figure 8-14. *Warning that shared folder duplication will not continue*

Repairing a Hard Drive

If you have a problem with one of the hard drives in your Windows Home Server, its status may appear as unhealthy, as shown in Figure 8-15. Fortunately, Windows Home Server has a wizard that may be able to fix the problem.

To repair a hard drive, perform the following steps:

1. In the Windows Home Server Console, click the Server Storage tab.

2. Click the unhealthy hard drive that you want to repair, and then click the Repair button above the list, or right-click the hard drive and select Repair from the context menu. This will launch the Repair Hard Drive Wizard, as shown in Figure 8-16.

Note The Repair button will be grayed out unless you have an unhealthy hard drive—only then will you be able to select to repair it.

Figure 8-15. *One of the hard drives is unhealthy.*

Figure 8-16. *Starting the Repair Hard Drive Wizard*

3. Click Next. You will see the Review the Repair Task screen, which shows information about what will happen during the repair process, as shown in Figure 8-17. The wizard performs the following tasks in an effort to repair the unhealthy drive:

  • The hard drive is scanned using the Chkdsk utility that is part of Windows in order to verify the integrity of the hard drive.

  • If an error is found, an attempt is made to correct and repair it.

  • Any duplicated shared folders using that hard drive are rebuilt, if necessary.

■**Caution** There is a possibility that repairing the hard drive will result in some data loss. However, chances are that the drive is corrupt anyway. You will probably want to proceed and hope that the drive can be repaired and that all of your data will remain intact.

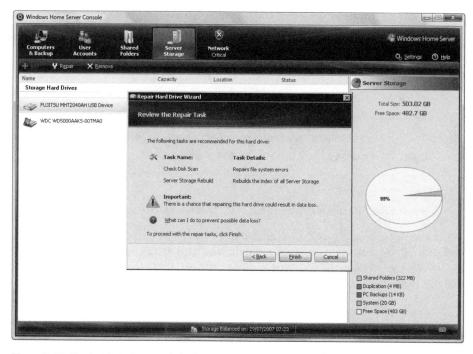

Figure 8-17. *Reviewing the repair tasks*

4. Click Finish to proceed with the repair tasks. You will then be presented with the Repair Hard Drive Status screen, as shown in Figure 8-18.

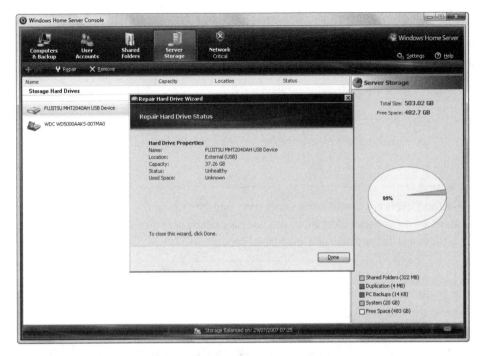

Figure 8-18. *Viewing the Repair Hard Drive Status screen*

Note   The repair tasks can take anywhere from a couple of minutes to several hours depending on the size of the hard drive and the amount of corruption on the drive itself.

---

5. Review the information presented, and then click Done to close the wizard.

In the example in Figure 8-18, the hard drive could not be repaired, and its status remains unhealthy. In this case, you could try removing the hard drive and then adding it (using the procedures described in the previous sections), to see if that solves the problem. But realize that this could result in data loss as well.

Summary

In this chapter, you learned how easy it is to increase the storage that your Windows Home Server uses. You also learned how to remove and repair hard drives as necessary. The next chapter covers sharing folders, which is another great feature of Windows Home Server.

CHAPTER 9

■ ■ ■

Shared Folders

If you want to store any digital data on your Windows Home Server and even share it with others, you use a shared folder. You may already be familiar with the concept of a shared folder from using a previous version of Windows. Basically, in versions of Windows other than Windows Home Server, you create a folder and assign permissions to it, including who has access to it and who can do what with it. For example, I can create a folder with some music in it and give certain people read access to the folder so that they may listen to the music; I also have write access to the folder, so that I can add any music I want to it at any time. Unless I give permission for others to see the contents of the folder, they cannot see it. All in all, the concept is not really that difficult, but sometimes setting the permissions on the folder can be complicated and time consuming, and it is quite easy to make a mistake and give someone permissions that you don't want them to have.

Although the concept of shared folders in Windows Home Server is very similar, all the complexity and risk have been eliminated so that it is incredibly simple and quick to create and remove shared folders and add and remove permissions whenever you need to. You can even ensure that the data is protected in case of a hardware failure.

The Shared Folders tab in the Windows Home Server Console, shown in Figure 9-1, lists all the current shared folders and displays information about them. From here you can also add and remove shared folders, and even change the permissions.

As you can see, the columns display the following information for each of the shared folders:

- *Name*: Shows the name of the shared folder

- *Description*: Shows the description for the shared folder, if it has one

- *Used Space*: Shows how much of the server storage space is being used by that folder

- *Duplication*: Shows whether Folder Duplication is on or off for the shared folder

- *Status*: Shows the health of the shared folder

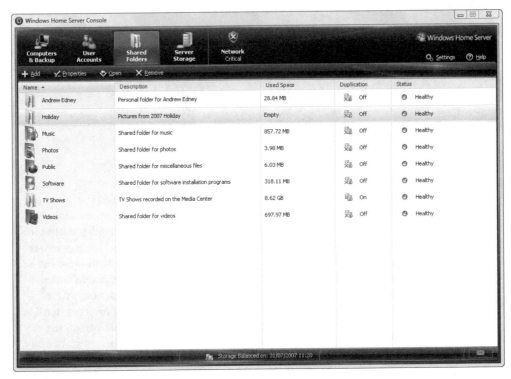

Figure 9-1. *The Shared Folders tab in the Windows Home Server Console*

When Windows Home Server was first installed, five shared folders were automatically created:

- Music

- Photos

- Public

- Software

- Videos

You may recall from earlier in the book that the Software shared folder contains copies of all the Windows Home Server software that you might need. All of the other folders are empty, but you can start adding your files to them whenever you are ready, as explained next. Following that, the chapter describes how to remove shared folders, change shared folder properties, duplicate shared folders, view the history of shared folders, access shared folders, and recover files from a shared folder.

Adding a Shared Folder

You can easily add a shared folder from the Shared Folders tab. To add a new shared folder, perform the following steps:

1. Click the Add button to open the Add a Shared Folder wizard, shown in Figure 9-2.

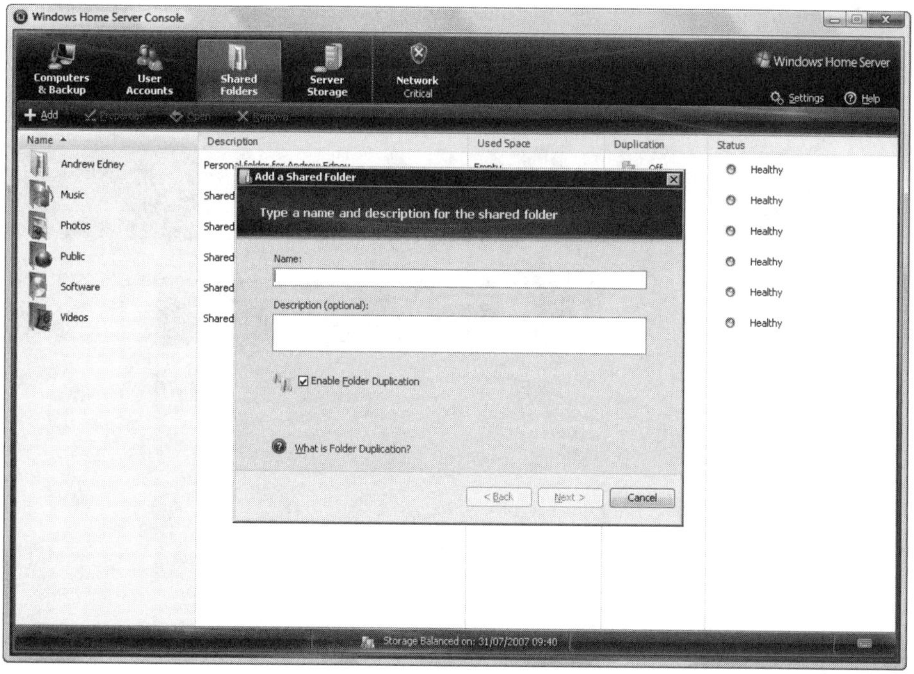

Figure 9-2. *Start the Add a Shared Folder wizard.*

2. Type a name for the new shared folder.

■**Note** The shared folder name can contain letters, numbers, spaces, and colon (:), dash (-), and underscore (_) characters. The shared folder name must also end with either a letter or a number, but not one of the characters.

---

3. Type a description for the new shared folder.

■**Tip** A folder description is completely optional but it makes sense to add one so that you can easily determine what the contents are. For example, if you want to have a number of folders of photos, you could call the folders *Photo1*, *Photo2*, and so on, but in the description you could put something like *Summer 2006 vacation*, *Christmas 2005*, and so on.

---

4. If you want to enable Folder Duplication for this folder as you create it, check the Enable Folder Duplication check box.

5. Click Next to continue.

6. The next screen of the wizard enables you to set the level of access for each user, as shown in Figure 9-3. You can choose among the following levels of access for each user:

Figure 9-3. *Setting access to the new folder*

- *Full*: The user is able to view, add, modify, and delete files in the shared folder.

- *Read*: The user is able to view files in the shared folder, but cannot add, modify, or delete any files.

- *None*: The user cannot view, add, modify, or delete any files in the shared folder. This is also the default setting for the Guest account.

Set the access for each user.

■**Note** Take a moment to double-check the access you have just set for each user before you continue.

---

7. Click Next to continue. The following actions then take place, the progress of which you can watch, as shown in Figure 9-4:

- The shared folder is added to Windows Home Server.

- Access is set for the shared folder.

- Folder duplication is enabled for that folder if you have enabled it.

Figure 9-4. *View the progress of adding the new shared folder.*

Note also that you are given an address you can enter to open the new shared folder in Windows Explorer (\\AE-WHS\TV Shows in this example).

8. Click Done to close the wizard and finish the process.

■**Caution** After a new shared folder has been created, users who have been given access may be denied access to the shared folder, receiving an "Access Denied" warning. If this happens, tell the user to log off and log back on again and access should be given. This should only happen when folder permissions are added or changed.

You will then be able to see the new shared folder immediately, as shown in Figure 9-5.

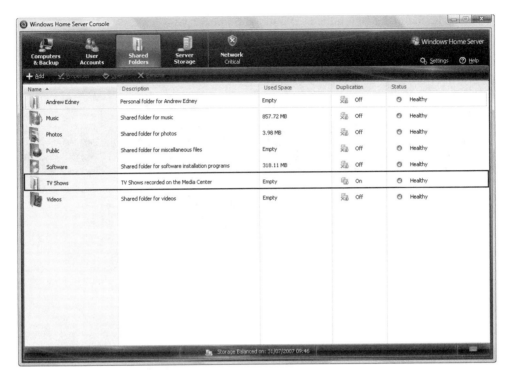

Figure 9-5. *Viewing the new shared folder*

Removing a Shared Folder

There may come a time when you want to remove one or more shared folders for whatever reason. As you can probably guess by now, this process is very simple.

To remove a shared folder, follow these few steps:

1. On the Shared Folders tab, select the folder you want to remove.

2. Click the Remove button. You will see a warning telling you that you are about to remove the shared folder and all of its contents, as shown in Figure 9-6.

■**Caution** All the contents of the shared folder will be deleted and cannot be recovered unless you have backed them up elsewhere, so be very careful when removing any shared folders.

Figure 9-6. *Confirm that you want to remove the shared folder and its contents.*

3. Click Finish to remove the shared folder and delete its contents.

■**Note** You cannot remove the original Windows Home Server shared folders (Music, Photos, Public, Software, and Videos) that were created during the installation of Windows Home Server.

Viewing and Changing Shared Folder Properties

You can view and even change the properties on most of the shared folders.

To view the properties of a shared folder, either select the folder and then click Properties or just double-click the shared folder. The first thing you see in the Properties dialog box is a view of the General tab, as shown in Figure 9-7.

On the General tab, you can change the name of the shared folder and the description, and also enable or disable Folder Duplication (described in the next section).

■**Note** You cannot change the name of any of the preinstalled Windows Home Server shared folders. However, you can change the description if you wish.

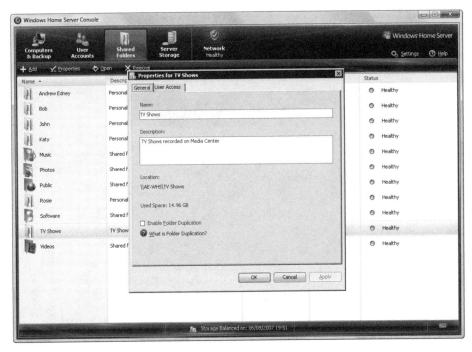

Figure 9-7. *Viewing the General tab of the shared folder*

The other tab is the User Access tab, shown in Figure 9-8.

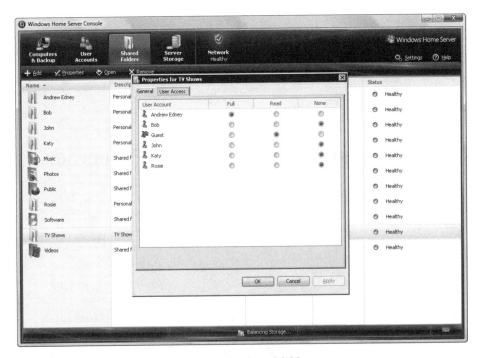

Figure 9-8. *Viewing the User Access tab of the shared folder*

On the User Access tab, you can change the permissions for any of the users for that shared folder. As listed in the "Adding a Shared Folder" section earlier, you can set any one of the following access levels for each user:

- *Full*: The user is able to view, add, modify, and delete files in the shared folder.

- *Read*: The user is able to view files in the shared folder, but cannot add, modify, or delete any files.

- *None*: The user cannot view, add, modify, or delete any files in the shared folder.

Enabling Folder Duplication

Folder Duplication is the process by which Windows Home Server protects your digital content in shared folders. If you have more than one hard drive in your Windows Home Server, you can enable Folder Duplication on a per shared folder basis.

Note You need more than one hard drive to enable Folder Duplication; it won't work with a single hard drive or even with a hard drive that has multiple partitions.

When you select a shared folder and enable Folder Duplication, that folder is automatically copied onto another hard drive within your Windows Home Server so that if one of the hard drives fails, you won't lose the shared folder. Each time you add or remove a file from that shared folder, both copies are automatically updated, so you never need to worry about them being out of sync.

Note Folder Duplication is switched off by default. You need to enable it on each folder that you want to protect.

To enable Folder Duplication for a shared folder, follow these steps:

1. On the Shared Folders tab, select the shared folder that you want to enable Folder Duplication for.

2. Click the Properties button to open the shared folder's Properties dialog box, as shown in Figure 9-9.

3. Check the Enable Folder Duplication box.

4. Click OK to finish.

Figure 9-9. *Enable Folder Duplication*

The shared folder is automatically duplicated to another hard drive in your Windows Home Server. Depending on the amount of data you have in the shared folder, Folder Duplication may take a while to complete, but you can carry on doing whatever you want to do as all magic takes place in the background.

■**Note** Every folder that you enable Folder Duplication for takes up twice as much server storage space as it takes without Folder Duplication enabled.

Troubleshooting Problems with Folder Duplication

From time to time you might experience some problems with Folder Duplication. The cause is usually either a faulty or missing hard drive or low disk space.

If you experience a problem, it might be displayed in a similar way to the example shown in the second row of Figure 9-10.

In this example, the status message is Failing (Check Health). At the same time, a Storage Status message balloon appears, as shown in Figure 9-11.

The problem experienced in this example is that the only additional hard drive connected to the Windows Home Server has failed, which caused Folder Duplication to fail. As you can see, the suggested resolution is to add another hard drive or to remove duplication for that folder.

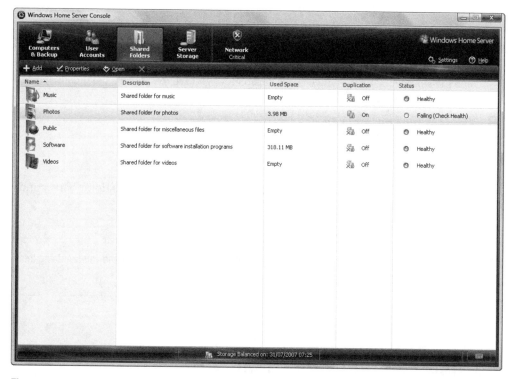

Figure 9-10. *A problem with the Photos shared folder*

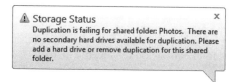

Figure 9-11. *A Storage Status message balloon*

To find out what might be causing a Folder Duplication problem, check the Network tab for more information.

Balancing Storage

The eagle-eyed among you have probably spotted at the bottom of the Windows Home Server Console, regardless of which tab you are on, three separate areas. The middle of the three areas usually says Storage Balanced On: *date* (where *date* is the actual date and time that the storage was balanced). What exactly is this? Well, this is the part of Drive Extender (introduced in Chapter 8) that handles Folder Duplication and moving files around.

Every time you add or remove something from a shared folder, the server storage will be balanced. First, you see a Balancing Storage message, as shown in Figure 9-12.

Figure 9-12. *Balancing storage*

Once the storage balancing process has completed, you see the Storage Balanced On *date* message, as shown in Figure 9-13.

Figure 9-13. *Storage balanced*

There is nothing that you need to do or worry about, because Windows Home Server and Drive Extender take care of everything for you.

■Note Don't worry if you see the Storage Balancing message a lot—it probably means you are doing lots of cool things with your data on Windows Home Server.

Viewing Shared Folder History

You might be curious to see how each of your shared folders has grown over time. To satisfy your curiosity, Windows Home Server has a feature that displays a graph of how each shared folder grows.

To view the shared folder history graph, perform the following steps:

1. On the Shared Folder tab, right-click the shared folder you want to view the history graph for.

2. Click View History from the context menu, as shown in Figure 9-14.

This displays the history graph for the selected folder, as shown in the example in Figure 9-15.

As you can see from the graph, you can choose from four History Range views:

- *One Week*: Displays the last seven days

- *One Month*: Displays the last four weeks

- *One Year*: Displays the last 12 months

- *Full History*: Displays the full history of the shared folder

---

■Tip You can display the history for the shared folder only if the history is actually available. For example, if the shared folder has been available for only two weeks, you cannot select the One Month or One Year view.

Figure 9-14. *Right-click a folder and choose View History to view its history.*

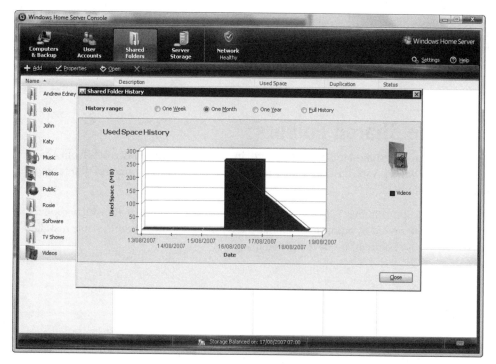

Figure 9-15. *A typical Shared Folder History graph*

To be able to view the history graph, the folder must have been created and used for at least a week; otherwise, you receive the message shown in Figure 9-16 and have to wait and try again at a later time.

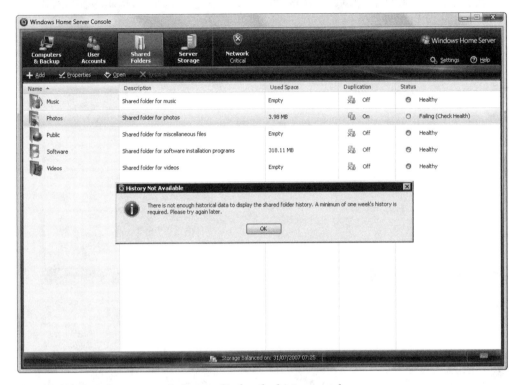

Figure 9-16. *There is not enough data to display the history graph.*

Accessing Shared Folders

It is very easy to access shared folders to view files in, add files to, or remove files from any shared folder for which you have the proper permission. There are a number of different ways to access shared folders:

- Double-click the Shared Folders on Server icon, shown in Figure 9-17, which appears on the Desktop of any computer that has the Windows Home Server Console installed on it (unless of course you have deleted the icon).

Figure 9-17. *The Shared Folders on Server icon on the Desktop*

- Right-click the Windows Home Server task tray icon and click Shared Folders from the context menu, as shown in Figure 9-18.

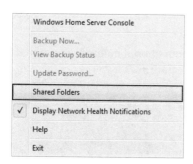

Figure 9-18. *Selecting Shared Folders from the context menu*

- In Windows Vista, click Start, type the address of the shared folder in the Start Search text box, and press Enter. For example, if I wanted to access the TV Shows shared folder I created earlier, I would type \\AE-WHS\TV Shows.

- In Windows XP, click Start, click Run, type the address (for example, \\AE-WHS\ TV Shows) in the Open text box, and click OK.

- In Windows Vista, click the Start button, click Network to open the Network window (see Figure 9-19), and double-click the computer icon that has the name of your Windows Home Server, such as the one highlighted in Figure 9-19. You may see a number of computers in the Network folder. Do not double-click the Windows Home Server whose icon looks like a server (the one in the middle in Figure 9-19) because this is for Remote Access, which is covered in Chapter 11.

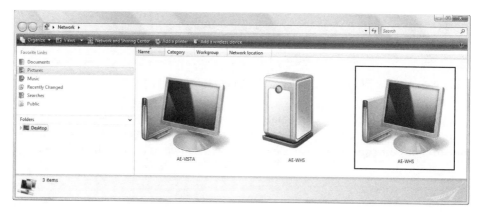

Figure 9-19. *Viewing the Windows Home Server in the Network folder*

- In Windows XP, click the Start button and click My Network Places. The shared folders that you have access to will be displayed.

Note Viewing the shared folders of your Windows Home Server using this method will not work if your computer is joined to a Windows domain.

When you have accessed the Shared Folders with your chosen method, you should see all the available folders in Windows Explorer, as shown in Figure 9-20.

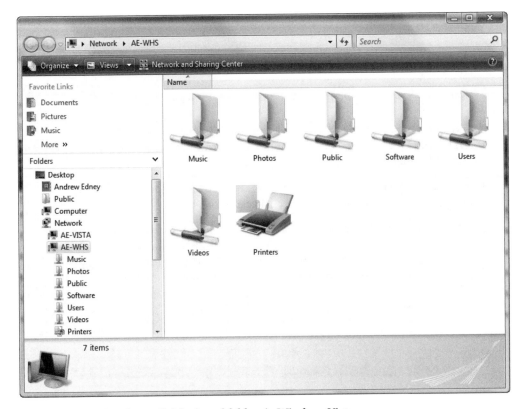

Figure 9-20. *Viewing the available shared folders in Windows Vista*

You can now double-click any shared folder to open it (as long as you have the correct permissions). You can add or delete content in that folder as you need to by simply dragging and dropping the content. You can even create new content directly into the folder.

Caution Do not attempt to manipulate the shared folders in any way from here. For example, do not try to create a new folder or change the folder permissions. If you want to do anything like this, you must do it from the Shared Folders tab in the Windows Home Server Console.

You can also access a specific shared folder from within the Windows Home Server Console. All you need to do is select the shared folder and then click the Open button. As long as you have permissions to that folder, it will open for you.

You can also access any of your shared folders remotely if you have enabled Remote Access. For more information on this method, and the other features of Remote Access, take a look at Chapter 11.

■**Tip** You can set up various programs on your home computers to automatically save files into your shared folders instead of having to copy or move files later on. For example, if you rip music CDs using Windows Media Player, you could have those rips stored directly into the Music folder, or you could have Word save your documents directly into your personal folder. The possibilities are endless—all you need to know is the location of the shared folder.

Recovering Files from Previous Versions

As you may remember from Chapter 7, if you accidentally delete a file, you can easily recover it if you have already made a backup. Well, there is another way to recover a file: from a shared folder. *Previous versions* are backup copies of folders and files that are created for you automatically.

■**Note** All Windows Home Server shared folders support previous versions.

To open a previous version, perform the following steps:

■**Note** These steps must be performed on a computer running Windows Vista or Windows XP with a minimum of Service Pack 2.

---

1. Double-click the Shared Folders on Server icon on the Desktop (or right-click the Windows Home Server task tray icon and select Shared Folders from the context menu).

2. Right-click the shared folder you want to use a previous version of and click Properties.

3. Click the Previous Versions tab, shown in Figure 9-21.

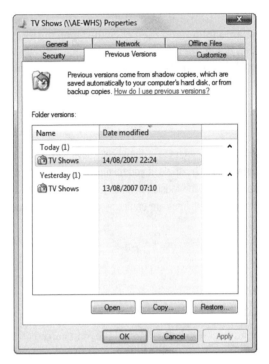

Figure 9-21. *View previous versions of a shared folder in Windows Vista.*

4. Select the version of the folder that you want to use from the available versions in the list and click the Open button.

■**Note** Windows Home Server automatically creates snapshots of the shared folders twice a day, at noon and at midnight.

---

5. Work your way through the contents of the Previous Version folder and locate the file or files you want to restore, and then copy and paste them onto your computer.

Summary

Now you know all there is to know about shared folders, including how to add them, delete them, access them, add to them, view their history, and even change their access permissions for other users of your Windows Home Server. You have also learned about Folder Duplication for shared folders and how to recover a file from a shared folder. You have even learned why that message about balancing storage keeps appearing. In the next chapter you will learn how to stream media from your shared folders to computers and other devices around your home.

CHAPTER 10

■ ■ ■

Media Streaming

Media streaming is the name given to the method of delivering from a single source to one or more devices digital media that can be played as it is being continually delivered, rather than being played locally on the device.

Within Windows Home Server, media streaming is also referred to as Media Library Sharing, which is in fact the process of enabling the digital content within specific shared folders to be streamed.

If you have a lot of digital media, such as videos, photos, and music, stored on your Windows Home Server that you share with the other users on your home network, you or the other users may want to access that content on a different device, perhaps in a room that doesn't have a computer. You can stream media content, specifically music, photos, and videos, from your Windows Home Server to other devices on your home network, such as an Xbox 360 or other supported digital media receiver (DMR), provided that they support Windows Media Connect (described in more detail later in the chapter).

Note DMRs are devices that can receive digital media streams from a computer over a network. Microsoft currently reports that the following DMRs are compatible with Windows Media Connect 2.0: the Xbox 360, Windows Vista, Roku Soundbridge Network Music Player (M1000 and M2000), and D-Link MediaLounge DSM-320 Wireless Media Player. For the latest list of supported devices, take a look at `http://www.microsoft.com/windows/windowsmedia/devices/wmconnect/faq.aspx#3_1`.

This chapter first demonstrates how to enable Media Library Sharing on your shared folders that can be used to stream content, which is necessary to stream your digital media content to different devices. It then introduces the technology that is used to stream content to different devices, Windows Media Connect. Finally, this chapter provides examples of streaming digital media to an Xbox 360 and a Windows Vista computer running Media Player 11. Windows Home Server can stream to other devices, of course, but the process is likely to be similar, and covering all devices is beyond the scope of this book. The examples in this chapter should give you a good idea of how to stream digital media to other devices, but if you are in any doubt, take a look at the documentation that came with your device or check online.

Not all of the available shared folders can be enabled for Media Library Sharing. In fact, only three shared folders can be enabled for it:

- Music

- Photos

- Videos

■**Note** Don't be confused by the fact that the process is called Media Library Sharing and that you are in fact enabling sharing on an already shared folder. You are actually enabling the shared folder to be configured for streaming.

By default, none of those three preconfigured folders is enabled for sharing. If you want to stream digital content from them, you have to enable Media Library Sharing on them first, as described next.

■**Caution** When you enable sharing for any or all of the media types, any device on your home network will be able to access the shared content, so make sure that you are happy sharing these files among everyone before you continue. Content can be accessed even by users without a Windows Home Server user account, so be very careful. If you have media content you want to be able to stream to certain users only, you should put it into a folder that only those users can access.

Enabling Media Library Sharing

To enable media streaming on any or all of the three shared folders that support Media Library Sharing, perform the following steps:

1. From the Windows Home Server Console, click the Settings button.

2. Click Media Sharing from the list in the left pane. You are presented with the three media types and their shared folders, along with radio buttons enabling you to switch on or off Media Library Sharing for each of them, as shown in Figure 10-1.

■**Note** The default setting for all three shared folders is Off.

---

3. Click the On radio button for each of the shared folders for which you want to enable Media Library Sharing.

4. Click OK to finish the task.

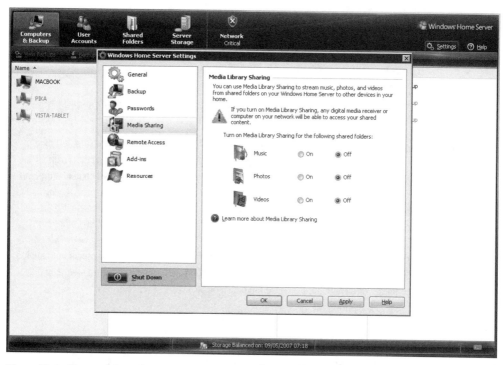

Figure 10-1. *Choose whether to turn on Media Library Sharing for the shared folders.*

When you first enable Media Library Sharing on one or more of the shared folders, the Windows Home Server Console may appear unresponsive for a few moments. This usually happens if you have a large number of digital files in those folders. If this does happen, just wait a moment or two and it should spring back to life.

■**Note** The only way to tell whether one of the shared folders is enabled for Media Library Sharing is to click the Settings button on the Windows Home Server Console and choose Media Sharing (which opens the window shown in Figure 10-1). You can't even tell whether it's enabled from the Shared Folders tab (which would have been useful!).

Disabling Media Library Sharing

Disabling Media Library Sharing is just as simple as enabling it. If you want to disable any or all of the folders, perform the following steps:

1. From the Windows Home Server Console, click the Settings button.

2. Click Media Sharing in the left pane.

3. Click the Off radio button for each of the shared folders for which you want to disable Media Library Sharing.

4. Click OK to finish the task.

COPY-PROTECTED MEDIA

If you have purchased music or videos from an online store, such as iTunes or Urge, chances are that the content you purchased is copy protected using digital rights management (DRM), technology that restricts your use of the content to the scope of the license. You may also have other copy-protected content stored on your home network.

Copy-protected media can be played back only on the device or computer used to purchase it—the one that has the license associated with it. This means that you cannot play that media back on any other computer or device.

Windows Home Server does not support the sharing and streaming of copy-protected media to multiple devices or computers on your network, but you can store the media on your Windows Home Server and play it back to the one computer or device that is licensed to play it back.

Streaming with Windows Media Connect

Windows Media Connect is software that you can download and install from Microsoft that enables you to stream digital media content from computers on your home network to DMRs. Those DMRs must be compatible with and support Windows Media Connect.

Windows Media Connect is installed automatically when you install Windows Home Server, so you don't have to do anything further to use your Windows Home Server to stream digital content.

■**Note** If you would like to read more about Windows Media Connect, including which DMRs are compatible with and support Windows Media Connect, take a look at http://www.microsoft.com/windows/ windowsmedia/devices/wmconnect/faq.aspx.

Streaming to an Xbox 360

If you have a Microsoft Xbox 360 in your home, you can use it as a media extender, which means that you can stream digital content to it from Windows Home Server. It is very easy to use your Xbox 360 to view streamed content. This section guides you through the steps of configuring and using your Xbox 360 as a media extender. First, follow these steps to access the Xbox 360 Dashboard, from which you can choose to listen to music, view pictures, and watch video streamed from Windows Home Server:

Note The Xbox 360 can display pictures that are stored as JPEG, BMP, GIF, PNG, and TIFF; play music that is stored as MP3, WAV, or WMA; and play videos stored as WMV. Any other formats will not work. You can find third-party software on the Internet to convert other formats to the formats that are playable on Xbox 360.

---

1. Make sure that your Xbox 360 is switched on and connected to your home network. This connection can be via a wired Ethernet connection or via the optional wireless adaptor.

2. Using the Xbox 360 controller, go to the Media blade, as shown in Figure 10-2.

Figure 10-2. *Open the Media blade on the Xbox 360 Dashboard.*

From the Media blade, you can choose which media you want to enjoy, as described in the following sections.

Listening to Music

To listen to music on your Xbox 360 streamed from the Music shared folder, follow these steps:

1. Select Music on the Media blade.

2. On the Music menu, select Computer, as shown in Figure 10-3.

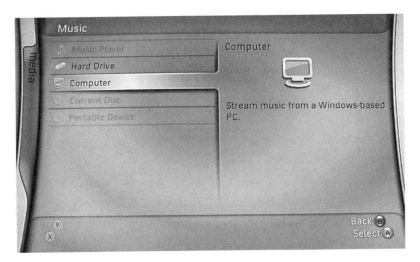

Figure 10-3. *Select Computer on the Music menu.*

3. If your Xbox 360 prompts you to download and install media sharing software, as shown in Figure 10-4, just click Yes, Continue, because the required software is built into Windows Home Server, so you don't need to do anything else.

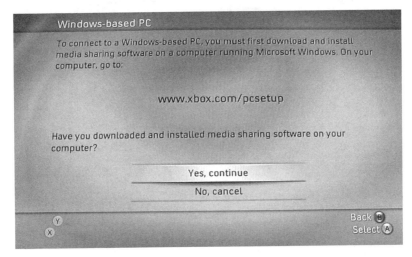

Figure 10-4. *Continue past the request to download Windows Media Connect.*

4. You then see the "Searching for Windows-based PCs" message, as shown in Figure 10-5. After the Xbox 360 searches your home network for computers running the Windows Media Connect software, you are presented with a list of available computers, as shown in Figure 10-6. Your Windows Home Server should be listed. Select it from the list.

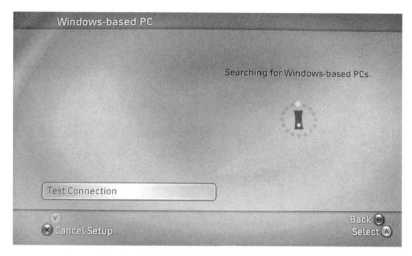

Figure 10-5. *Searching for your Windows Home Server*

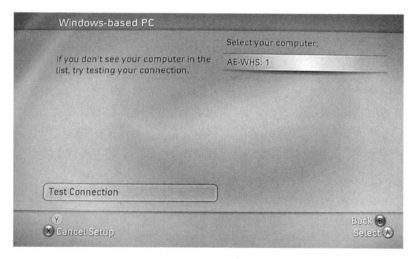

Figure 10-6. *Select your Windows Home Server.*

5. The Xbox 360 connects to your Windows Home Server and displays a list of available music, as shown in Figure 10-7. Scroll through the list of available music and choose something specific to listen to, or choose to play all the available music by clicking Play All Music.

Tip If you want to listen to something particular, you can search by album, artist, saved playlist, song, or genre, by using the corresponding tabs.

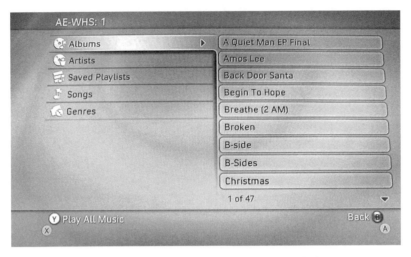

Figure 10-7. *Choose from among the music that is available for streaming.*

Viewing Pictures

To view pictures on your Xbox 360 streamed from the Photos shared folder, follow these steps:

1. Select Pictures on the Media blade.

2. On the Pictures menu, select Computer, as shown in Figure 10-8.

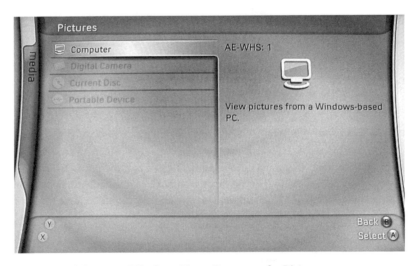

Figure 10-8. *Select your Windows Home Server on the Pictures menu.*

3. As shown in Figure 10-9, you can either choose to play a slideshow of all of your pictures, or select the Photos folder. If you select the Photos folder, you can click any available folder to view its contents, as shown in Figure 10-10.

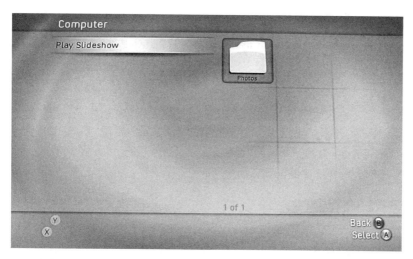

Figure 10-9. *Choose between playing a slideshow and viewing the top-level Photos folder.*

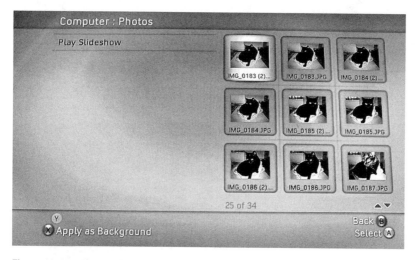

Figure 10-10. *Choose from among the available photos that can be streamed.*

Watching Videos

To watch videos on your Xbox 360 streamed from the Videos shared folder (or the Pictures shared folder, if applicable), follow these steps:

■**Note** You cannot watch video files with the .avi file extension on Xbox 360. If you want to view these files, you need to convert them to WMV (Windows Media Video) files using third-party software.

---

1. Select Videos on the Media blade.

2. On the Video menu, select Computer, as shown in Figure 10-11.

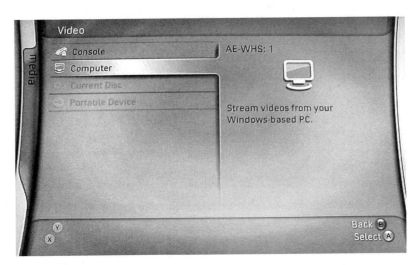

Figure 10-11. *Select your Windows Home Server from the Video menu.*

3. Select the location of your videos, as shown in Figure 10-12.

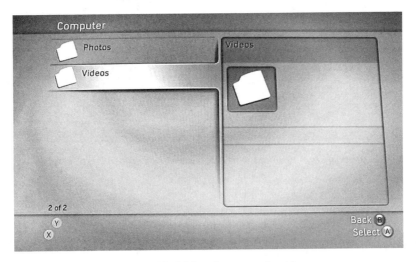

Figure 10-12. *View the available folders that contain videos.*

■**Note** As Figure 10-12 shows, I have videos stored in both the Videos shared folder and the Photos shared folder.

4. Select a video to view, as shown in Figure 10-13.

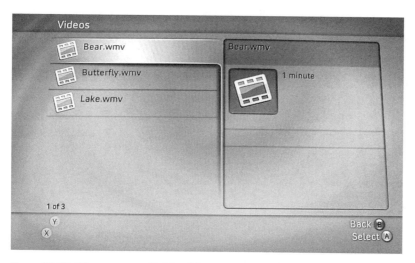

Figure 10-13. *Choose an available video to view.*

■**Tip** Sometimes your videos may not appear in the folders viewable on your Xbox 360. This appears to be a bug with Windows Home Server that has yet to be fixed. To resolve this issue, simply turn off Media Library Sharing for the Videos shared folder and then turn it back on.

Disconnecting Your Xbox 360

To disconnect your Xbox 360 from your Windows Home Server, follow these steps:

■**Note** You don't need to disconnect your Xbox 360 from your Windows Home Server unless you want to connect it to another Windows Media Connect–enabled computer on your network. If you don't want to connect it to another computer, then leave the connection in place so that you can easily access your digital content in the future. Remember, though, that Windows Home Server supports Media Library Sharing to a maximum of ten devices.

---

1. Go to the System blade, shown in Figure 10-14.

2. Click Computers.

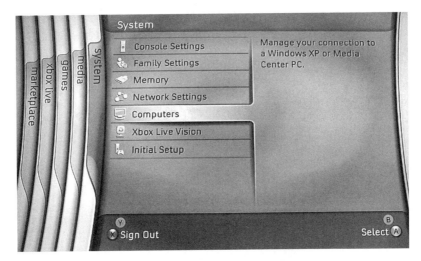

Figure 10-14. *Click Computers on the System blade of the Xbox 360.*

3. Click Windows-based PC to confirm that you are still connected to your Windows Home Server, as shown in Figure 10-15.

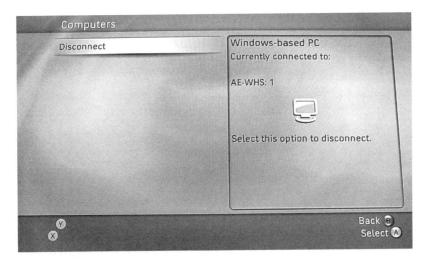

Figure 10-15. *Select your Windows Home Server and disconnect.*

4. Click Disconnect.

Streaming to Windows Media Player 11

You can use Windows Media Player 11, which comes preinstalled with Windows Vista, to listen to and view your streaming media content from your Windows Home Server.

■Note Windows Media Player 11 on Windows XP cannot be used to view or listen to your streaming media; only Windows Media Player 11 on Windows Vista is supported.

To use Windows Media Player 11 to listen to your streaming content, perform the following steps:

1. Launch Windows Media Player 11 from the Start menu or from any other shortcut or link you have available.

2. Click the Library tab at the top of Media Player, as shown in Figure 10-16.

Figure 10-16. *Click the Library tab in Media Player.*

3. From the drop-down list, click Media Sharing, as shown in Figure 10-17.

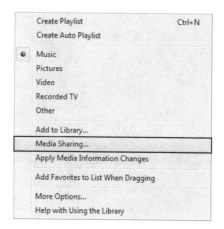

Figure 10-17. *Click Media Sharing from the Library drop-down list.*

4. In the Media Sharing dialog box, shown in Figure 10-18, check the Find Media That Others Are Sharing check box.

5. Click OK to finish. (You may be asked to give your permission for the change, depending on your settings.) You should be able to see your Windows Home Server share, as shown in Figure 10-19. In this example, it is User 1 on ae-whs.

6. Click one of the available views, such as Artist, to see the shared songs, as shown in Figure 10-20. This displays all the songs sorted by artist.

7. Choose what you want to listen to by double-clicking a song, and Windows Media Player will take care of the rest for you.

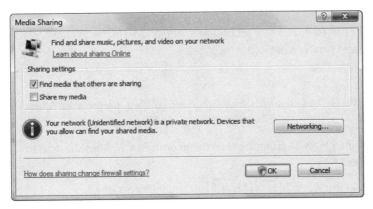

Figure 10-18. *Check the Find Media That Others Are Sharing check box.*

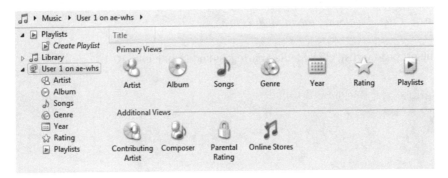

Figure 10-19. *Locate your Windows Home Server share.*

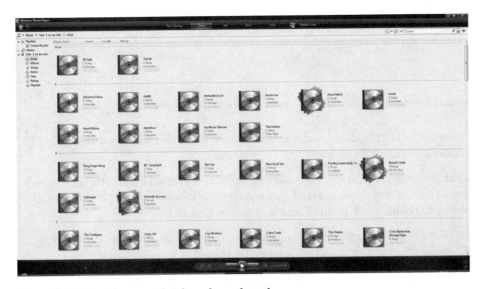

Figure 10-20. *View the songs that have been shared.*

You can also use Media Player to view your pictures or watch your videos. Select the type of content you want to view by clicking the Category icon in the top-left corner and selecting either Music, Pictures, or Video, as shown in Figure 10-21. Don't bother to select Recorded TV or Other Media, because they are not supported by Windows Home Server.

Figure 10-21. *Selecting a different category*

Summary

In this chapter you learned how to enable streaming using Media Library Sharing on your Windows Home Server. You also learned how to configure and view your streaming content both on an Xbox 360 and on Windows Media Player 11 running on Windows Vista. Streaming your digital media content using your Windows Home Server makes it easy for your home network users to view, watch, and listen to your shared content on other devices that support Windows Media Connect.

■■■

CHAPTER 11

Remote Access

Remote Access is the facility provided by Window Home Server that enables you to easily access via an Internet browser your files, home computers, and even the Windows Home Server itself when you are away from home.

You can view the contents of any shared folders you have access to, download any files to the computer you are using, and even upload files to a shared folder to access them at a later time. You can even take over any supported computer on your home network and use it as though you were sitting in front of it; for example, you can start any application, print, and so on.

This chapter will explain how to check your broadband router to ensure that it is compatible with Windows Home Server. It will also walk you through how to set up and configure each element of Remote Access, including choosing a domain name to be used for easy access to your Windows Home Server. There are also steps covering how to configure your compatible home computers for Remote Access, and also how to use the various Remote Access capabilities, including uploading and downloading files.

Checking Broadband Router Compatibility

Before you start configuring your Windows Home Server for Remote Access, take a few minutes to check that your broadband router is compatible for automatic configuration by Windows Home Server. If it isn't, don't worry—you can just configure it manually; it's just quicker and easier to have it done for you.

Fortunately, Microsoft provides a very useful tool for checking whether the broadband router is compatible for automatic configuration. The Internet Connectivity Evaluation Tool is quick and easy to use, doesn't require you to download and install anything, and, best of all, it's free!

Tip The Internet Connectivity Evaluation Tool is not specifically for use with Windows Home Server. You can use the tool to check any Internet router to discover what it can do and whether it supports certain technologies.

To use the Internet Connectivity Evaluation Tool, follow these steps:

Note To perform the tests, you must be using a computer that can connect to the Internet and that is running either Windows Vista or Windows XP.

1. From your Internet browser, go to the following URL: `http://www.microsoft.com/windows/using/tools/igd`.

2. On the Internet Connectivity Evaluation Tool start screen, shown in Figure 11-1, read through all the instructions that are displayed onscreen to ensure that you know about the tests.

3. Check the I Have Read and ACCEPT the Terms of the License Agreement check box.

4. Click the Continue button.

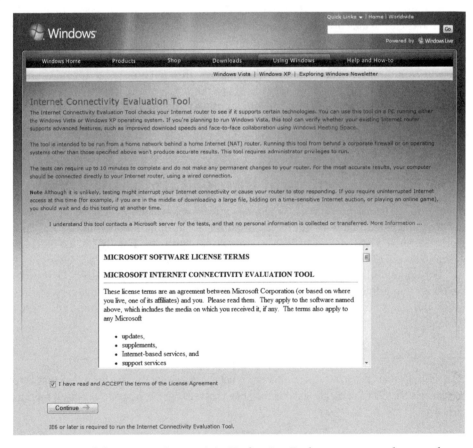

Figure 11-1. *Read the Internet Connectivity Evaluation Tool start screen and accept the License Agreement.*

5. Click the Start Test button, shown in Figure 11-2, to begin the various tests.

Figure 11-2. *Click Start Test to start the tests.*

You can monitor the progress of the testing of each element, as shown in Figure 11-3. The following tests will be performed on your broadband router:

- Basic Internet Connectivity Test

- Network Address Translator Type

- Traffic Congestion Test

- TCP High Performance Test

- UPnP Support Test

- Multiple Simultaneous Connection States Test

■**Note** Detailed information on each test and what constitutes a success is presented to you for review while each test is being performed.

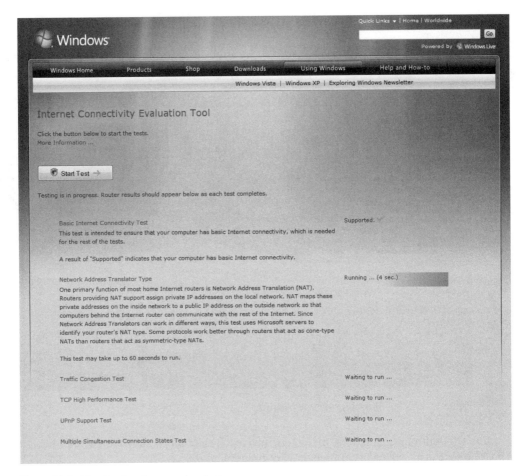

Figure 11-3. *Monitoring the running tests*

When all the testing has completed, you can scroll down to the bottom of the page and click View Detailed Report to view a more detailed report, as shown in Figure 11-4.

■**Note** You can click each Test line to expand or hide the details and results of each test.

You should now know whether your broadband router can be configured automatically for you. As shown in Figure 11-4, my broadband router does not support Universal Plug and Play (UPnP), so I will have to configure it manually, as explained in the following section, which covers both automatic and manual configuration of the router for Remote Access.

Figure 11-4. *Viewing a detailed report of the testing*

Configuring Remote Access

Out of the box, the Remote Access facilities within Windows Home Server are disabled as an added security measure, so if you want to use them, you need to first enable them.

Enabling Web Site Connectivity

When you enable Web Site Connectivity, the following three network ports are opened on the Windows Home Server Firewall so that incoming requests from the Internet can be routed to your Windows Home Server:

- Port 80, for HTTP requests

- Port 443, for HTTPS requests (the secure version of HTTP via Secure Sockets Layer, or SSL, which basically means that the connection is encrypted to provide additional security)

- Port 4125, for Remote Desktop

To enable web site connectivity, perform the following steps:

1. On the Windows Home Server Console, click the Settings button.

2. Click Remote Access in the left pane.

3. Click the Turn On button in the Web Site Connectivity area, as shown in Figure 11-5.

Note You cannot set up the router or the domain name that will be used for Remote Access to your Windows Home Server, or change any web site settings, until you turn on Web Site Connectivity.

Figure 11-5. *Turn on Web Site Connectivity.*

Automatically Configuring the Router

The next step is to set up and configure your broadband router for Remote Access. This stage configures (or attempts to configure) persistent port forwarding from your router to your Windows Home Server for the three network ports mentioned earlier. This means that any time data on one of those ports is received by the router, it will be forwarded to the Windows Home Server automatically.

■**Note** Your router must support UPnP to be automatically configured. If it doesn't support UPnP, then you need to manually add port forwarding to your router; see the next section, "Manually Configuring the Router."

To attempt to automatically configure your router, perform the following steps:

1. Click Setup next to the Router option, as shown in Figure 11-6.

2. You are informed that Windows Home Server will attempt to configure port forwarding for your router, as shown in Figure 11-7. Click OK to continue.

Figure 11-6. *Click Setup to start the router configuration.*

Figure 11-7. *Click OK to attempt to configure port forwarding.*

If port forwarding can be automatically configured for your router, it will be done now and you can skip to the "Setting Up the Domain Name" section of this chapter. However, if your router does not support UPnP, it cannot be configured automatically and you will see the failure message shown in Figure 11-8.

Figure 11-8. *The router doesn't support UPnP and thus cannot be configured automatically.*

3. Click OK to clear the message and proceed to the following section.

Manually Configuring the Router

If your router doesn't support UPnP or cannot be configured automatically, don't worry, you can manually configure port forwarding on your router, as follows:

■**Caution** Configuring port forwarding on your particular router may be different from the steps that are described next, so check your router documentation before you continue, to ensure that you don't make any mistakes.

---

1. Connect to your router (you may need to check your documentation to find out how to do this).

2. Click the Firewall icon to access the firewall settings on the router.

■**Note** The following example is using the BT (British Telecom) Home Hub router.

---

3. Click Firewall Settings so that you can make changes to the firewall, as shown in
Figure 11-9.

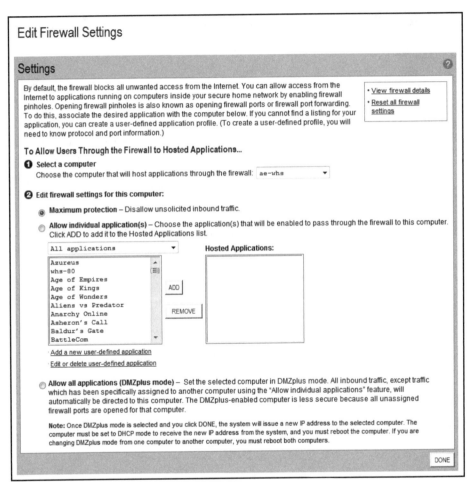

Figure 11-9. *Editing the firewall settings on the BT Home Hub router*

4. It is very unlikely that there will already be an application defined that allows the three
specific network ports (80, 443, and 4125) through the firewall, so you need to add a
new user-defined application. Click the Add a New User-defined Application link to
display the Edit Application dialog box, shown in Figure 11-10.

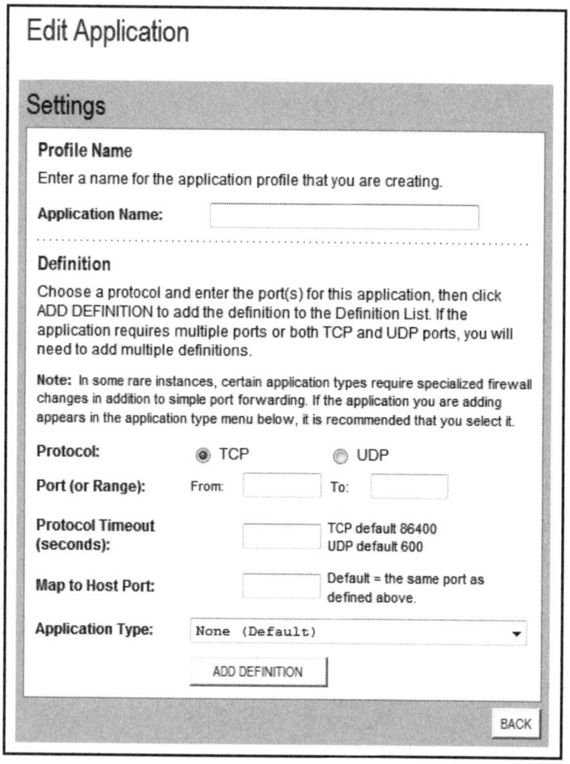

Figure 11-10. *Add a new user-defined application to the firewall.*

5. Enter a name in the Application Name box (for example, Windows Home Server Remote).

6. With TCP selected as the protocol, enter **80** in both the From and To boxes for the Port (or Range).

7. Click the Add Definition button to add that port range.

8. Again, with TCP selected as the protocol, enter **443** in both the From and To boxes for the Port (or Range).

9. Click the Add Definition button to add that port range.

10. Again, with TCP selected as the protocol, enter **4125** in both the From and To boxes for the Port (or Range) section.

11. Click the Add Definition button to add that port range.

    You should now have those three ports (80, 443, and 4125) displayed in the Definition List, as shown in Figure 11-11.

Protocol	Port (or Range)	Host Port	Timeout (sec)	
TCP	80	80	86400	REMOVE
TCP	443	443	86400	REMOVE
TCP	4125	4125	86400	REMOVE

Definition List

Figure 11-11. *Check for the ports in the Definition List.*

12. Click Back to return to the Edit Firewall Settings screen (see Figure 11-9). You should see the new application listed.

13. Select the computer you want to host applications through the firewall from the drop-down list. In my case, the Windows Home Server is listed as ae-whs.

14. Click the Allow Individual Application(s) radio button, select the new application (Windows Home Server Remote) from the box below it, and then click Add. Windows Home Server Remote should now be listed as a hosted application for ae-whs, as shown in Figure 11-12.

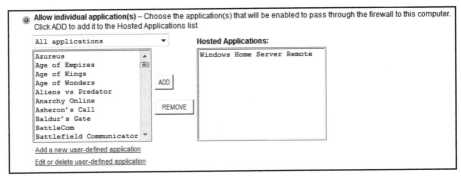

Figure 11-12. *Check that Windows Home Server Remote is now a hosted application.*

15. Click Done to complete the manual process.

16. Close down the connection to your router by closing the web page.

Setting Up the Domain Name

This step enables you to select a personalized domain name for your Windows Home Server, which makes it easier for you to remember the URL to connect to your Windows Home Server when you are away from home. For example, if available, I could use edneyfamily.homeserver.com. The only part of the domain name I need to choose is the edneyfamily part.

■**Note** Because the personalized domain name is used to access your Windows Home Server over the Internet, it has to be unique, so think of something that is easy for you to remember. Make sure you think of a couple of different possibilities just in case the domain name you want has already been taken by someone else.

To configure your domain name, follow these steps:

1. Click Setup next to the Domain Name option, as shown in Figure 11-13. This launches the Domain Name Setup Wizard, as shown in Figure 11-14.

Figure 11-13. *Click Setup to start the domain name setup.*

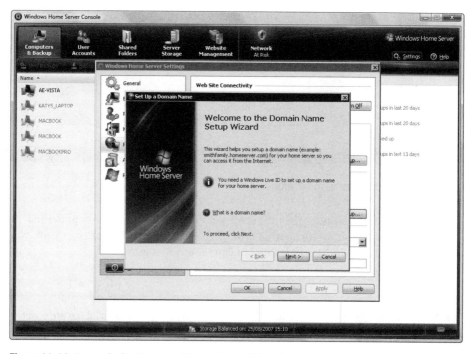

Figure 11-14. *Launch the Domain Name Setup Wizard.*

> ■**Note** You need a Windows Live ID to set up a domain name. If you don't have one, see the "Creating a Windows Live ID" section later in the chapter for information on how to do this.

2. Click Next to continue.

3. You must sign in to Windows Live to continue. Enter your Windows Live ID e-mail address and password to sign in to Windows Live, as shown in Figure 11-15.

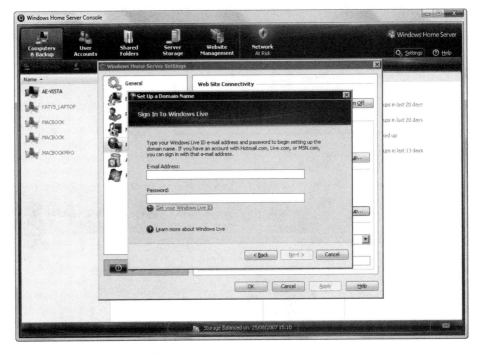

Figure 11-15. *Sign in to Windows Live.*

4. Click Next to continue. The next screen of the wizard is the Privacy Statement and Agreement, as shown in Figure 11-16. Read the Windows Home Server Privacy Statement and the Windows Live Custom Domains Addendum.

> ■**Note** Before you accept the agreement, it is a good idea to read it and make sure you are comfortable with its terms. If you do not agree, however, you cannot use the Remote Access facilities of Windows Home Server.

5. Click the I Accept button (assuming you accept).

6. Click Next to continue.

Figure 11-16. *You must accept the Privacy Statement and Agreement to continue.*

7. Type in the domain name you would like to use in the Domain Name box, as shown in Figure 11-17. The domain name can contain a maximum of 63 characters and can consist of letters, numbers, or hyphens. The name must begin and end with a letter or a number.

Figure 11-17. *Type in the domain name you would like to use.*

Note You can register only one domain name per Windows Live ID you have.

8. Click the Confirm button to check that the domain name is available to use. If it is not available, you will see the message shown in Figure 11-18. Just choose another one and try again.

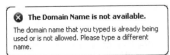

The Domain Name is not available.
The domain name that you typed is already being used or is not allowed. Please type a different name.

Figure 11-18. *The domain name is not available.*

9. When you find an available domain name, it will be displayed on the screen. Click Finish. You will see confirmation that the domain name has been set up, as shown in Figure 11-19.

Figure 11-19. *The domain name is now set up.*

Tip Make a note of the URL so that you can access your Windows Home Server. It will be `http://`*domainname*`.homeserver.com` followed by either `/home` for the home page over port 80 or `/remote` for the Remote Access login page over port 443 (which will start with `https://` instead of `http://`).

10. Click Done to complete the process.

Windows Home Server will now perform a series of tests to ensure everything is working. These tests include the following:

- Verifying the Internet connection to Windows Live

- Updating Windows Live Custom Domains

- Verifying that your web site is accessible from the Internet

- Verifying that Remote Access is accessible from the Internet

If you want to see the status of these tests, as shown in Figure 11-20, click the Details button, which now appears in the Domain Name section, as shown in Figure 11-21.

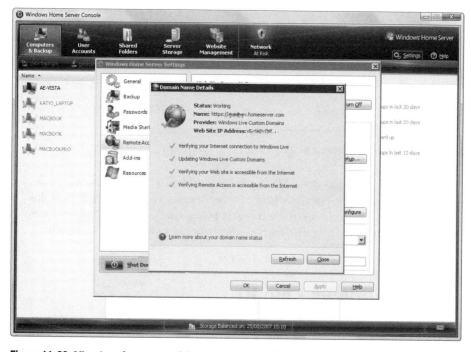

Figure 11-20. *Viewing the status of the various tests*

Along with the new Details button, there is also a button called Change, which just runs through the domain name setup again, and one called Unconfigure, which just unconfigures the domain name setup.

Figure 11-21. *New options available in the Domain Name section*

Unconfiguring the Domain Name

If you want to remove the domain name you just configured, you can do so simply by clicking the Unconfigure button, shown in Figure 11-21.

■**Caution** If you click the Unconfigure button, you are given no warning about what you are about to do. The domain name is just unconfigured, and you need to configure it again to use Remote Access.

Configuring Web Site Settings

The final section of the Remote Access area is Web Site Settings. This area enables you to set the web site home page and the web site headline, as shown in Figure 11-22.

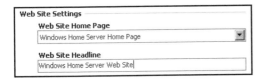

Figure 11-22. *Changing the web site settings*

The Web Site Home Page drop-down list enables you to choose between the Windows Home Server Home Page and the Windows Home Server Remote Access Page. The Web Site Headline setting enables you to change the text that appears—the default is Windows Home Server Web Site. You can change it to anything you want (for example, The Edney Family Home Server).

Creating a Windows Live ID

Having a Windows Live ID is a prerequisite for creating a domain name for use with Windows Home Server.

To create a Windows Live ID, just follow these steps:

1. Using Internet Explorer or any other Internet browser, visit `https://accountservices.passport.net/ppnetworkhome.srf?lc=2057`, which is the Windows Live ID web site.

2. Select the type of Windows Live ID you want to create by clicking the Get Started Now link below it, as shown in Figure 11-23. For the sake of this example, I will select Sign Up for a Limited Account.

3. Create an e-mail address (which can contain only letters, numbers, periods, hyphens, and underscores) and password to use as Windows Live ID credentials, as shown in Figure 11-24. As noted, you can't send or receive e-mail using this address—it's only for use when you sign in.

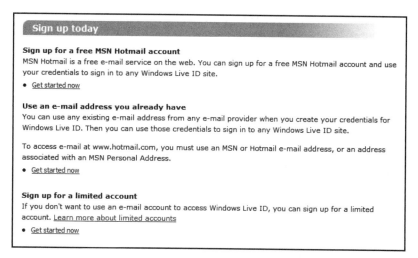

Figure 11-23. *Select one of the available choices of Windows Live ID.*

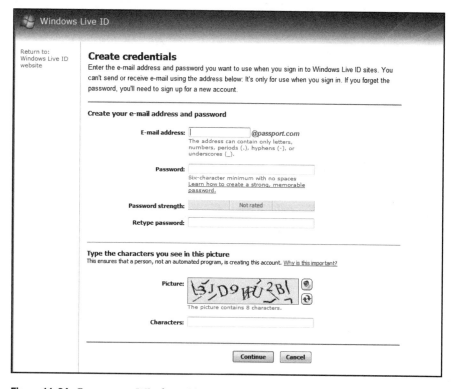

Figure 11-24. *Create your Windows Live ID.*

■**Note** The password must be a minimum of six characters in length. As you type the password, you can see from the password strength visual how strong your password actually is.

4. Type in the characters that are displayed in the picture. This is used as a security mechanism to stop automated programs from creating accounts.

5. Click the Continue button.

6. The next screen, shown in Figure 11-25, contains links to the terms of use and online privacy statement. Type in your e-mail address that you just created and click the I Accept button to continue.

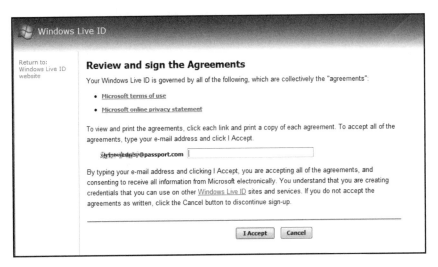

Figure 11-25. *Review and accept the agreement for a Windows Live ID.*

7. The last screen confirms that you have created your Windows Live ID, as shown in Figure 11-26. Click the Continue button to complete the process.

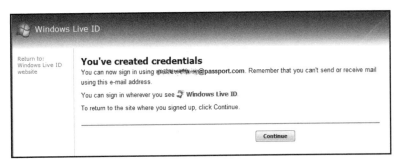

Figure 11-26. *Your Windows Live ID has been created.*

You can now use this newly created Windows Live ID for creating the Windows Home Server domain.

■**Tip** You can also use this Windows Live ID for any other purpose that requires a Windows Live ID.

Enabling Users for Remote Access

Now that you have enabled Remote Access on your Windows Home Server and have configured the domain name and your router, the final step is to enable any of your user accounts
for Remote Access.

■**Note** By default, all user accounts have Remote Access disabled, for security reasons.

---

1. On the Windows Home Server Console, click the User Accounts icon.

2. Double-click the user you want to enable for Remote Access, which will open the Properties dialog box for that user, as shown in Figure 11-27.

■**Note** You cannot enable the Guest account or Windows Home Server Administrator account for Remote
Access. You must use a normal user account.

---

3. Check the Enable Remote Access for This User check box and click OK to close the user
   account Properties dialog box.

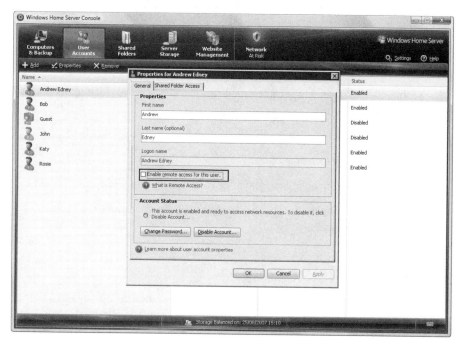

Figure 11-27. *Enable Remote Access for a user account.*

4. If the user account does not have a strong password, the message shown in Figure 11-28 is displayed. If you get this message, click Yes to change the password to a strong password. For more information on changing passwords and what a strong password must contain, take a look at Chapter 6.

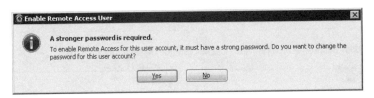

Figure 11-28. *The current password is not strong enough for Remote Access.*

5. Repeat the steps for each user that you wish to grant Remote Access.

You will now be able to see in the User Accounts list which user accounts have Remote Access allowed, as shown in Figure 11-29.

Figure 11-29. *Confirming that the user account has Remote Access allowed*

Disabling Users for Remote Access

If you want to disable Remote Access for any given user, the process is just as straightforward as enabling Remote Access. Follow these steps:

1. On the Windows Home Server Console, click the User Accounts icon.

2. Double-click the user you want to enable for Remote Access, which opens the Properties dialog box for that user.

3. Remove the check from the Enable Remote Access for This User check box.

4. Click OK to close the user account Properties dialog box.

5. Repeat the steps for each user for whom you wish to remove Remote Access.

You can then also confirm that those users are now shown in the User Accounts list as Not Allowed under Remote Access.

Testing Remote Access

It is a very good idea to test Remote Access before you go somewhere away from home, just to ensure it's actually working. If these tests are successful, coupled with the domain testing that has already been successful, you should be able to access your Windows Home Server from a location away from home.

■**Note** For help on troubleshooting Remote Access problems, take a look at the "Troubleshooting Remote Access" section later in this chapter.

You can perform the following tests from any computer on your home network:

- *Test connectivity to the Windows Home Server home page over port 80*: In Internet Explorer, type the following URL in the Address box: **http://***servername***/home**, where *servername* is the name of your Windows Home Server. For example, in my case it would be http://ae-whs/home. If the test is successful, you should see the Windows Home Server Web Site page, as shown in Figure 11-30.

Figure 11-30. *The Windows Home Server Web Site home page*

- *Test connectivity to the Windows Home Server Remote Access page over port 443*: In Internet Explorer, type the following URL in the Address box: **https://***servername***/remote**, where *servername* is the name of your Windows Home Server. So, in my case it would be https://ae-whs/remote. If the test is successful, you should see the Windows Home Server Remote Access page, as shown in Figure 11-31.

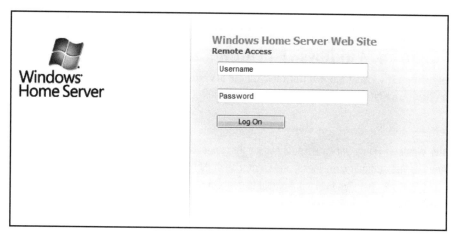

Figure 11-31. *The Windows Home Server Remote Access page*

Configuring Computers for Remote Access

You can use Windows Home Server Remote Access to connect to your home computers when you are away from home. Before you can use this feature, though, you have to ensure that the computers you want to be able to connect to have the Remote Desktop capability switched on.

REMOTE DESKTOP

The Remote Desktop capability uses the Remote Desktop Protocol (RDP) to connect one computer to another using Microsoft Terminal Services. RDP is based on, and an extension of, the ITU T.120 family of protocols. RDP is a multichannel-capable protocol that allows for separate virtual channels for carrying device communication and presentation data from the server, as well as encrypted client mouse and keyboard data. RDP provides an extensible base and supports up to 64,000 separate channels for data transmission and provisions for multipoint transmission.

For more information on RDP, take a look at `http://msdn2.microsoft.com/en-us/library/aa383015.aspx`.

■**Note** Not all home computers are compatible with the Windows Home Server Remote Access facility. Your home computers need to be running Windows Vista Ultimate, Vista Business, Vista Enterprise, Windows XP Professional, Windows XP Tablet Edition, or Windows Media Center 2005. Any other version of Windows is not supported, which means you won't be able to use Remote Access to connect to a computer running another version.

Configuring Windows Vista for Remote Access

Configuring Windows Vista for Remote Access is very simple. Perform the following steps on each Windows Vista computer you want to enable for Remote Access:

■**Note** Windows Home Server Remote Access for connecting to Windows Vista computers works only on Windows Vista Ultimate, Business, and Enterprise editions. If you have a computer running any other edition of Windows Vista, you will not be able to connect remotely to it using Windows Home Server Remote Access.

1. Click the Start button and then click Control Panel.

2. Click System and Maintenance.

3. In the System section, click Allow Remote Access.

4. In the System Properties dialog box, click the Remote tab and ensure that the Allow Connections from Computers Running Any Version of Remote Desktop (Less Secure) radio button is selected, as shown in Figure 11-32.

Figure 11-32. *Enable Remote Desktop on a Windows Vista computer.*

5. Click OK to close the dialog box.

6. Click the back arrow to return to the Control Panel.

7. Click Security.

8. Click Windows Firewall.

9. Click Change Settings.

10. In the Windows Firewall Settings dialog box, click the Exceptions tab.

11. Scroll down through the list of exceptions and ensure that the Remote Desktop entry has a check mark next to it, as shown in Figure 11-33.

12. Click OK to close the Windows Firewall Settings dialog box.

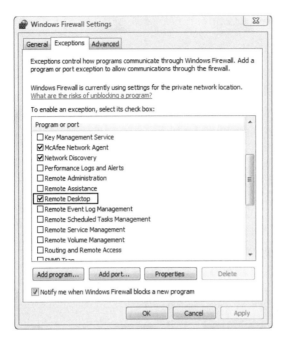

Figure 11-33. *Confirm that Remote Desktop is allowed through Windows Firewall.*

Configuring Windows XP for Remote Access

Configuring Windows XP Professional for Remote Access is also very simple. Perform the following steps on each Windows XP Professional computer you want to enable for Remote Access:

■Note Windows Home Server Remote Access for connecting to Windows XP computers works only on Windows XP Professional, Windows XP Tablet Edition, and Windows Media Center 2005. If you have a computer running any other edition of Windows XP, you will not be able to connect remotely to it using Windows Home Server Remote Access.

---

1. Click the Start button and then click Control Panel.

2. Double-click the System icon (in Classic View) to launch the System Properties dialog box.

3. Click the Remote tab and ensure that the Allow Users to Connect Remotely to This Computer box is checked, as shown in Figure 11-34.

4. Click OK to close the System Properties dialog box.

5. In the Control Panel, double-click the Windows Firewall icon.

6. In the Windows Firewall dialog box, click the Exceptions tab.

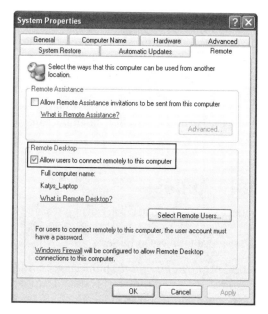

Figure 11-34. *Enable Remote Desktop on a Windows XP Professional computer.*

7. Scroll down through the list of exceptions and ensure that the Remote Desktop entry has a check mark next to it, as shown in Figure 11-35.

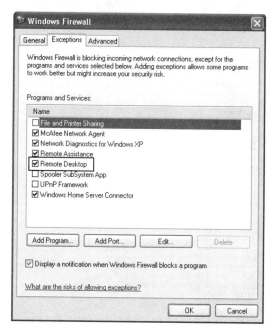

Figure 11-35. *Confirm that Remote Desktop is allowed through Windows Firewall.*

8. Click OK to close the Windows Firewall dialog box.

Configuring Windows Home Server for Remote Access

You do not need to do any special configuration to your Windows Home Server to use the Remote Access facilities. However, as an aside, if you enabled Remote Desktop on your Windows Home Server, you can then access it from any one of your home computers that has the Remote Desktop Connection client on. This can make life easier for you later on if you need to do something on the Windows Home Server that you cannot do using the Windows Home Server Console and you don't want to connect the keyboard, monitor, and mouse (assuming you have ports).

Logging On Using Remote Access

From any computer in the world that is connected to the Internet, you can access your Windows Home Server remotely.

There are two different ways to log on to your Windows Home Server:

- From an Internet browser, type the URL **http://***domainname***.homeserver.com/home**, where *domainname* is the domain name you created earlier. This should connect to your Windows Home Server Web Site home page, as shown in Figure 11-36. Click the Log On button. This actually takes you to the same screen that you are taken to directly by using the second method, the Windows Home Server Remote Access page.

Figure 11-36. *The Windows Home Server Web Site home page*

- From an Internet browser, type the URL **https://***domainname***.homeserver.com/remote**, where *domainname* is the domain name you created earlier. This should connect to your Windows Home Server Remote Access page, shown in Figure 11-37, although you first might receive the warning described next.

■Caution Connecting to your Windows Home Server using the http:// address means that your connection is in the clear (not encrypted) and thus is considered riskier.

■Tip Connecting to your Windows Home Server via https:// means that the connection from the computer you are using and your Windows Home Server is encrypted, which essentially means that it is more secure.

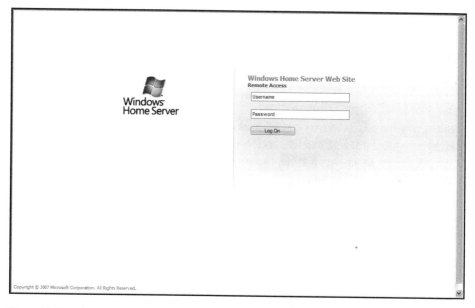

Figure 11-37. *The Windows Home Server Remote Access page*

As mentioned, you might receive a warning shown in Figure 11-38, telling you that there is a problem with the web site's security certificate. This is to be expected because, to securely communicate with the browser, your Windows Home Server uses a self-certified certificate that is not recognized as being from a trusted certificate authority.

During the installation of the Windows Home Server Connector software, the Windows Home Server security certificate is added to the trusted certificate list on your home computer, so the warning about the certificate appears only on computers that you have not installed the Windows Home Server Connector software on.

■Tip If you use a laptop when you are away from home and you want to use it for Remote Access to your Windows Home Server, ensure that you have installed the Windows Home Server Connector software on it.

Don't worry; just click Continue to This Website to carry on.

There is a problem with this website's security certificate.

The security certificate presented by this website was not issued by a trusted certificate authority.

Security certificate problems may indicate an attempt to fool you or intercept any data you send to the server.

We recommend that you close this webpage and do not continue to this website.

✓ Click here to close this webpage.

✗ Continue to this website (not recommended).

⊙ More information

Figure 11-38. *Warning about the security certificate used on your Windows Home Server*

■Note During the beta testing phase of Windows Home Server, Microsoft said that there may be something released in the future that will resolve the security certificate issue, so keep your eyes on the Windows Home Server web site and any updates that may become available.

All that you need to do now is enter your username and password, and then click the Log On button. As stated earlier, the account you are using to log on to the Windows Home Server Remote Access facility must have been enabled for Remote Access first.

■Note As an added security measure to stop someone from trying to continually guess your password, the IP address of the computer trying to log on is tracked and if the number of logon attempts from that IP address is greater than the threshold in a given period of time, the next logon attempt is delayed.

Using Remote Access

Now that you have logged on and connected to your Windows Home Server web site, you will see the Home tab of the Windows Home Server Web Site Remote Access home page, as shown in Figure 11-39.

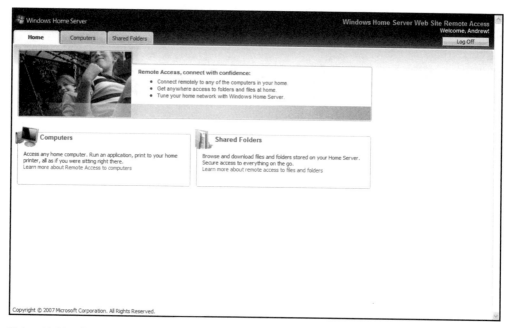

Figure 11-39. *The Windows Home Server Web Site Remote Access home page*

As you can see, there are three tabs:

- *Home*: The main home page where you can access the Computers and Shared Folders areas.

- *Computers*: Enables you to access any of your home computers that have Remote Access enabled and are supported. You can also access your Windows Home Server and make settings changes and anything else that can be performed using the Windows Home Server Console. You can also access this tab by clicking Computers on the Home tab.

- *Shared Folders*: Enables you to browse any shared folders you have access to, upload and download files, and more. You can also access this tab by clicking Shared Folders on the Home tab.

Accessing Your Computers

You can remotely access any of your home computers that are supported and have been configured for Remote Access. You can also access your Windows Home Server to make configuration changes, check on backups, view network messages, and more.

Note Using Remote Access to access any of your home computers is only supported when using Internet Explorer. If you use any other web browser, you will not be able to remotely connect to your home computers.

When you click the Computers tab, you are presented with the Computers web page, as shown in Figure 11-40.

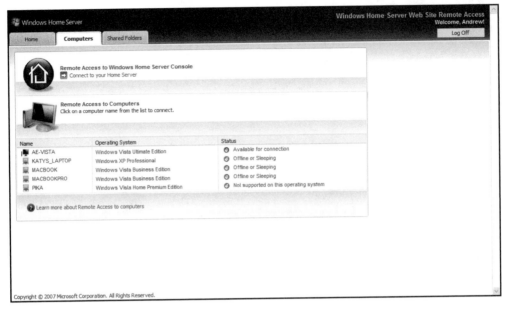

Figure 11-40. *The Computers Web page*

From here, you can see all of your home computers, along with details of the operating system they are running and the status of those computers. The possible status messages include the following:

- *Available for connection*: The computer is switched on and you are able to connect to it (unless it is blocked by a third-party firewall).

- *Connection disabled*: The computer is switched on but you are not able to connect to it because Remote Access has not been enabled, or it is blocked by a third-party firewall.

- *Offline or Sleeping*: The computer is either switched off, not connected to your home network, or is sleeping.

- *Not supported on this operating system*: The version of the operating system does not allow you to use Remote Access via Windows Home Server.

This page also includes the link that enables you to connect to your Windows Home Server, discussed next.

Connecting to Your Windows Home Server

While you are away from home, you might need to connect to your Windows Home Server to check the status of backups, view any Network Health messages, do administrative-type tasks, and more.

You can connect to your Windows Home Server by following these steps:

1. On the Computer tab, click Connect to Your Home Server. This launches the familiar Windows Home Server Console logon screen, only this time through the web browser, as shown in Figure 11-41.

Note You don't have a Password Hint button when trying to connect via the web site, so make sure you remember what the Windows Home Server Administrator password is before continuing.

Figure 11-41. *Access the web-based Windows Home Server Console logon screen.*

2. Enter your Windows Home Server Administrator password.

3. Click OK to continue logging on.

You are presented with the familiar Windows Home Server Console screen, as shown in Figure 11-42. You can now perform most of the tasks you need to exactly as though you were using the Windows Home Server Console from one of your home computers.

Note You cannot open any of the shared folders from here. You need to use the Shared Folders tab on the Remote Access web site if you want to open any shared folders.

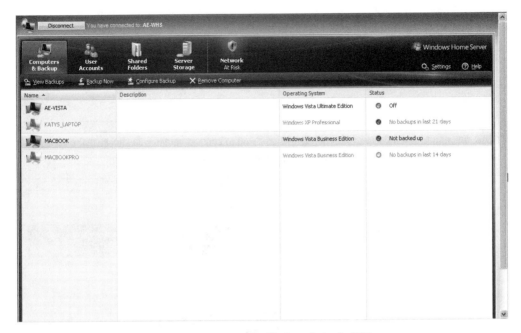

Figure 11-42. *The Windows Home Server Console displayed via the Web*

When you have finished using the Windows Home Server Console, click the Disconnect button in the top-left corner of the screen to return to the Remote Access web site.

■**Caution** Make sure that you use the Disconnect button to close down the Windows Home Server Console screen and that you do not use the Shut Down button from the Settings menu; otherwise, you will shut down your Windows Home Server and lose your Remote Access facilities until such time as you can power back up the Windows Home Server.

Connecting to One of Your Home Computers

As mentioned earlier, you can connect to one of your home computers and use it as though you were sitting in front of it. Therefore, you can start an application, print something, and pretty much do anything you could do if you were sitting in front of it at home.

■**Note** To be able to connect to one of your home computers, the computer must be switched on and connected to your home network; otherwise, you won't be able to connect to it. It also must be running one of the supported operating systems and have been configured for Remote Access.

You can connect to one of your home computers by following these steps:

1. On the Computers tab, look through the list of computers until you find the one you want to connect to, and make sure that it is listed as Available for Connection.

2. Click the computer name to open the Connection Options dialog box, shown in Figure 11-43.

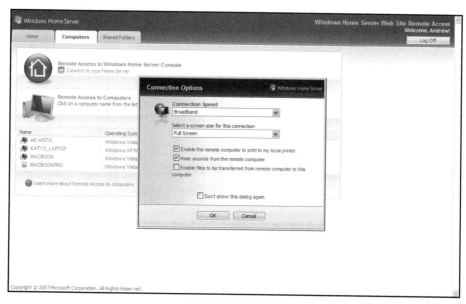

Figure 11-43. *Open the Connection Options dialog box to choose your connection options.*

3. Choose the connection speed from the drop-down list: either Broadband or Modem.

4. Select a screen size for the connection from the drop-down list, ranging from Small to Full Screen. This is the size of the screen you want the remote connection displayed at. The size of the screen affects the speed of screen refreshes.

5. Check the Enable the Remote Computer to Print to My Local Printer check box if you want to send something from your remote computer to your local printer (the one connected to the machine you are currently using, assuming it has one connected).

6. Check the Hear Sounds from the Remote Computer check box if you want to hear any sounds from the remote computer on the local computer; for example, if you want to play some music on the remote computer.

7. Check the Enable Files to Be Transferred from Remote Computer to This Computer check box if you want to allow files to be transferred to the computer you are on.

8. Click OK to continue. A remote connection will now be attempted. If it is successful, you should see a logon screen similar to the one shown in Figure 11-44.

Figure 11-44. *Enter your password in the Windows Vista logon screen.*

9. Enter the password for the user account on the computer you are trying to establish the connection to.

You should now be able to use your home computer and perform any tasks that you wish. When you are ready to stop the remote connection, choose Start ➤ Disconnect, which will disconnect the remote session and return you to the Remote Access web site.

Accessing Your Shared Folders

From the Shared Folders tab, you can access any of the shared folders from your Windows Home Server, as long as you have the correct permissions. Depending on your permissions, you will be able to upload and download files, delete files, and even rename them, all of which are described in this section. You can also search for a file even if you cannot remember which shared folder it is stored in, as also explained in this section.

When you click the Shared Folders tab, you see the list of shared folders, as shown in Figure 11-45.

Figure 11-45. *The Shared Folders tab view*

From here, you can click any of the displayed shared folders to see its contents.

Downloading a File

You can easily download one or more of your files from any shared folder on your Windows Home Server that you have access to, as follows:

1. Click the folder that you want to open to view its contents.

2. Place a check in the box for each file that you want to download to the computer you are currently using, as shown in Figure 11-46.

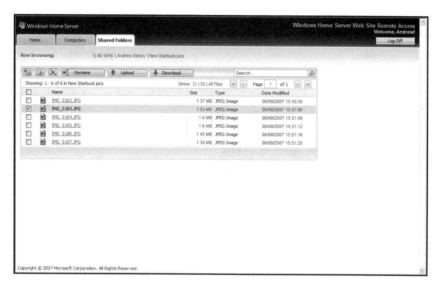

Figure 11-46. *Select which files to download.*

3. When you have selected all the files that you want to download, click the Download button. If you select more than one file, the multiple files are then prepared and placed in a compressed zip folder for you, to reduce the size of the file to be downloaded and thus the amount of time it will actually take to download.

4. When the File Download dialog box appears, as shown in Figure 11-47, click the Save button and select the location on the computer you are using where you want the zip file to be placed.

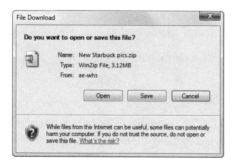

Figure 11-47. *Click Save in the File Download dialog box.*

■**Note** The zip file is automatically named with the name of the folder that the files were stored in. For example, in Figure 11-47 it is named New Starbuck pics.zip.

5. Open the downloaded zip file to gain access to the compressed files within it, or just double-click the individual file if that is all you downloaded.

Uploading a File

You can also upload a file to any shared folder that you have write permissions to. To upload a file that will be stored in whichever shared folder you are currently viewing, follow these steps:

1. From the shared folder that you wish to upload a file to, click the Upload button to open the Upload dialog box, shown in Figure 11-48.

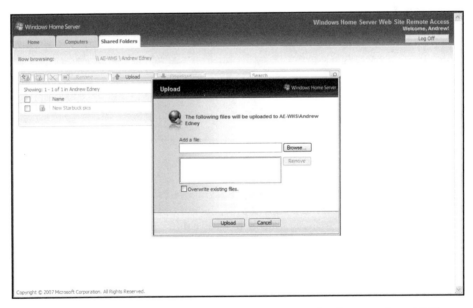

Figure 11-48. *Use the Upload dialog box to choose a file to upload to your shared folder.*

2. Click the Browse button and then search for and double-click the file you want to upload.

3. Repeat this process for each file that you wish to upload.

■**Note** If you change your mind about one or more of the files in the list you are about to upload to the shared folder, just click the file or files to highlight them and then click the Remove button to remove them from the upload list.

4. If a version of a file already exists in the shared folder, it won't be overwritten unless you place a check in the Overwrite Existing Files check box.

■**Caution** Use the Overwrite Existing Files check box with caution because it will overwrite all files with the same name from your upload list. So if you have a file that you don't want overwritten as well as some files that you do want overwritten, it is advisable to upload them separately.

---

5. Click the Upload button to begin the uploading process to your shared folder. You can see that the files are being uploaded, as shown in Figure 11-49.

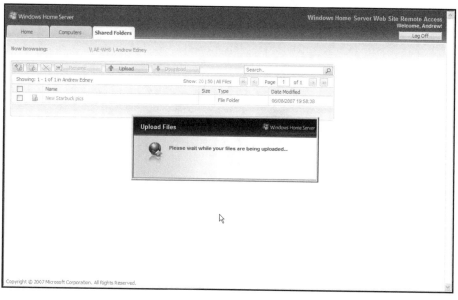

Figure 11-49. *Wait while the files are being uploaded to the shared folder.*

■**Note** The amount of time it will take to upload the files to your shared folder will depend on a number of factors, including the speed of the Internet connection on the computer you are uploading from, the speed of the Internet connection that your Windows Home Server is connected to, the number and size of the files your are uploading, and more.

Once the uploading process has completed, the files will be displayed in the shared folder.

Renaming a File or Folder

You may decide to rename a file or folder to something more meaningful than it is currently called. For example, instead of having a photo called IMG_0183.jpg, you could rename it to indicate what it depicts, such as the name of the person or place, or whatever.

To rename any file or folder in the folder you are currently viewing, perform the following steps:

1. Check the box of the file or folder that you want to rename.

2. Click the Rename button.

3. Type a new name for the file or folder, as shown in Figure 11-50.

4. Click OK to finish.

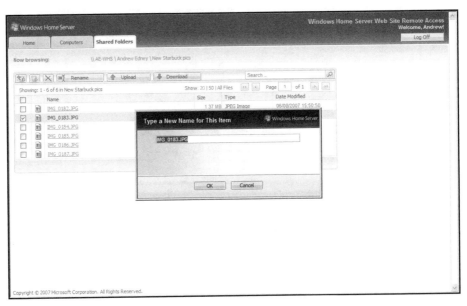

Figure 11-50. *Type the new name for the file or folder and click OK.*

Creating a New Folder

You may decide that you want to create a new folder in which to store your files. For example, you may be on vacation and decide that you want to upload the digital photos that you have taken, in which case you can create a new folder for the vacation and upload the photos.

Note You cannot create a folder in the root directory. You can create a new folder only within an existing shared folder. If you want to create a new top-level folder, you must use the Windows Home Server Console.

To create a new folder in the folder you are currently viewing, perform the following steps:

1. Click the New Folder icon, as shown in Figure 11-51.

Figure 11-51. *Click this icon to create a new folder.*

2. Type a name for the new folder, as shown in Figure 11-52.

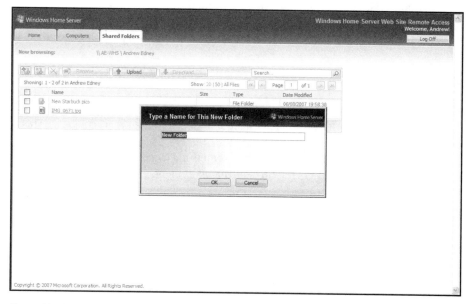

Figure 11-52. *Type a name for the new folder.*

3. Click OK to create the new folder.

The new folder will now appear in your Windows Home Server and you can start uploading files to it as you see fit.

Deleting a File or Folder

If you decide you want to delete a file or a folder from your Windows Home Server remotely, just follow these steps:

1. Select the file or folder that you want to delete by checking the relevant box or boxes.

2. Click the Delete button, as shown in Figure 11-53. You will be asked to confirm the deletion, as shown in Figure 11-54.

Caution Be sure that you want to delete the file or folder, because once it has been deleted, it's gone!

Figure 11-53. *Click this icon to delete a file or folder.*

Figure 11-54. *Confirm the deletion by clicking OK.*

3. Click OK to confirm the deletion, or click Cancel if you change your mind.

Searching for a File

Finding the file you are looking for is easy if you can remember exactly which folder it is stored in, but sometimes, especially if you have a lot of folders and files, this is not easy. This is where searching comes into play.

To search for a file, just type its name (or something close if you can't remember it) in the Search box, shown in Figure 11-55, and click the magnifying glass to begin the search.

Figure 11-55. *Searching for a file*

The results of the search will be displayed, and you can select the file you want from the search results.

Logging Off

When you have finished whatever it is that you are doing using Remote Access, you should log off. To do this, just click the Log Off button and your session will end. You can now close down the Internet browser session.

Viewing Remote Access Connections

If you have the Windows Home Server Console open and someone is connected to your Windows Home Server using Remote Access, you can see who it is. In the bottom-left part of the Windows Home Server Console, when someone is connected, Remote Access: *username* (where *username* is the person's username) appears, as shown in Figure 11-56.

Figure 11-56. *Viewing who is connected via Remote Access*

■Note Viewing who is connected to your Windows Home Server is provided for information purposes only. You cannot see what they are doing and you cannot stop them from using Remote Access without stopping Remote Access while they are connected.

Troubleshooting Remote Access

If you are having trouble with Remote Access, there are a number of troubleshooting steps you could take. Here are some examples:

- Confirm the version of the operating system of the home computer you are trying to connect to.

- Confirm that Remote Desktop is enabled on the home computer you are trying to connect to.

- Confirm that Remote Desktop is allowed through Windows Firewall on the computer you are trying to connect to.

- If you are using a third-party firewall, ensure that TCP port 3389 is allowed. You may need to check the documentation that came with your firewall to enable this.

- Confirm that your broadband router is configured.

If you have checked everything, and the tests that you performed to ensure that you could connect from within your home were successful, but the tests from outside of your home were not successful, then your ISP might be blocking either port 80 or port 443, or both. The easiest way to check this is to contact your ISP and ask them. If they are blocking you, there are ways around this, and you can search for these ways on the Internet.

■Caution Be very careful if you decide to use a method to get around your ISP blocking those ports. Doing so could be considered a breach of your contract and you could be liable. Because of this fact, the locations of these methods and how to use them will not be mentioned in the book.

Enabling JavaScript

You may find that you need to enable JavaScript on your home computers to use the Remote Access web site. The following steps should be performed in Internet Explorer 7:

1. Open Internet Explorer 7.

2. Choose Tools ➤ Internet Options.

3. Click the Security tab.

4. Click Internet to select the Internet zone.

5. Click the Custom Level button.

6. Scroll down to the Scripting section (it will be quite a way down the list).

7. Click Enable under Active Scripting.

8. Click OK to close the Security Settings dialog box and then click OK to close the Internet Options dialog box.

9. Restart Internet Explorer 7.

■**Tip** Always check the help documentation for any additional troubleshooting steps, and don't forget the wealth of information and advice on the Windows Home Server forums.

Summary

In this chapter, you learned about the Remote Access facility provided by Windows Home Server. You learned how to check whether your broadband router could be automatically configured to support Remote Access. You also learned how to enable Remote Access, manually configure your broadband router, and create a Windows Home Server domain name, along with creating a Windows Live ID. You then learned how to use the Remote Access facilities and how to troubleshoot things if they go wrong.

Remote Access is a great feature that is relatively easy to configure and use and provides great benefit if you are away from home but really need to access your home network.

■■■

CHAPTER 12

Home Network Health Monitoring

Windows Home Server has a feature called Network Health that monitors the health of computers on your home network, including the Windows Home Server itself, and notifies you in a few different ways if it finds a problem. Unfortunately, Network Health works only with computers running Windows Vista, so if all of your computers are running Windows XP, Network Health will monitor only your Windows Home Server.

This chapter introduces the Network Health feature, with particular attention given to the notifications that Network Health issues and what they mean. Understanding how Network Health functions is useful to you because it saves you from having to go to each of your Windows Vista home computers and check such things as antivirus and firewall status.

■**Caution** Network Health monitors the health of your Windows Home Server and only those computers on your home network that are running Windows Vista as the operating system. Any other computers on your home network will be ignored, so you need to manually check those at regular intervals by performing a visual inspection at each computer.

Viewing Network Health Notifications

There are two locations where you can see the Network Health notifications for your Windows Home Server and your Windows Vista computers:

- The Windows Home Server icon in the task tray on any computer that has the Windows Home Server Connector installed

- The Network button in the Windows Home Server Console

Viewing Network Health in the Task Tray

If you have the Windows Home Server Connector software installed on your computer, you can easily see the status of the network just by looking at the color and appearance of the

Windows Home Server task tray icon. You will see one of three different icons, as shown and described in the following table.

Icon	Description
	Green indicates a healthy network that requires no further action.
	Yellow indicates that there is an "at risk" issue that you should address as soon as possible.
	Red indicates that there is a "critical" issue that needs your immediate attention.

Caution You should investigate and address issues identified with a yellow icon as soon as possible, although they do not necessarily require that you drop everything immediately to check them out. However, for issues identified with a red icon, you should stop whatever you are doing, if possible, and investigate and resolve the issue so that it does not cause you any additional problems.

Sometimes, specific messages appear that tell you about an issue that needs to be addressed, such as the antivirus software status message, shown in Figure 12-1.

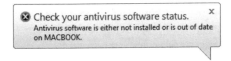

Figure 12-1. *Warning about an antivirus issue with one computer*

Another warning message you could see is the "Your Home Network Health Is Critical" warning, shown in Figure 12-2.

Figure 12-2. *Warning that your home network health is critical*

If you see that message, you should open the Windows Home Server Console immediately and investigate the issue or issues and plan to resolve them before you do anything else.

If you do not want Network Health notifications to appear on your computer, you can easily switch them off. To do this, right-click the Windows Home Server task tray icon and click the Display Network Health Notifications option to remove the check mark that is shown in Figure 12-3.

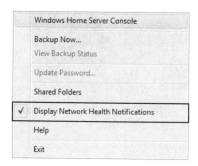

Figure 12-3. *Choosing whether to display Network Health notifications*

Note Unchecking the Display Network Health Notifications option only stops the display on your computer; it does not stop the notifications from appearing in the Windows Home Server Console. You can easily choose to display them again on your computer by checking the option at any time.

Viewing Network Health on the Network Button in the Windows Home Server Console

When the Windows Home Server Console is open, you see the Network button at the top of the screen. This button includes above the word Network an icon whose color indicates the health status of your network, in the same way as the Windows Home Server task tray icon. The button also includes below the word Network a text status notification that corresponds to the color of the icon: Healthy (green), At Risk (yellow), or Critical (red).

The following table shows and describes the three possible icons you will see on the Network button, which are very similar to the corresponding Windows Home Server task tray icons.

Icon	Description
	Green indicates a healthy network that requires no further action.
	Yellow indicates that there is an "at risk" issue that you should address as soon as possible.
	Red indicates that there is a "critical" issue that needs your immediate attention.

To see the specific network health issues, click the Network button. This displays the Home Network Health dialog box, which shows a list of any items that need your attention, as shown in Figure 12-4.

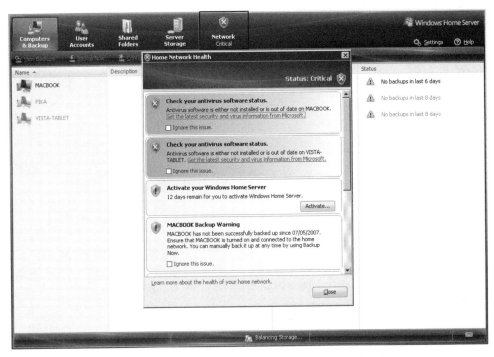

Figure 12-4. *Viewing network health issues in the Home Network Health dialog box*

Again, each item is color coded to make it easier for you to tell which ones need your immediate attention and which have a lower priority. Most of the Network Health items include an Ignore This Issue check box below them. If it is an issue you know about, don't want to fix, or can't fix for whatever reason, you can check this box, which will gray it out so that you are no longer notified of the problem, as shown in Figure 12-5. If an issue does not have an Ignore This Issue check box, it is an issue that you just cannot ignore (for example, the need to activate your Windows Home Server). Once all the issues have either been dealt with or ignored, the network status will revert back to Healthy.

■Note Even if you choose to ignore an issue by checking the box, it still appears in the list until it is resolved, so it would be wise to try and resolve it so that you don't end up with lots of ignored issues.

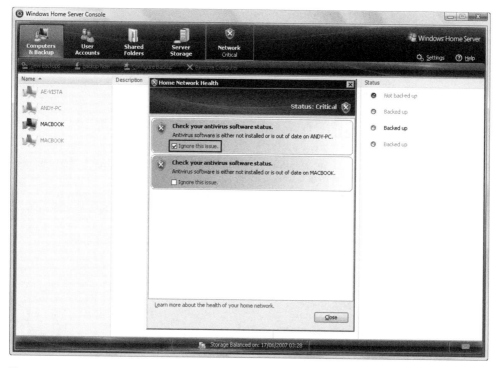

Figure 12-5. *Choosing to ignore a Network Health notification*

Examining the Windows Home Server Notifications

This section describes the Network Health notifications that are specific to the Windows Home Server. It is important to note that the list of notifications is likely to be continually updated as Microsoft releases patches and fixes and discovers any other important security information. For the latest list of notifications, take a look at the help file that comes with the Windows Home Server Connector. The following sections have been adapted from the help file that came with the RTM version.

Server Hard Drive

There are different health status messages related to the Windows Home Server hard drives. Table 12-1 shows some of them.

Table 12-1. *Server Hard Drive Health Status Messages*

Health Status	Description
Yellow	Less than a certain % (x) of the space is available for server storage. If your total server storage is 100 GB or less, x = 12% 101-200 GB, x = 10% 201-500 GB, x = 7% 501-1000 GB, x = 4% 1001-2000 GB, x = 3% 2001 GB or more, x = 2%.
Yellow	Shared folder duplication has stopped for one or more shared folders because the server storage is low.
Yellow	One or more of the Windows Home Server hard drives has failed. It is important to note that this message applies to S.M.A.R.T. (Self-Monitoring, Analysis and Reporting Technology) hard drives only.
Red	Less than a certain % (x) of the space is available for server storage. If your total server storage is 100 GB or less, x = 3% 101-200 GB, x = 3% 201-500 GB, x = 2% 501-1000 GB, x = 2% 1001-2000 GB, x = 1% 2001 GB or more, x = 1%.
Red	One or more of the Windows Home Server hard drives has failed.

Product Activation

If you have not yet activated your Windows Home Server, you will receive a couple of status messages, which are listed and described in Table 12-2.

Table 12-2. *Windows Home Server Product Activation Status Messages*

Health Status	Description
Yellow	15 days or less remain to activate Windows Home Server before it will stop functioning.
Red	10 days or less remain to activate Windows Home Server before it will stop functioning.

If you want to activate your Windows Home Server, you are given the option from within the Network Health status message, or you can use one of the other two methods described in both Chapters 3 and 5.

Windows Update

If you have set Windows Update to be On for your Windows Home Server, any updates will automatically be downloaded and installed. However, occasionally, an update that is released will require your authorization before the installation can take place. Table 12-3 shows the status message.

Table 12-3. *Windows Update Status Message*

Health Status	Description
Red	An update for your Windows Home Server requires your specific approval before it can be installed.

Shared Folder Duplication

If you have Folder Duplication enabled for shared folders, you may see the status messages shown in Table 12-4.

Table 12-4. *Shared Folder Duplication Status Messages*

Health Status	Description
Yellow	A shared folder contains one or more files with a path name longer than 260 characters and so these file or files cannot be duplicated.
Yellow	There is not enough server storage space for folder duplication to take place.

Evaluation Period Expiration

If you are running an evaluation copy of Windows Home Server, you can use it for 120 days only, and you may see the status messages shown in Table 12-5.

Table 12-5. *Evaluation Period Expiration Status Messages*

Health Status	Description
Yellow	30 days or less remain before your evaluation copy of Windows Home Server will stop functioning.
Red	15 days or less remain before your evaluation copy of Windows Home Server will stop functioning.

■**Caution** If your copy of Windows Home Server expires, you will not be able to access the files or backups stored on it. If you want to continue to use the features of Windows Home Server, you can upgrade the 120-day evaluation copy to a full-blown copy of Windows Home Server.

Examining the Windows Vista Computer Notifications

This section describes the Network Health notifications that are specific to Windows Vista computers that have the Windows Home Server Connector installed. Any other Windows computers on your home network will only report their backup status, which itself is not really a Network Health issue. It is important to note that the list of notifications is likely to be continually updated as patches and fixes are released and any other important security information comes to light. For the latest list of notifications, take a look at the help file that comes with the Windows Home Server Connector. The following sections have been adapted from the help file.

■**Note** *ComputerName* refers to the actual name of the computer; for example, in Figure 12-4 earlier in the chapter, one of the messages related to one of my computers called Vista-Tablet. Being able to identify easily which computer has a Network Health issue is another reason why it is extremely useful to give your computers useful names rather than 1, 2, 3, and so on.

Windows Firewall Status

Table 12-6 lists and describes the status message for Windows Firewall.

Table 12-6. *Windows Firewall Status Message*

Health Status	Description
Red	*ComputerName* has the Windows Firewall turned off.

Windows Update Status

Table 12-7 shows the status messages for Windows Update.

Table 12-7. *Windows Update Status Messages*

Health Status	Description
Yellow	*ComputerName* has updates to install for Windows.
Red	*ComputerName* has been configured to never check for Windows Updates.

Virus Protection Status

Table 12-8 shows the status message for virus protection of your computers.

Table 12-8. *Virus Protection Status Message*

Health Status	Description
Red	*ComputerName* does not have antivirus software. The antivirus software is not installed, is turned off, or is out of date.

■**Caution** If you see a red status warning relating to virus protection, you should immediately investigate and, if necessary, remove that computer from your home network until you have resolved the issue, which may mean updating (or installing) the antivirus software. It is a very bad idea to run a networked computer that does not have adequate virus protection on it. One infected computer on your network jeopardizes your entire network.

Antispyware Protection Status

Table 12-9 shows the status message for antispyware protection of your computers.

Table 12-9. *Antispyware Status Message*

Health Status	Description
Red	*ComputerName* does not have antispyware software. The antispyware software is not installed, is turned off, or is out of date.

■**Note** Windows Vista comes with antispyware software known as Windows Defender preinstalled, so there is no reason to not have it running if you have no other software performing that function. For more information on Windows Defender, take a look at the Windows help files and search using the term Defender.

Backup Status

Table 12-10 shows the status messages for your computer backups.

Table 12-10. *Backup Status Messages*

Health Status	Description
Yellow	*ComputerName* has not been successfully backed up for at least five days.
Yellow	The most recent backup for *ComputerName* was not successful.
Yellow	*ComputerName* has a new hard-drive volume. Do you want to automatically back up this new volume?
Red	*ComputerName* has not been successfully backed up for least 15 days.

■**Note** For more information on backing up your home computers with Windows Home Server, take a look at Chapter 7.

Summary

In this chapter you learned about the different types of Network Health notifications and where you can view them. You should take these notifications seriously and resolve them as soon as you possibly can, or immediately in the case of any critical notification.

CHAPTER 13

Add-Ins

Add-ins are additional features or functionality that can be easily added to Windows Home Server. The additional features or functionality can even make changes to the look and feel of the Windows Home Server Console, which may include adding new tabs for you to control the application. Add-ins effectively extend the capability of your Windows Home Server, and the possibilities for new add-ins are endless.

At the time of writing, Microsoft has not officially released any add-ins, but several third parties have already written and released quite a few add-ins, as discussed later in the chapter in the section "Finding More Information on Add-Ins." First, this chapter explains where in the Windows Home Server Console you can view available and installed add-ins, how to install add-ins, and how to uninstall add-ins.

Viewing Add-Ins

Click the Settings button on the Windows Home Server Console and then click Add-ins to open the screen shown in Figure 13-1.

Figure 13-1. *The Add-ins settings on the Windows Home Server Console*

As you can see, there are two available tabs, Installed and Available. The Installed tab lists all of the add-ins that are currently installed and operational on your Windows Home Server. The Available tab lists any add-ins that are available to install. In this example, no add-ins are currently available or installed, so let's change that and install one, as described next.

Installing an Add-In

In order to use an add-in, you must first install it. For this example, I am installing the Whiist Website Management Add-in for Windows Home Server, written by Andrew Grant. This particular add-in allows you to create and manage web sites on your Windows Home Server. After you install Whiist, it adds a new Website Management option to your Windows Home Server Console, enabling you to easily create new web sites and links for users in your network. For more information on Whiist, including the download link, visit http://www. andrewgrant.org/whiist.

Installing an add-in is fairly straightforward:

■**Note** The specific steps required for each add-in might be slightly different, so make sure you check the documentation that comes with the add-in, just to make sure you don't miss an important step.

---

1. Download a copy of the add-in for Windows Home Server that you want to install and use, and save it wherever you usually save your downloaded items, or insert a CD or DVD with the add-in on any computer on your network that has the Windows Home Server Connector software installed.

2. Right-click the Windows Home Server task tray icon and click Shared Folders, as shown in Figure 13-2, or double-click the Shared Folders on Server icon on the Desktop, shown in Figure 13-3. Either method connects you to the Shared Folders area on your Windows Home Server.

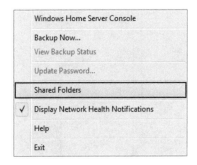

Figure 13-2. *Right-click the Windows Home Server task tray icon and select Shared Folders.*

Figure 13-3. *Double-click the Shared Folders on Server icon on your Desktop.*

3. When the Shared Folders window opens, as shown in Figure 13-4, double-click the Software folder.

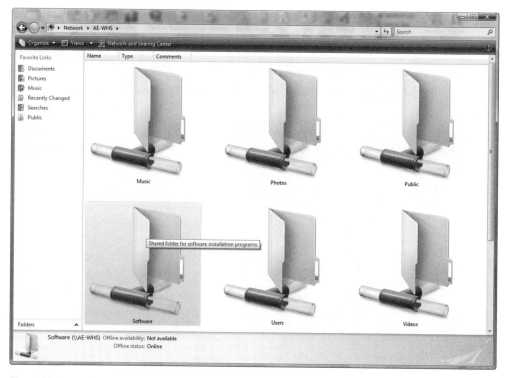

Figure 13-4. *Double-click the Software shared folder on your Windows Home Server.*

4. In the Software folder, double-click the Add-Ins folder, shown in Figure 13-5. The Add-Ins folder contains any add-ins you currently have installed on your Windows Home Server. As shown in Figure 13-6, I don't have any add-ins currently installed on my Windows Home Server, so the only file currently in the folder is ReadMe.txt.

■**Note** If you are curious about what the ReadMe.txt file contains, this is it: *Copy Windows Home Server Add-in files (.msi) to this folder. For more information about Add-ins, open the Windows Home Server Console Help and search for "Add-ins."*

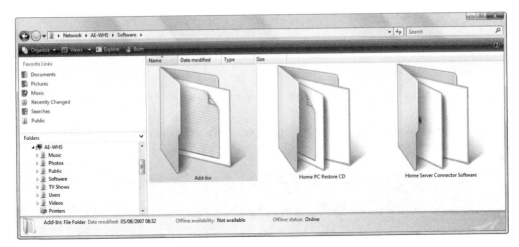

Figure 13-5. *Double-click the Add-Ins folder in the Software shared folder.*

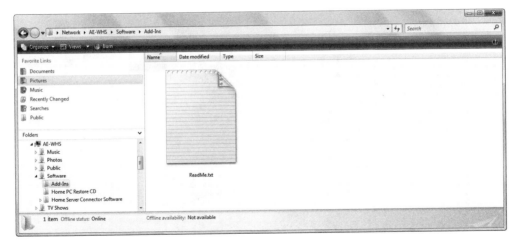

Figure 13-6. *An Add-Ins folder with no add-ins*

5. Copy the add-in (it is likely to be called *something*.msi) to the Add-Ins folder. Before you continue, make sure that you can see the add-in or add-ins in the Add-Ins folder, similar to the example shown in Figure 13-7, in which I have copied Whiist and two other add-ins (PhotoSync for Windows Home Server, by Ed Holloway, and mControl, by Embedded Automation, Inc.).

6. Close the Add-Ins folder when you have confirmed that the add-in appears in the folder.

7. Launch the Windows Home Server Console.

8. Click the Settings button on the Windows Home Server Console to open the Settings screen.

9. Click Add-ins in the left pane.

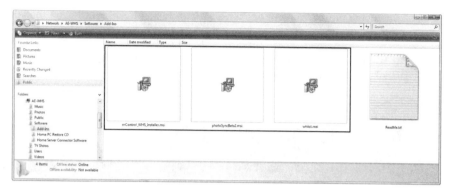

Figure 13-7. *Check that the new add-in appears in the Add-Ins folder.*

10. Click the Available tab. You should now see the new add-in listed, as shown in the example in Figure 13-8.

Figure 13-8. *View the Available tab to make sure that your add-in is listed.*

■Tip Before continuing, check to make sure that the add-in or add-ins listed are the ones you expect to be there. For example, I am installing the Whiist – Website Management Plugin add-in, and that is what is listed, along with a couple of other add-ins, so I am happy to continue the installation process. If the add-in or add-ins that you copied to the Add-Ins folder are not listed on the Available tab, try restarting the Windows Home Server Console, because that refreshes the list on the Available tab.

11. Click the Install button on your chosen add-in to install it. Depending on the add-in you are installing, the installation process may take a moment or two.

12. You are then presented with the Installation Succeeded dialog box, shown in Figure 13-9. Click OK to close the Windows Home Server Console.

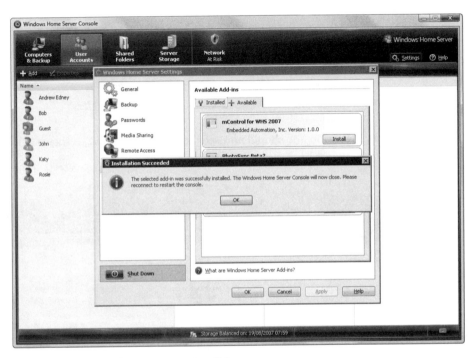

Figure 13-9. *The installation was successful.*

13. After the Windows Home Server Console closes, you see a message advising you that your computer has lost its connection to the Windows Home Server, as shown in Figure 13-10. Don't worry, this is supposed to happen; just click OK to clear the message.

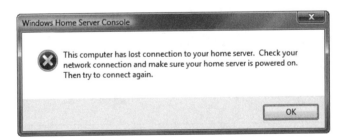

Figure 13-10. *Click OK to dismiss this message.*

14. Reconnect as usual to the Windows Home Server via the Console.

15. Click the Settings button and choose Add-ins; you should see the new add-in appear on the Installed tab, as shown in Figure 13-11.

Figure 13-11. *Confirm that the new add-in is installed.*

Tip If the add-in does not appear on the Installed tab, click the Available tab and see if it is still appears there. If it does, then just repeat the installation process and try again.

16. Click OK to close the Settings window.

Note If the new add-in includes a new Windows Home Server Console tab, it should now be visible and selectable. For example, as shown in Figure 13-11, the Whiist add-in has added a new Website Management icon.

Now that the add-in has been installed, you can start using it. You may need to perform additional configuration steps on the add-in before you can use it, so make sure you read the instructions that came with the add-in.

Uninstalling an Add-In

To uninstall an add-in, following these steps:

1. Launch the Windows Home Server Console.

2. Click the Settings button on the Windows Home Server Console to open the Settings screen.

3. Click Add-ins in the left pane.

4. On the Installed tab, click Uninstall for the add-in you want to remove, as shown in Figure 13-12. Depending on the add-in you are uninstalling, the uninstallation process may take a moment or two.

Figure 13-12. *Click Uninstall for the add-in you want to uninstall.*

5. In the Uninstallation Succeeded dialog box, shown in Figure 13-13, click OK to close the Windows Home Server Console.

6. After the Windows Home Server Console closes, you see a message advising you that your computer has lost its connection to the Windows Home Server. Don't worry, this is supposed to happen; just click OK to clear the message.

7. Reconnect as usual to the Windows Home Server via the Console.

Figure 13-13. *The uninstallation of the add-in has been successful.*

8. If you now click the Settings button and choose Add-ins, you should see that the add-in you chose has disappeared from the Installed tab. If you click the Available tab, it now reappears there, giving you the option to reinstall it at a later date.

9. Click OK to close the Settings window.

You should now see that any additional tabs that may have been included as part of the add-in have also been removed.

■**Note** If you do not intend to reinstall the add-in in the future, you should delete the MSI file from the Add-Ins folder in the Software shared folder on your Windows Home Server. Not only will this keep the list of available add-ins to only those you may want to reinstall, but it will also save disk space on the Windows Home Server itself.

Finding More Information on Add-Ins

As mentioned earlier in this chapter, at the time of writing, Microsoft has not released any add-ins, but several third parties have written and released many add-ins.

As time goes on, there will be more and more add-ins available that extend the functionality of Windows Home Server. Some of them may be invaluable to you, and others may not interest you at all. Everyone has different interests, and different "digital home" requirements.

A really good place to go and see information on the latest add-ins is the add-ins page on the We Got Served blog, as shown in Figure 13-14, which can be viewed at http://www.wegotserved.co.uk/windows-home-server-add-ins/.

Figure 13-14. *The WHS Add-ins list on the We Got Served blog*

This list is growing all the time, so it really is worth checking it out—you never know, you might find something you like.

If you are interested in developing your own add-ins for Windows Home Server, there is a software development kit (SDK) for Windows Home Server that can help you to do so. Take a look at Appendix C for more information on the SDK.

Additionally, software companies may release Windows Home Server–specific versions of software either as add-ins or as a separately installable applications.

■**Note** Read through all the documentation that comes with either the add-in or the application to ensure that you know what it does, how to install and configure it, and how to use and control it.

During the Windows Hardware Engineering Conference (WinHEC) on May 15, 2007, Bill Gates announced that the following eight Microsoft Partners would be releasing software and add-ins for Windows Home Server:

- *Diskeeper Corporation* (http://www.diskeeper.com): Diskeeper will support Windows Home Server in its consumer line of products to improve PC and application performance and efficiency.

- *Embedded Automation, Inc.* (http://www.embeddedautomation.com): mControl software will help consumers manage home lighting systems, security cameras, climate control, and audio-visual components.

- *F-Secure Corporation* (http://www.f-secure.com): Software features from its server and consumer lines will be combined to create a strong solution for protecting Windows Home Server's consumers against computer viruses and other threats from the Internet and mobile networks.

- *Iron Mountain* (http://www.ironmountain.com): Iron Mountain plans to provide Internet-based records management and data protection services for Windows Home Server consumers.

- *Lagotek Corporation* (http://www.lagotek.com): Its Home Intelligence Platform for home automation will be expanded to embrace and support Windows Home Server.

- *PacketVideo Corporation* (http://www.packetvideo.com and http://www.twonkyvision.com): Its DLNA and UPnP software will enable media streaming from Windows Home Server to entertainment devices in the home.

- *Riptopia* (http://www.riptopia.com): Riptopia's CD Loading Service and Angel DJ for Windows Home Server will convert and load a customer's entire CD collection for storage and protection on Windows Home Server.

- *SageTV* (http://www.sagetv.com): Its software enables Windows Home Server to provide a complete, "always on" digital entertainment experience for enjoyment of personal media and online content on any TV or PC screen in the home. SageTV is an AMDLive partner.

■**Note** This list will continue to grow as time goes on, so keep your eyes on the Microsoft Windows Home Server web site for more information.

Summary

In this chapter you learned about add-ins and how to install and remove them from your Windows Home Server. You also found out where you can look to find a list of different add-ins, and what some Microsoft Partners are planning to do in terms of software for Windows Home Server.

■■■

CHAPTER 14

Additional Resources

If you want to find out more about Windows Home Server or have questions that you need answers to, but you don't know where to look, this chapter directs you to some of the additional resources that are available to help you. This is by no means a definitive list, and you should always use your favorite search engine as well to look for anything specific, but these resources are a good starting point.

■**Caution** The Internet by its very nature is changing all the time, so by the time you read this some of the resources may not be available or may have changed location. Also keep in mind that Windows Home Server is new to the market, so there will be considerably more resources available in the future than there are at the time of this writing. You can locate new resources, or resources listed here that might have changed location, by using a search engine.

Microsoft Windows Home Server Web Site

Obviously, if you want to read the latest information on Windows Home Server, your first port of call should be the Windows Home Server page of the Microsoft web site, shown in Figure 14-1.

This web site contains all the latest information on Windows Home Server, its features, availability, and much more. The URL is http://www.microsoft.com/windows/products/winfamily/windowshomeserver/default.mspx.

Figure 14-1. *The Microsoft Windows Home Server web site*

Official Windows Home Server Blog

During the Windows Home Server beta program, the Windows Home Server product team launched the official Windows Home Server blog, shown in Figure 14-2.

This blog contains lots of really useful insights into Windows Home Server, the development process, what changes are happening with the product, and more. It is frequently updated by various members of the product team. This book was even mentioned on it at one point. The URL for the blog is `http://blogs.technet.com/homeserver`.

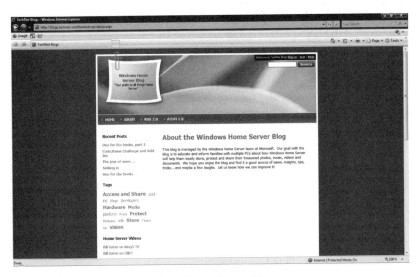

Figure 14-2. *The Official Windows Home Server blog*

Official Windows Home Server Forums

Another really useful place to search for answers and even to pose your own questions is the official Windows Home Server forums, shown in Figure 14-3.

There are a number of different forums here, including a FAQ and Known Issues forum, a forum dedicated to Windows Home Server software, one dedicated to hardware, and even a Suggestions forum, where you can post your suggestions for how to make Windows Home Server even better than it already is.

There are thousands of posts here, so if you are having a particular issue or are looking for an answer to a question, no matter how obscure, you can use the Search facility to see if it has already been covered.

■**Note** You should always try to give something back to the Windows Home Server community. If someone has posed a question that you know the answer to, or if you think you can help, then you should take the time to respond to the post. This also helps the community to grow and, who knows, one day someone might answer a question that you have posted.

The URL for the Windows Home Server Forums is `http://forums.microsoft.com/ windowshomeserver/default.aspx?siteid=50`.

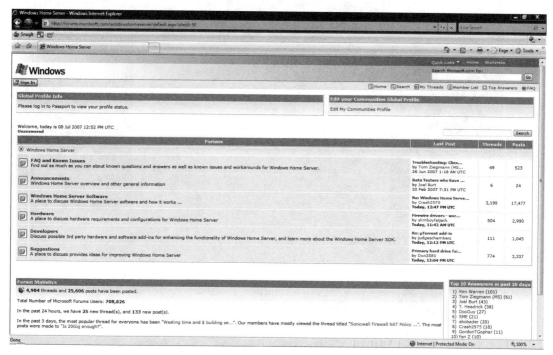

Figure 14-3. *The Official Windows Home Server forums*

We Got Served Blog

The We Got Served blog, shown in Figure 14-4, is one of the biggest and most useful Windows Home Server blogs out there at the time of writing. It is run by Terry Walsh in the UK and has been going since the early days of the Windows Home Server beta. It contains lots of useful information and posts and is a great community site.

The URL for the We Got Served blog is `http://www.wegotserved.co.uk`. You can also subscribe to an RSS feed of this blog.

Note RSS stands for Really Simple Syndication and is content that is frequently updated and published by web sites and can be subscribed to so that you don't have to continually visit that web site to see if there are any changes. You can use Internet Explorer, Outlook 2007, or any RSS reader of your choice to subscribe to an RSS feed.

Figure 14-4. *We Got Served blog*

MS Windows Home Server Blog

Another really useful site is the MS Windows Home Server blog, shown in Figure 14-5. Again, like the We Got Served blog, this site has been going since the early days of Windows Home Server and provides a great resource for anyone who wants to know more about Windows Home Server. It is run by Philip Churchill out of the UK.

The URL for the MS Windows Home Server blog is `http://mswhs.com`. You can also subscribe to an RSS feed of this blog.

Figure 14-5. *MS Windows Home Server blog*

Summary

In this chapter you discovered just a few of the additional resources that are available for Windows Home Server out there on the Internet. These are just the tip of the iceberg—just do a search for Windows Home Server in your favorite search engine to see just what I mean. Some of the resources out there are official, such as the Microsoft web site, blog, and forums, and some, like the We Got Served blog and the MS Windows Home Server blog, are run by dedicated Windows Home Server enthusiasts. Take some time to go visit these sites and see what a fantastic job they are doing.

APPENDIX A

■■■

Networking Primer

The idea behind this appendix is to give you a gentle introduction to some of the more common networking concepts that have been mentioned throughout this book. If you are already comfortable with those concepts, then feel free to skip this appendix. This appendix doesn't provide huge amounts of detail on the various networking elements, but it should provide enough information to help your general understanding of networking.

Toward the end of this appendix, you will also find coverage of some useful command-line tools for troubleshooting network problems. This is a little more advanced than you might be expecting, but I included it anyway because some of these tools were used in Chapter 4 for troubleshooting problems with the Windows Home Server Connector.

Cables

If you have a wired network, you need cabling to connect your devices. For example, you need a cable to connect your computer to your cable modem. Even if you have a wireless network, there is a good chance you have something connected via a network cable.

The cheapest and most common form of home network cabling is known as Category 5 (CAT5) cabling, shown in Figure A-1.

Figure A-1. *CAT5 Ethernet cable*

CAT5 is an Ethernet cable standard defined by the Electronic Industries Alliance and Telecommunications Industry Association. It is the fifth generation of twisted-pair Ethernet cabling. CAT5 contains four pairs of unshielded twisted copper wire, can transmit data at speeds up to 100 Mbps (also known as Fast Ethernet), and has a recommended maximum length of 100m (328 feet). A slightly newer version, called CAT5e (or CAT5 enhanced), supports data transmission at speeds up to 1000 Mbps (also known as Gigabit Ethernet).

CAT5 and CAT5e cables use one wire pair for transmission in each direction. This means that the "transmit" pair is connected to the "receive" pair at the other end. When the cables are connected to a switch or a hub (which are covered later in this appendix), the crossover is done internally to that device.

8P8C is the physical interface used to terminate the cables. In English, it is the plug-like end of each cable. This is often confused with RJ45, and is often actually referred to as RJ45 even though "true" RJ45 is used for telephony. Of course, you do not have to buy ready-made cables. You could always make your own if you felt daring.

Network Interface Cards

Network interface cards (NICs) are required if you want to set up any sort of network, be it wired or wireless. They are used to connect your computer to your network. They come in a variety of different formats and speeds. The aim of this section is to help you understand what NICs are so that you can make an informed decision about what you need for your network.

Each NIC has its own unique address, known as a Media Access Control (MAC) address. The MAC address is used to direct data to the correct destination—think of it as though each NIC has its own ZIP code.

NICs for Wired Networks

Most home networks that are wired use either a 10 Mbps or a 100 Mbps network card in each computer. Obviously, 100 Mbps is considerably faster than 10 Mbps, but you may not actually need anything faster than 10 Mbps if you do not intend to stream media—although, from a cost perspective, you would be wiser to go for the faster cards. Besides, it is very difficult these days to actually find a 10 Mbps card, as most cards are actually 10/100 Mbps switchable. This means that the card will detect the speed of your network and adjust accordingly. 1000 Mbps (Gigabit Ethernet) network cards are becoming more popular and considerably cheaper than they used to be—and are considerably faster. It is a good idea to get the fastest card possible if you plan to stream various media content across your network, because, along with "normal"computer use, this has the potential to slow down your network.

The type of computer you want to network determines what type of card you should buy. If you are using a desktop computer, and the motherboard does not have a built-in network card, then you need to buy a PCI network card. This card slots into one of the spare PCI slots in your computer. You then connect the network cable to the port on the back of the card. Figure A-2 shows a typical PCI network card.

Figure A-2. *A PCI network card*

If you are using a laptop computer that does not have a built-in network adapter, you need to buy a PCMCIA network card. This slots into the PCMCIA slot. You then connect the network cable to that.

NICs for Wireless Networks

If you want to network computers in different rooms of your house, but you do not want to run cables everywhere, then you need to use wireless. Wireless has become so cheap and easy to set up that some computer shops now only carry wireless equipment. As mentioned, wireless is great if you do not want to have cables all around your home. The most important thing to remember when selecting your wireless equipment is that what you buy must be compatible with the rest of your system—for example, the speed!

There are many wireless formats available, such as 802.11a, 802.11b, 802.11g, 54g, 125g, and so on. Some of these formats are better than others, and some are now hard to find. There is a really useful table showing the differences in some of the formats and standards at http://en.wikipedia.org/wiki/IEEE_802.11. Today, the most common are the 802.11g and 54g formats.

As with the wired cards, wireless cards also come in different varieties. If you have a desktop computer, you can buy a PCI wireless card. These cards look like a standard PCI network card but have an aerial instead of an Ethernet plug, as shown in Figure A-3. One version has in the back of the card a PCI cradle for a PCMCIA card that can be removed. This option can be quite useful because you can use the PCMCIA card on your laptop and then swap it to your desktop if required (assuming you do not want both machines connected to the network at the same time).

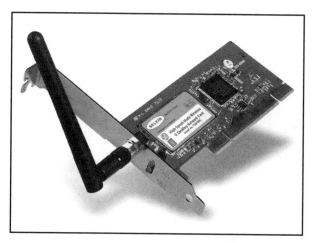

Figure A-3. *A PCI wireless network card*

If you are using a laptop that does not have a built-in wireless adapter, you can buy a wireless PCMCIA card (see the example in Figure A-4). As with the wired card, this can be slotted into the PCMCIA slot.

The other option available for both desktop and laptop users is to buy a USB wireless adapter. These are very cheap and, again, can be used on different devices as long as you do not want to use them at the same time.

■**Note** You cannot connect your Windows Home Server to the network wirelessly; you can only connect it using a wired connection.

Figure A-4. *A PCMCIA wireless network card*

Hubs and Switches

A hub is usually used to connect two or more computers on a network. Hubs come in a variety of sizes, one of the most popular being four ports, as in the example shown in Figure A-5.

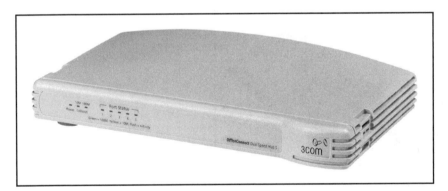

Figure A-5. *A typical small network hub*

Hubs are very cheap, quite small, and very useful for connecting a small number of computers on the same network. They just route network traffic onwards and can be used to extend your network.

Switches, on the other hand, are more expensive, but this is for a good reason. They provide much higher performance than a hub. If you plan to have more than four computers on your network or plan to use applications that generate significant amounts of network traffic, then a switch would be a much better investment. Switches are also used to divide a network into different segments. Figure A-6 shows an example of a switch.

Figure A-6. *A typical small network switch*

Routers

A router is a device that routes data throughout your network—hence the name. Routers act like relay stations; they pass data between points on the journey. Routers are often used to connect your network to another network, such as the Internet via your ISP.

Routers can be both wired and wireless, and even the wireless routers have to have at least one wired connection. An example wireless router is shown in Figure A-7.

Figure A-7. *A typical wireless network router*

Routers often contain additional security settings, such as a firewall and the ability to set up specific routes and settings for your network. Routers are very cheap and easy to configure.

Firewalls

A firewall is probably the single most important security component you will have on your network. If you do not currently have one, get one now. Outside the computing world, a firewall refers to something that keeps a fire from spreading from one area to the next. In computing terms, a firewall does the same thing for your network and computers; it filters information coming from another network, such as the Internet, and stops anything from passing onto your network without permission (as demonstrated in Figure A-8).

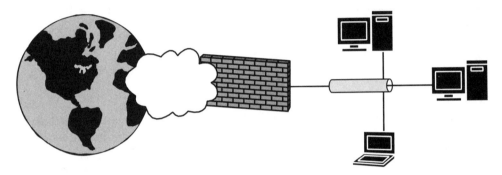

Figure A-8. *A firewall guarding your network*

A firewall can be a piece of software, such as Windows Firewall (which is part of the Windows XP SP2 and Windows Vista operating systems) or a third-party vendor product, or it can be a separate piece of hardware. Hardware firewalls are more common in large companies. For the home, a software firewall should be sufficient.

Firewalls use different methods to control the network traffic passing in or out of your network, including the following:

- *Packet filtering*: This method examines each packet of data that goes through the firewall and checks it against a set of rules (also called filters). If there is a rule to allow it, the data passes through. Otherwise, it is stopped.

- *Proxy*: The firewall acts as the "middle man." For example, your computer asks the firewall to retrieve information from a web site on the Internet, and then that information is passed back to your computer. This means that your computer never actually requests information from the Internet directly; the proxy server requests the information, so your computer is never "on the Internet."

- *Stateful inspection*: This method compares certain parts of the packet against a database of trusted information.

The following sections describe firewall filters and rules, identify the threats that firewalls protect your network against, and give an overview of Windows Firewall, which comes preinstalled on Windows computers (depending on your operating system).

Firewall Filters/Rules

Firewall filters, commonly referred to as rules, are a very important component of any firewall. These are added and removed in order to apply certain conditions, depending on your specific requirements.

Firewall rules should be set up to allow only what is needed to pass through. The last rule should always be to deny everything, so that if a rule has not been specifically added, then anything that reaches the firewall is stopped. The rules may include the following:

- IP address

- Domain name

- Protocol

- Port number

The protocol rule is very useful. For example, if you want to allow web traffic through, you just add a rule for the HTTP protocol. These protocols are predefined to make things easier for you. Table A-1 lists a number of the more common protocols, along with explanations of what they are used for.

Table A-1. *Network Protocols and Their Purposes*

Protocol	Purpose
HTTP	Used for web pages
FTP	Used for file transfers
UDP	Used for audio and video, among others
SMTP	Used for e-mail

Threats Protected Against

Probably the biggest threat to your network is from either a hacker or a malicious program. Using a firewall is not a 100-percent effective deterrent, but it is certainly better than nothing and should stop the average "attack." An unprotected computer can be hijacked within minutes of first connecting to the Internet.

Malicious programs come in many forms, including viruses, worms, and Trojan horses. Once a computer has been infected, it can be used without your knowledge. For example, if you use online banking, all of your details could be recorded and passed on to someone else!

Windows Firewall

Windows Firewall is a fairly simple to use firewall that pretty much does what you need without your intervention. When you select Windows Firewall from Security Center (if you are using a Windows XP or Windows Vista computer), you see a page telling you the status of the firewall. On a Windows Home Server, you only need to select Windows Firewall from the Control Panel. If you click the Change Settings button, you can also see the status of the firewall, as well as enable or disable it or make changes to it, as shown in Figure A-9.

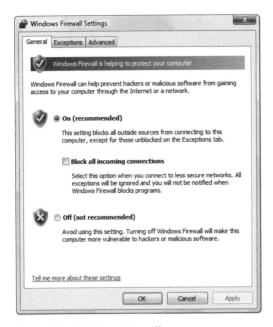

Figure A-9. *Windows Firewall*

If you click the Exceptions tab, any exceptions that have been added, either manually or by Windows Firewall on your behalf, are displayed, as shown in Figure A-10.

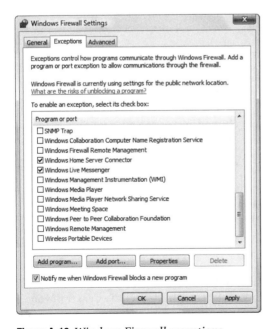

Figure A-10. *Windows Firewall exceptions*

On this tab, you can add a program or a port, edit an existing exception, or even delete an entry.

■**Note** A port is a virtual way in or out of a computer through a firewall. Think of it as a doorway for a specific thing only. For example, if you wanted to allow web traffic through the firewall, you would open port 80, which is the port for HTTP.

If you click Add Port, you are presented with the Add a Port dialog box, shown in Figure A-11. Just enter a name and the relevant port number, specify whether it is TCP or UDP, and click OK.

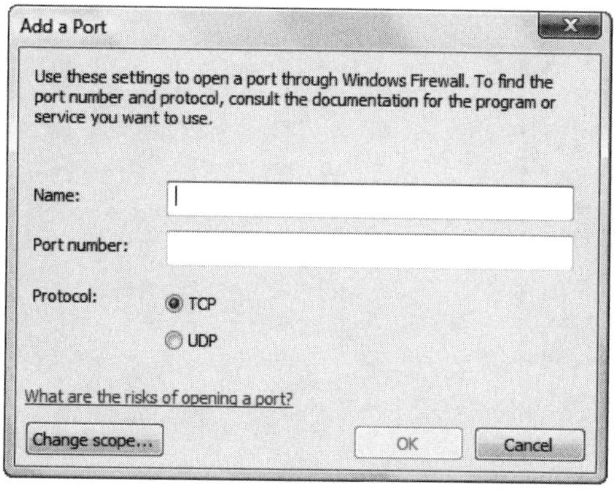

Figure A-11. *Adding a port to the exceptions*

You may have noticed that there is a button called Change Scope on a number of Windows Firewall screens. When you click this button, the Change Scope dialog box is displayed, as shown in Figure A-12. This option enables you to specify the set of computers for which the port or program is unblocked. You can choose Any Computer, My Network, or Custom List (and provide a list of IP addresses).

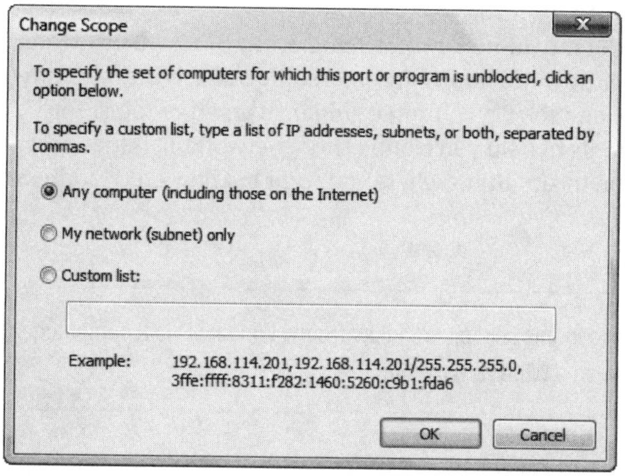

Figure A-12. *Changing the scope of port unblocking*

The last tab, Advanced (see Figure A-13), contains the network connection settings, a link to ICMP and security logging settings, and a button that enables you to restore Windows Firewall to its default setting.

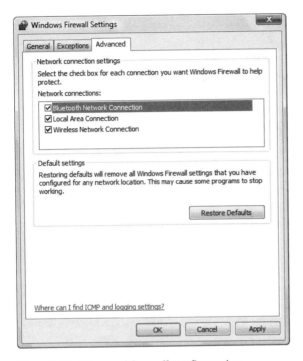

Figure A-13. *Advanced firewall configuration*

The check boxes under Network Connections enable you to select which network connection Windows Firewall is used for. A check in the box means it is being used.

Windows Command-Line Tools

The remainder of this appendix is considerably more advanced than what you have just read. It is included here to provide you with a little more information on some of the Windows command-line tools mentioned in Chapter 4 and to give you some guidance on other tools. You can use these Windows command-line tools to help you troubleshoot networking issues. You can also use them to give you information in situations where you want to know an IP address of a certain piece of equipment.

Note The commands and screenshots shown in this section are taken from a Windows Vista computer; the basic commands are pretty much the same on a Windows XP computer.

Ipconfig

The ipconfig tool displays the TCP/IP network configuration information of your computer and can be used to refresh DHCP and DNS settings. If you use the tool without specifying any parameters, it displays the IP address, subnet mask, and default gateway for any installed network adapters.

■**Note** *DHCP* stands for Dynamic Host Configuration Protocol, which is a communications protocol that automatically assigns IP addresses to devices that support it. *DNS* stands for Domain Name System, which is used to map an IP address to a computer name. An *IP address* is like a phone number and is used to find a particular computer. A *subnet mask* is used to break up a larger network into a smaller network. Finally, a *default gateway* is used as the access point to another network—for example, your home network accessing the Internet.

Syntax

The following is the syntax that can be used with ipconfig to perform different functions:

```
ipconfig [/all] [/renew [adapter]] [/release [adapter]]
[/renew6 [adapter]] [/release6 [adapter]] [/flushdns] [/displaydns]
[/registerdns] [/showclassid adapter] [/setclassid adapter [ClassID]]
```

Parameters

The following are the parameters that can be used with ipconfig to perform different functions:

/all: Displays the full TCP/IP configuration for all adapters. Adapters can be physical interfaces, such as network cards, or logical interfaces, such as dial-up connections.

/renew [adapter]: Renews the DHCP configuration for all adapters. You can specify an adapter by using the adapter parameter and using the adapter name. You can use this parameter only if the adapter is set up to use DHCP. This is specific to IPv4.

/release [adapter]: Used to discard the current DHCP configuration for all adapters or for a specific adapter if using the adapter parameter. This is specific to IPv4.

/renew6 [adapter]: Renews the DHCP configuration for all adapters. You can specify an adapter by using the adapter parameter and using the adapter name. You can use this parameter only if the adapter is set up to use DHCP. This is specific to IPv6.

/release6 [adapter]: Used to discard the current DHCP configuration for all adapters or for a specific adapter if using the adapter parameter. This is specific to IPv6.

/flushdns: Used to flush and then reset the DNS client resolver cache. This can also be used to remove entries that have been added to DNS dynamically.

/displaydns: Used to display the contents of the DNS client resolver cache.

/registerdns: Used to initiate a manual dynamic registration for the DNS names and IP addresses that are configured at a computer. The DNS settings in the advanced properties of the TCP/IP protocol determine which names are registered in DNS.

/showclassid *adapter*: Displays the DHCP class ID for a specific adapter. To display the IDs for all adapters, use the asterisk (*) wildcard in place of *adapter*.

/setclassid *adapter* [*ClassID*]: Used to configure the DHCP class ID for a specific adapter. To set the IDs for all adapters, use the asterisk (*) wildcard in place of *adapter*.

/?: Displays help (as shown in Figure A-14).

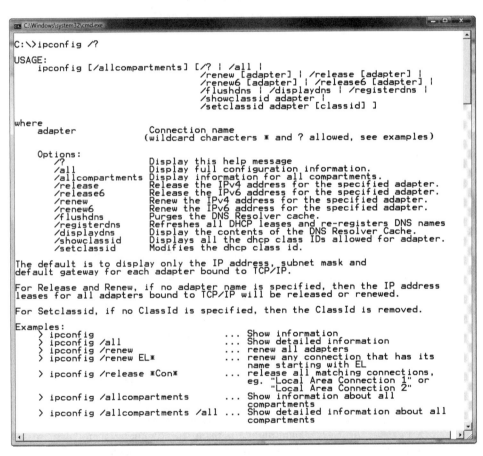

Figure A-14. *The output from ipconfig, at first glance, looks daunting until you look at the detail.*

Ipconfig is the tool within Windows XP and Windows Vista that replaced winipcfg from Windows 95, Millennium, and 98. It would be useful to keep a copy of your ipconfig information, in case you need it at a later stage. You can do this from a DOS prompt by typing **ipconfig /all >ipconfig.txt**. Figure A-15 shows the results.

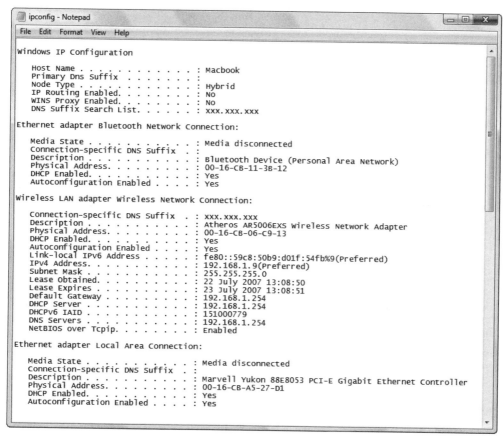

Figure A-15. *An example ipconfig text file*

Ping

Ping is a tool that is used to verify IP connectivity to another computer by sending ICMP Echo Request messages. You can use ping to test both the IP address and computer name you are trying to contact. If you can ping the IP address but not the computer name, then there might be a name resolution issue. This is the best tool to use to troubleshoot connectivity and should probably be your first step. You can see the list of parameters for ping by typing **ping** at a command prompt, as shown in Figure A-16.

```
C:\Windows\system32\cmd.exe

C:\>ping

Usage: ping [-t] [-a] [-n count] [-l size] [-f] [-i TTL] [-v TOS]
            [-r count] [-s count] [[-j host-list] | [-k host-list]]
            [-w timeout] [-R] [-S srcaddr] [-4] [-6] target_name

Options:
    -t              Ping the specified host until stopped.
                    To see statistics and continue - type Control-Break;
                    To stop - type Control-C.
    -a              Resolve addresses to hostnames.
    -n count        Number of echo requests to send.
    -l size         Send buffer size.
    -f              Set Don't Fragment flag in packet (IPv4-only).
    -i TTL          Time To Live.
    -v TOS          Type Of Service (IPv4-only).
    -r count        Record route for count hops (IPv4-only).
    -s count        Timestamp for count hops (IPv4-only).
    -j host-list    Loose source route along host-list (IPv4-only).
    -k host-list    Strict source route along host-list (IPv4-only).
    -w timeout      Timeout in milliseconds to wait for each reply.
    -R              Use routing header to test reverse route also (IPv6-only).
    -S srcaddr      Source address to use (IPv6-only).
    -4              Force using IPv4.
    -6              Force using IPv6.

C:\>
```

Figure A-16. *Typing ping without qualifiers or switches displays the syntax.*

Syntax

The following is the syntax that can be used with ping to perform different functions:

```
ping [-t] [-a] [-n count] [-l size] [-f] [-i TTL] [-v TOS]
[-r count] [-s count] [-j host-list] [-k host-list]
[-w timeout] [-R] [-S srcaddr] [-4] [-6] target_name
```

Parameters

The following are the parameters that can be used with ping to perform different functions:

-t: Specifies that ping continues sending messages to the destination address until it is stopped. To stop and display statistics press Ctrl+Break; to stop and quit press Ctrl+C.

-a: Used to display the reverse name resolution on the destination IP address to show the hostname.

-n count: Used to specify the number of Echo Request messages sent. The default number is 4.

-l size: Used to specify the Data field length in bytes in the Echo Request messages. The default size is 32 and the maximum size is 65,527.

-f: Used to specify that the Echo Request messages are sent with the Don't Fragment flag in the IP header set to a value of 1.

-i *TTL*: Used to specify the value in the TTL field in the IP header. The default is the default TTL value for the host. For Windows XP hosts, the value is typically 128 and the maximum is 255.

-v *TOS*: Used to specify the value for the Type of Service (TOS) field in the IP header. The default is 0 and the maximum is 255.

-r *count*: Used to specify that the Record Route option in the IP header is used to record the path taken by the Echo Request message and Echo Reply message. Each hop in the path adds an entry. The *count* must be a minimum of 1 and a maximum of 9.

-s *count*: Used to specify that the Internet Timestamp option in the IP header is used to record the time of arrival for the Echo Request message and Echo Reply message for each hop. The *count* must be a minimum of 1 and a maximum of 4.

-j *host-list*: Used to specify that the Echo Request messages use the Loose Source Route option in the IP header with the set of intermediate destinations specified in *host-list*. With loose source routing, successive intermediate destinations can be separated by one or more routers. The maximum number of entries in the *host-list* is 9.

-k *host-list*: Used to specify that the Echo Request messages use the Strict Source Route option in the IP header with the set of intermediate destinations specified in *host-list*. With strict source routing, the next intermediate destination must be directly reachable. The maximum number of entries in the *host-list* is 9.

-w *timeout*: Used to specify the amount of time, in milliseconds, to wait for a reply to be received.

-R: An IPv6 parameter used to specify a routing header to test reverse route.

-S *srcaddr*: An IPv6 parameter used to specify the source address to use.

-4: Forces the ping to use IPv4.

-6: Forces the ping to use IPv6.

target_name: Used to specify the amount of time, in milliseconds, to wait for either a response or the timeout. The default timeout is 4000 milliseconds (or 4 seconds).

/?: Displays help (help is also shown by just typing ping, as shown in Figure A-16).

Figure A-17 shows an example of pinging a specific IP address. As you can see, the computer in question was switched on and available, so it responded to the ping.

Figure A-18 shows an example of pinging a specific computer name. The computer in question was switched on and available, so it responded to the ping. In fact, notice that it is in fact the same machine as the other ping.

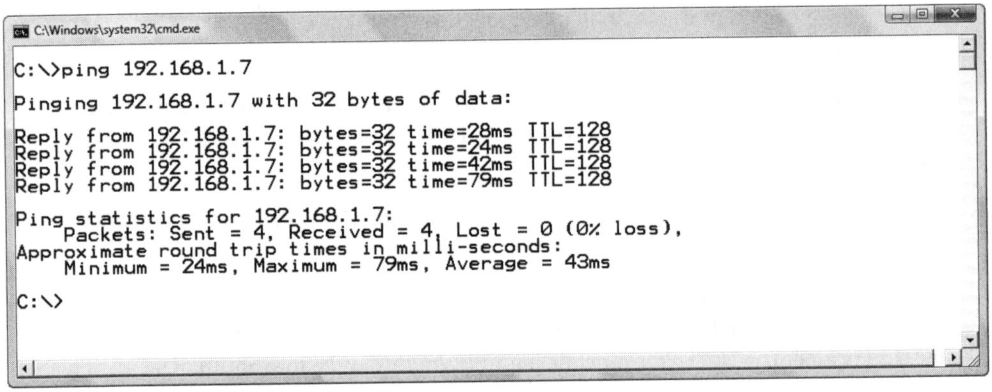

```
C:\Windows\system32\cmd.exe

C:\>ping 192.168.1.7

Pinging 192.168.1.7 with 32 bytes of data:

Reply from 192.168.1.7: bytes=32 time=28ms TTL=128
Reply from 192.168.1.7: bytes=32 time=24ms TTL=128
Reply from 192.168.1.7: bytes=32 time=42ms TTL=128
Reply from 192.168.1.7: bytes=32 time=79ms TTL=128

Ping statistics for 192.168.1.7:
    Packets: Sent = 4, Received = 4, Lost = 0 (0% loss),
Approximate round trip times in milli-seconds:
    Minimum = 24ms, Maximum = 79ms, Average = 43ms

C:\>
```

Figure A-17. *An example of pinging an IP address*

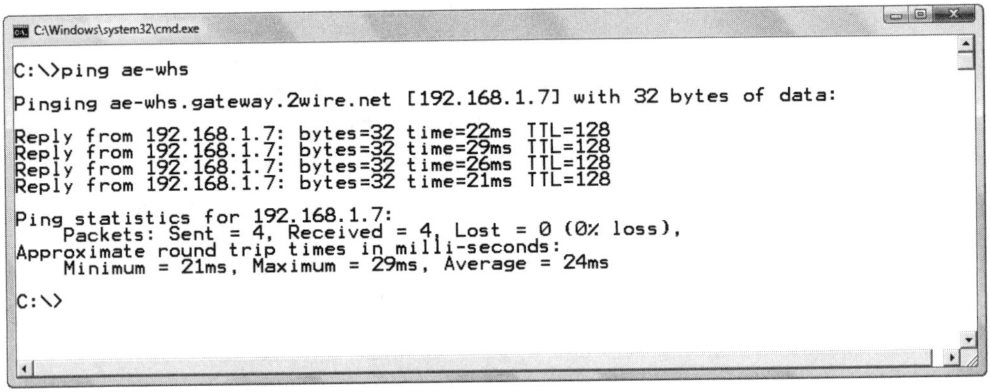

```
C:\Windows\system32\cmd.exe

C:\>ping ae-whs

Pinging ae-whs.gateway.2wire.net [192.168.1.7] with 32 bytes of data:

Reply from 192.168.1.7: bytes=32 time=22ms TTL=128
Reply from 192.168.1.7: bytes=32 time=29ms TTL=128
Reply from 192.168.1.7: bytes=32 time=26ms TTL=128
Reply from 192.168.1.7: bytes=32 time=21ms TTL=128

Ping statistics for 192.168.1.7:
    Packets: Sent = 4, Received = 4, Lost = 0 (0% loss),
Approximate round trip times in milli-seconds:
    Minimum = 21ms, Maximum = 29ms, Average = 24ms

C:\>
```

Figure A-18. *An example of pinging a computer name*

Always try to ping the device that is furthest away, and then work backward. For example, if you want to ping a computer that you know is connected to a router, try pinging the computer first. If that doesn't work, try pinging the router next, because the problem may be with the router. This seems a little backward, but often it is the quickest way. However, make sure you try to ping your own computer and your router as well.

Tracert

The tracert tool displays the path taken between computers—for example, between your computer and another one. It works by sending ICMP Echo Request messages to the destination with increasing Time to Live (TTL) values. The path that is displayed when using the tool is the list of near-side router interfaces in the path between the source and destination. The near-side router interface is the closest one to the sending host used in the path.

You can see the list of parameters for tracert by typing **tracert** at a command prompt, as shown in Figure A-19. Tracert is considered an advanced tool and the results that it provides might be confusing to you if you are not sure how it works and what it is showing you.

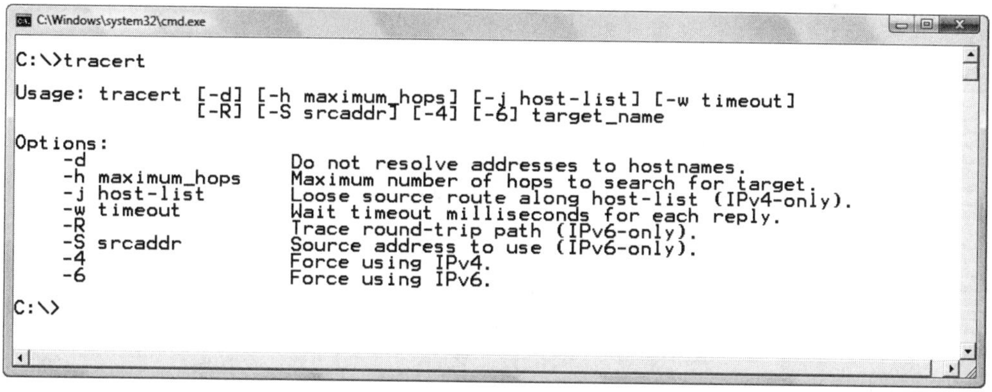

Figure A-19. *Typing tracert without qualifiers or switches displays the syntax.*

Syntax

The following is the syntax that can be used with tracert to perform different functions:

tracert [-d] [-h *maximum_hops*] [-j *host-list*]
[-w *timeout*] [-R] [-S *srcaddr*] [-4] [-6] *target_name*

Parameters

The following are the parameters that can be used with tracert to perform the functions described:

-d: Prevents the resolution of IP addresses of intermediate routers to their names. This can increase the speed in which results are displayed.

-h *maximum_hops*: Specifies the maximum number of hops to search for the destination. The default number is 30 hops.

-j *host-list*: Specifies that the messages use the Loose Source Route option in the IP header with the set of intermediate destinations specified in *host-list*. A host list is a series of IP addresses separated by spaces. The maximum number in the list is 9.

-w *timeout*: Specifies the amount of time, in milliseconds, to wait for either a response or the timeout. An asterisk (*) is displayed if the response is not received. The default time-out is 4000 milliseconds (or 4 seconds).

-R: An IPv6 parameter used to trace a round-trip path.

-S *srcaddr*: An IPv6 parameter used to specify the source address to use.

-4: Forces the ping to use IPv4.

-6: Forces the ping to use IPv6.

target_name: Specifies the destination either by an IP address or by a hostname.

-?: Displays help (help is also displayed by just typing tracert, as shown in Figure A-19).

Figure A-20 shows a standard tracert to Microsoft.com.

```
C:\Windows\system32\cmd.exe

C:\>tracert microsoft.com

Tracing route to microsoft.com [207.46.197.32]
over a maximum of 30 hops:
  1     1 ms     1 ms     1 ms  home [192.168.1.254]
  2    13 ms    17 ms    13 ms  esr18.kingston6.broadband.bt.net [217.47.159.141]
  3    15 ms    15 ms    15 ms  217.47.159.30
  4    15 ms    15 ms    18 ms  217.41.217.13
  5    18 ms    15 ms    15 ms  217.41.171.65
  6    52 ms    15 ms    15 ms  217.41.171.74
  7    55 ms    16 ms    24 ms  217.41.171.58
  8    14 ms    14 ms    15 ms  217.47.46.59
  9    15 ms    15 ms    15 ms  core1-pos12-1.kingston.ukcore.bt.net [62.6.40.90]
 10    14 ms    17 ms    17 ms  core1-pos0-15-0-8.ealing.ukcore.bt.net [62.6.201.73]
 11    33 ms    25 ms    34 ms  62.6.200.106
 12    14 ms    15 ms    14 ms  t2c1-ge13-0-0.uk-eal.eu.bt.net [166.49.168.21]
 13   116 ms   111 ms   145 ms  t2c1-p5-0-0.us-ash.eu.bt.net [166.49.164.65]
 14   169 ms   234 ms   208 ms  8057.microsoft.com [206.223.115.17]
 15   132 ms   109 ms   130 ms  ge-0-3-0-57.ash-64cb-1b.ntwk.msn.net [207.46.41.57]
 16   102 ms   103 ms   103 ms  ge-0-0-0-0.ash-64cb-1a.ntwk.msn.net [207.46.41.33]
 17   259 ms   190 ms   183 ms  so-7-2-3-0.wst-64cb-1b.ntwk.msn.net [207.46.35.97]
 18   185 ms   243 ms   178 ms  ten9-3.cpk-76c-1a.ntwk.msn.net [207.46.35.37]
 19     *        *        *     Request timed out.
 20   174 ms   174 ms   174 ms  207.46.197.32

Trace complete.

C:\>
```

Figure A-20. *The tracert command offers feedback on every stage of an IP connection.*

Figure A-21 shows a `tracert -d` to Microsoft.com. Notice that this time only the IP addresses are displayed.

```
C:\Windows\system32\cmd.exe

C:\>tracert -d microsoft.com

Tracing route to microsoft.com [207.46.197.32]
over a maximum of 30 hops:
  1     1 ms     2 ms     1 ms  192.168.1.254
  2    16 ms    18 ms    15 ms  217.47.159.141
  3    14 ms    13 ms    15 ms  217.47.159.30
  4    97 ms    18 ms    14 ms  217.41.217.13
  5    97 ms    15 ms    14 ms  217.41.171.65
  6    14 ms    15 ms    14 ms  217.41.171.74
  7    17 ms    15 ms    15 ms  217.41.171.58
  8    66 ms    68 ms    44 ms  217.47.46.59
  9    15 ms    15 ms    14 ms  62.6.40.90
 10    30 ms    14 ms    17 ms  62.6.201.73
 11    97 ms    15 ms    15 ms  62.6.200.106
 12   113 ms    14 ms    15 ms  166.49.168.21
 13   200 ms   103 ms   101 ms  166.49.164.65
 14   102 ms   103 ms   108 ms  206.223.115.17
 15   103 ms   104 ms   107 ms  207.46.41.57
 16   103 ms   101 ms   109 ms  207.46.41.33
 17   176 ms   172 ms   174 ms  207.46.35.97
 18   173 ms   174 ms   174 ms  207.46.35.37
 19     *        *        *     Request timed out.
 20   199 ms   182 ms   176 ms  207.46.197.32

Trace complete.

C:\>
```

Figure A-21. *Output from the tracert -d switch*

Summary

This appendix has given you a little more insight into the world of networking and some of the tools that you can use to troubleshoot your network. It has barely scratched the surface, though, so if you want to learn more about any of the concepts mentioned here, or about any other networking concepts, there are some really great networking books available, and also some really great web sites with very detailed information that can be of use.

APPENDIX B

■■■

Build Your Own Windows Home Server

The more adventurous among you might decide to actually build your own Windows Home Server rather than buy one. If you feel up to this challenge (actually, it is not that much of a challenge), this brief appendix lists the components that you need to build your own Windows Home Server. This appendix does not show you how to connect all the components together. The procedure should be pretty straightforward, and you should get instructions with each of the components. If you want more integrated instructions, do a search on the Internet. There are lots of really good guides on how to put everything together—just make sure you are looking at the same type of hardware! One such guide can be found on the We Got Served blog at `http://www.wegotserved.co.uk/2007/02/11/how-to-build-your-new-home-server/`.

■**Note** As Chapter 1 pointed out, buying a ready-made Windows Home Server does have several advantages. For example, the hardware is prebuilt to work with the Windows Home Server software, the software is included, and you get support from the computer manufacturer.

Although every computer system is composed of numerous different components, you don't necessarily have to buy each component separately to build your Windows Home Server, which might save you a bit of money. For example, if you buy a motherboard with integrated graphics and sound, then you don't need to buy a separate graphics card and sound card. Normally, if you were building yourself a decent home computer, depending on what you planned to do with it, you probably would consider buying a high-spec graphics card so that you could play the latest games or watch the latest movies (some of the higher-spec cards support playing of Blu-ray discs). Likewise, you probably would consider buying a decent sound card, again depending on what you wanted to do with it and what existing equipment you wanted to connect it to, such as an amplifier and speakers.

For a Windows Home Server, as you have read throughout this book, you don't necessarily need the best and latest hardware. Why, for example, would you want to spend a few hundred dollars on the latest graphics card when you will hardly ever have your Windows Home Server connected to a monitor? Certainly in that scenario, integrated graphics on the motherboard would be more than sufficient.

■**Note** The type and quality of equipment you need depends quite heavily on what you intend to do with your Windows Home Server. This appendix assumes that you want to use it only as a Windows Home Server and that you will probably make it "headless" to keep it hidden out of the way.

Windows Home Server Software

Unfortunately, you won't be able to just go into any computer store and buy the Windows Home Server software. It is going to be available for purchase only through either the OEM (original equipment manufacturer) channel or the system builder channel. That doesn't mean you won't be able to buy it. Far from it—many places sell OEM software these days; just do a search on the Internet and I am sure you will find Windows Home Server available somewhere.

■**Note** If you would like to sample the delights of Windows Home Server before you decide whether to purchase it, you can order the 120-day evaluation edition from the Microsoft Windows Home Server web site at http://www.microsoft.com/windowshomeserver.

Motherboard

The motherboard is the part of the system to which you essentially attach everything, including the memory, processor, hard drives, and so on. The type of motherboard that you should buy depends a lot on what type of components you want to use and the size of the machine you want to build. By size, I mean the actual physical dimensions of the box. If you want to make it as small as possible so that you can easily tuck it out of the way somewhere, then you might want to look at smaller motherboards. Usually these have limited expansion possibilities, but this probably won't be of major concern for this project.

■**Tip** To read about the different motherboard form factors, take a look at http://en.wikipedia.org/wiki/Comparison_of_computer_form_factors.

Also, you need to ensure that the motherboard you buy is compatible with the processor you intend to buy (see the next section for more information). For example, if you plan to use an Intel-based processor, then you must buy a motherboard that supports Intel-based processors, specifically the processor type you are buying. If you are in any doubt, take a look at the manufacturer's web site; this sort of information is usually very easy to find.

Processor

As pointed out in Chapter 1, the *Windows Home Server Getting Started* guide mentions that future versions of the product may be supported only on 64-bit processors. With this in mind, you should seriously consider buying a 64-bit processor to at least future-proof your new machine for a while.

The minimum supported processor is a 1 GHz Pentium 3 (or equivalent), but frankly these are so old now that if you are buying new components, you should look for something a lot better. If you are using old components, then you could get away with something this "slow," but the faster the processor, the better the overall experience will be.

■**Note** Whichever processor you decide to buy, make sure that it will work with the motherboard that you choose. Sometimes it is easier to pick the processor first and then choose a motherboard. Also, make sure that you have a sufficiently effective fan or cooling unit for the processor—this should come with the processor when you buy it. This is particularly important if you are placing the Windows Home Server out of the way, such as in a closet.

Memory

In its simplest form, a Windows Home Server is just a file server. Therefore, its memory requirements are not very high. Both the minimum and recommended memory requirement is 512 MB. Personally, I would never build a box with less than 1 GB of RAM these days, even if it is not going to be used for memory-intensive functions. The price of RAM is currently quite reasonable, so consider what your future needs might be.

Make sure that you buy RAM that is suitable for your motherboard. You may also need to install the memory in pairs; for example, to have 1 GB of RAM, you may need to use two 512 MB pieces. Check the motherboard manual for more information on adding memory, just to be safe.

■**Tip** If you are unsure of the type or amount of memory that is supported on the motherboard, search the Internet. Numerous good sites are out there that can advise you. One that I often use is `http://www.crucial.com`.

Graphics Card

As mentioned earlier in this appendix, unless you plan to do more with your Windows Home Server than just use it as a Windows Home Server, you really don't need to buy the latest and greatest graphics card. It's not as if you are planning on playing Quake 3 on it—are you?

If you have purchased a motherboard with onboard graphics capabilities, you don't need to buy anything else. If the motherboard doesn't have onboard graphics, then all you really need is a very basic graphics card for those times when you need to connect a monitor to the Windows Home Server, but make sure that the connections on the graphics card are compatible with the connections on the monitor that you plan to use; otherwise, you may need to buy an adaptor.

■Note If you are going to buy a graphics card, make sure that Windows 2003–compatible drivers are available for it; otherwise, it may not work.

Sound Card

As with the graphics card, you really don't need to worry too much about a sound card unless you want to listen to something on your Windows Home Server—and if you do, why not just stream it to one of your home computers? Most modern motherboards come with onboard sound, so you probably don't need to buy a sound card. If your motherboard doesn't include onboard sound, you can buy a basic sound card, but if you want to listen to files stored on your Windows Home Server, why not just stream them to one of your home computers?

■Note If you decide to buy a sound card, make sure that Windows 2003–compatible drivers are available for it; otherwise, it may not work.

DVD Drive

If you plan to install any software directly onto the Windows Home Server, then you need some sort of media drive. Most modern software these days is distributed on a DVD, so avoid buying just a CD-ROM drive. DVD drives are not much more expensive than CD-ROM drives, and you really don't want to reduce the capability of your new computer before you have even finished building it.

Unless you plan to play Blu-ray discs on the Windows Home Server, you should buy a standard DVD drive. Given the costs, I highly recommend buying a dual-layer DVD writer; they are really cheap and enable you to both read DVDs and write DVDs if necessary (always good for doing backups if needed). And a dual-layer DVD writer enables you to write up to 8.5 GB per blank DVD, which is quite a lot of data. Don't forget to buy some blank discs as well.

Case

When you have all of your components gathered together, you need to put them together in a case. The size and type of case you should use depends on what components you have purchased and possibly where you want to put the Windows Home Server.

■Tip Some cases come with a power supply as part of the package. If you are going to buy such a case, make sure that the power supply is sufficient to run all the components you intend to use. This shouldn't be an issue if you intend to use your Windows Home Server only as a Windows Home Server. If the case doesn't come with a power supply, make sure you select a power supply that will fit the case you have chosen.

Network Interface Card

Obviously, a network interface card (NIC) is a fundamental element of any Windows Home Server. Without one, you won't be able to connect to your home network, which is the whole point of building a Windows Home Server.

The minimum requirement is a 100 Mbps Ethernet NIC, but if your network supports a higher speed, you should buy a compatible NIC, such as a Gigabit Ethernet card, that can provide faster access speeds and quicker transfer of your files. Again, most modern motherboards have a built-in Ethernet network card, so check this before you spend money on a card you may not need. And don't forget to buy some extra Ethernet cables if you need them. There is nothing worse than going to connect a piece of hardware only to find that you don't have a spare cable or one that is long enough to reach wherever you plan to keep your Windows Home Server.

■Note Windows Home Server does not support wireless, so don't bother looking at a wireless connection.

Hard Drives

As you have read, the components for building your own Windows Home Server largely consist of components that will "just do," because you don't really need to spend much money or buy the latest and greatest.

When it comes to hard drives, however, it's a completely different story. If you think that some of the primary functions of a Windows Home Server are to store and share your digital content, and also to back up your home computers, the more storage space you have, and the faster the hard drives are, then the better the experience is for you and your family.

The recommendation from Microsoft for hard drives is at least two internal hard drives, with 300 GB as the primary (system) partition. Depending on the amount of digital content you want to store and share, this may be perfectly sufficient. But hard drive prices are quite low these days, so you might want to consider putting in a couple of 500 GB hard drives, and in terms of speed and reliability, you should look at SATA II hard drives. Obviously, any supported hard drive type will do, but if you are buying new drives, why not go for the latest and greatest? After all, this is why you spent as little as you could on other components. And don't forget that you can also add USB or FireWire external hard drives as well.

■**Note** Having more than one hard drive in your Windows Home Server means that you can duplicate shared folders across the drives so that if one drive fails, you won't lose any of your important digital data. Make sure, though, that whatever hard drive types you decide on, they are supported by the motherboard. It's no good to buy SATA II hard drives only to find that your motherboard supports IDE drives only.

Summary

This brief appendix has given you an idea of what components you need to build your own Windows Home Server. It really is not as difficult as you might think. However, if the thought of picking out all the components is intimidating, or you just want an easier alternative (and a warranty, not to mention having a Windows Home Server that conforms to certain requirements, such as power efficiency, noise levels, and more), then buying a ready-made Windows Home Server is probably the route for you.

■ ■ ■

Basics of the SDK

The Windows Home Server software development kit (SDK) is used by developers and enthusiasts to create applications and add-ins for Windows Home Server. This appendix takes a brief look at the SDK, including where you can obtain it and what it contains. This appendix does not teach you how to program or how to develop your own applications and add-ins for Windows Home Server, but it does point you in the right direction of where to look for information.

■**Note** As covered in Chapter 13, an add-in is something that extends the functionality and capability of your Windows Home Server. The possibilities for these add-ins are endless.

The SDK is located in the MSDN Library at `http://msdn2.microsoft.com/en-us/library/aa496121.aspx`. Figure C-1 shows the SDK for Windows Home Server welcome page, which provides a brief explanation of what the SDK includes. As this page states, you can use the SDK to learn how to use the Windows Home Server application programming interface (API) to build applications and add-ins. The SDK itself contains the API files for Windows Home Server:

- *Microsoft.HomeServer.SDK.Interop.v1.dll*: Used to extend the Windows Home Server platform

- *HomeServerExt.dll*: Used to extend the Windows Home Server Console

The SDK also contains some detailed documentation on the API files and some programming examples and tutorials. Specifically, the SDK contains the *SDK Developer's Guide* and the *Windows Home Server API Reference*.

■**Note** To understand and get the most out of the documentation and examples, you must understand programming.

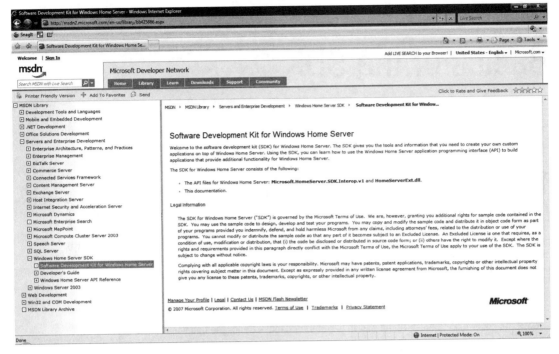

Figure C-1. *MSDN Library for Windows Home Server SDK*

SDK Developer's Guide

The *Developer's Guide* included in the SDK contains three very useful sections to help you start using the SDK:

- *Getting Started*: Explains what you need to begin developing applications and add-ins for Windows Home Server

- *API Overview*: Explains how the API for Windows Home Server works

- *Programming Tutorial*: Provides an example that shows most of the Windows Home Server functionality

You can access these sections by clicking the + sign next to Developer's Guide in the left pane of the MSDN Library.

Getting Started

As the "Getting Started" section explains, to use the SDK and start to develop your applications and add-ins, you need to ensure that you have the correct development software installed on your computer:

- You need to use the Visual Studio 2005 IDE (Integrated Development Environment).

- You need to develop your applications and add-ins using the Visual C# 2005 programming language. (You can use another programming language, such as Visual Basic .NET 2005, but the examples within the SDK documentation are written specifically for Visual C# 2005.)

- You need to ensure that the .NET Framework 2.0 is installed, as previous versions of the .NET Framework are not supported.

Note The .NET Framework 2.0 is installed automatically when you install any version of Visual Studio 2005, so you don't need to worry about installing it separately.

If you don't have a copy of Visual C# 2005, you can download Visual C# 2005 Express Edition for free. The link for this free download is http://msdn2.microsoft.com/en-us/express/aa700756.aspx. As you can see in Figure C-2, you need to click the Download button to choose the software you want to download and use.

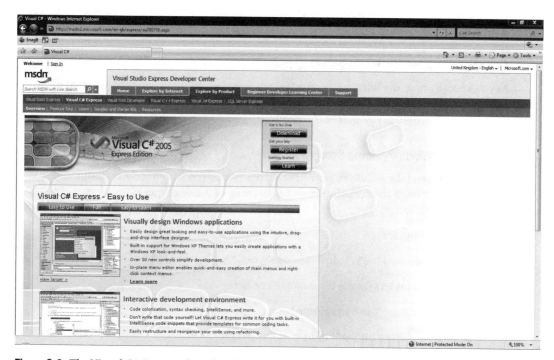

Figure C-2. *The Visual C# Express download site*

Once you have clicked the Download button, you are presented with a list of available tools that you can download, including Visual C# 2005. All you have to do is select the language version you want to download from the relevant drop-down list and then save the file to your computer and run it. Make sure you follow all the instructions to install it. Make sure as well to register, because you will need a registration key; registering also enables you to get quite a lot of other free materials, such as online training, images, and more.

You also need to copy the two Windows Home Server API DLL files to the computer on which you just installed, or already have installed, Visual C# 2005. Those files are located on Windows Home Server in the %ProgramFiles%\Windows Home Server\ directory (where %ProgramFiles% is the system drive—for example, C:\Program Files).

API Overview

As the "API Overview" section explains, there are three different ways that you can extend Windows Home Server:

- Extend the Windows Home Server Console

- Extend the Windows Home Server platform

- Extend the Windows Home Server Console and platform together

You can also use the Windows Server 2003 API to add additional functionality, but that is outside the scope of this appendix.

Extending the Windows Home Server Console

As you know by now, the Windows Home Server Console contains a series of tabs that provide different views and different functionality specific to each view. You can create new tabs with new custom functionality as part of the application you want to create.

Extending the Windows Home Server Platform

You can also extend the Windows Home Server platform itself. The Windows Home Server API provides an easy route to access information on many of the Windows Home Server objects, including the following:

- Client computers

- Shared folders on the Windows Home Server

- Application folders on the Windows Home Server

- Hard disks on the Windows Home Server

- Managed volumes on the Windows Home Server

- Backup jobs on the Windows Home Server

- Notifications on the Windows Home Server

- UPnP certified routers on the Windows Home Server network

Programming Tutorial

The "Programming Tutorial" section of the *Developer's Guide* contains some very useful examples that demonstrate common operations of the Windows Home Server. These examples are split into two sections:

- *Extending the Windows Home Server Console*: Contains an example creating a Windows Home Server add-in and demonstrates how to write code that adds to the Windows Home Server Console a Console tab and a Settings tab. You can access this section directly at `http://msdn2.microsoft.com/en-us/library/bb425860.aspx`.

- *Extending the Windows Home Server*: Contains several examples that demonstrate how to write code that retrieves information about some common Windows Home Server objects. You can access this section directly at `http://msdn2.microsoft.com/en-us/library/bb425853.aspx`.

Take a look at both of these tutorials. They are very detailed and contain simple steps that you can follow to create your own add-ins.

Windows Home Server API Reference

The *Windows Home Server API Reference* contains the class library for the following namespaces:

- *Microsoft.HomeServer.Extensibility*: Contains the interfaces used to extend the Windows Home Server Console

- *Microsoft.HomeServer.SDK.Interop.v1*: Contains the classes and interfaces used to extend the Windows Home Server platform

You can examine each of these namespaces in detail by expanding their navigation links in the left pane.

Code2Fame Challenge

During the beta phase of Windows Home Server, Microsoft launched a competition called the Code2Fame Challenge. The challenge was to develop "cool" software and hardware add-ins for Windows Home Server that would simplify the digital lifestyles of families everywhere.

There was over $50,000 in cash and prizes up for grabs, not to mention that Microsoft would put information about the winners and their add-ins on both the Windows Home Server web site and the Windows Home Server Blog.

This was a really good idea to get people interested in, and developing add-ins for, Windows Home Server, especially because Microsoft was not launching any "official" add-ins for Windows Home Server in time for the official launch of the product. The only real problem with the competition was that is was open only to U.S. residents. This was surprising for many reasons, not least of which were that different language versions of Windows Home Server would be available and that a huge pool of talented developers exists outside the United States.

The Code2Fame Challenge web site, shown in Figure C-3, is at `http://www.microsoft.com/windows/products/winfamily/windowshomeserver/partners/challenge.mspx`.

Figure C-3. *Code2Fame Challenge web site*

Take a look at the various add-ins out there—you never know, you might just be using one developed by one of the winners.

Additional Resources

As with any product, the longer the SDK is around, the more information and resources that will become available. In addition to the MSDN Library for Windows Home Server, there is also the Windows Home Server Developer Forum, at http://forums.microsoft.com/ WindowsHomeServer/ShowForum.aspx?ForumID=1407&SiteID=50. This is a great place to ask questions, talk about add-ins and other development, and just generally communicate with other developers.

Also, keep your eyes on the Windows Home Server Blog and don't forget that there is a wealth of useful (and sometime useless) information on the Internet.

Summary

During this brief introduction to the Windows Home Server SDK, you learned what the SDK contains and what the requirements are for developing add-ins with the SDK, and you were given a very brief introduction to the Windows Home Server API. Obviously, an entire book could be dedicated to the SDK and how to develop different applications for your Windows Home Server. If you are interested in developing your own applications, take the time to work through the great examples and tutorials in the MSDN Library.

Index

Find it faster at http://superindex.apress.com/

You Need the Companion eBook

Your purchase of this book entitles you to buy the companion PDF-version eBook for only $10. Take the weightless companion with you anywhere.

We believe this Apress title will prove so indispensable that you'll want to carry it with you everywhere, which is why we are offering the companion eBook (in PDF format) for $10 to customers who purchase this book now. Convenient and fully searchable, the PDF version of any content-rich, page-heavy Apress book makes a valuable addition to your programming library. You can easily find and copy code—or perform examples by quickly toggling between instructions and the application. Even simultaneously tackling a donut, diet soda, and complex code becomes simplified with hands-free eBooks!

Once you purchase your book, getting the $10 companion eBook is simple:

❶ Visit **www.apress.com/promo/tendollars/**.

❷ Complete a basic registration form to receive a randomly generated question about this title.

❸ Answer the question correctly in 60 seconds, and you will receive a promotional code to redeem for the $10.00 eBook.

2855 TELEGRAPH AVENUE | SUITE 600 | BERKELEY, CA 94705

Offer valid through 04/08.